ERRATA

Page 126: In paragraph commencing **In the autumn of. . .** , delete reference to Philipp Fahrbach junior. Delete also reference in Index (p. 199).

Page 133: Final paragraph. New evidence shows that Eduard Strauss conducted a performance of the waltz **Seid umschlungen Millionen** at the Exhibition on 13 September 1892.

Page 180: **Sympathie, Polka française** should read **Sympathieklänge, Polka française.**

Page 182: Opp. 356–61 should read 356–60. The waltz **Bei uns z'Haus** is entirely independent of **Der Carneval in Rom.**

The Strauss Family

*To my parents, who had to frogmarch
me to my first Strauss concert . . .*

Illustrations not otherwise credited are courtesy of the Archives of the Johann Strauss
Society of Great Britain, or from the author's private collection. Picture research by
Peter Kemp, who also took the photographs of Am Dreimarkstein No. 13, the
original gravestones of Joseph Lanner and Johann Strauss father, and the
'Fledermaus Villa' in Hietzing.

Cover design and art direction by Pearce Marchbank Studio
Cover photography by Julian Hawkins

Printed and bound in Austria.

© Peter Kemp 1985 & 1989.
First published by The Baton Press in 1985.
This edition published in 1989 by Omnibus Press, a division of Book Sales Limited.

Hardback
Order No. OP44585
ISBN 0.7119.1405.2

Softback
Order No. OP45194
ISBN 0.7119.1726.4

Exclusive Distributors:
Book Sales Limited,
8/9 Frith Street,
London W1V 5TZ,
England.
Music Sales Pty Limited,
120 Rothschild Avenue,
Rosebery,
Sydney,
NSW 2018,
Australia.
Music Sales Corporation,
225 Park Avenue South,
New York,
NY10003,
U.S.A.
To The Music Trade Only:
Music Sales Limited,
8/9 Frith Street,
London W1V 5TZ,
England.

The Illustrated Lives of the Great Composers.

The Strauss Family

Peter Kemp

A token of our appreciation
from
United Closures and Plastics,
Bridge of Allan —
The "cap-it-all" of Scotland!

Omnibus Press
London/New York/Sydney/Cologne

Other titles in the series

CONTENTS

FOREWORD

WITH GREAT pleasure I have read this new book, and consider it has a worthy place among a modern generation of biographies, the authors of which do not tire of casting aside the 'glorifying rose-tinted fairy-tales' about my family, in favour of well-researched verifiable facts. For no fairy-tale is so gripping, no myth so fascinating, as the story that life itself writes.

One cannot isolate the music of my ancestors from the era of its creation. It is, like all music, a product of its time and a signpost to the future. Again and again one can see from the growing worldwide interest in my family and its musical achievements that Strauss music is not imprisoned in the nineteenth century but, especially today, spreads hope and joyfulness among people of all ages. I must leave the explanation and interpretation of this phenomenon to those who are more competent. I can only gaze in wonder at the fact that two generations of my family should have produced such a wealth of talent. Among those who know me, it is no secret that my favourite family composer is Josef Strauss. What a tragedy that he lived less than forty-three years!

I have known Peter Kemp for many years as an accurate and reliable writer who has shown a profound and enthusiastic interest in the music and history of my family and its contemporaries. Since 1974 he has proved his ability in the field of research with a series of articles for *Tritsch-Tratsch*, the journal of the Johann Strauss Society of Great Britain, in which he has examined in detail compositions by my family like *Frühlingsstimmen*, *Die Emancipierte*, *Unter Donner und Blitz*, the *Aschenbrödel* ballet and other works. Having read these articles and a number of his notes for record sleeves and concert programmes, and having observed his development as a highly creditable Strauss researcher, I am by no means surprised at the emergence of this book.

In closing, I feel sure that both the casual reader and the keen Strauss student will find this book valuable, interesting and informative.

Dr. Eduard Strauss

Dr. EDUARD STRAUSS
Vienna, *November 1984*

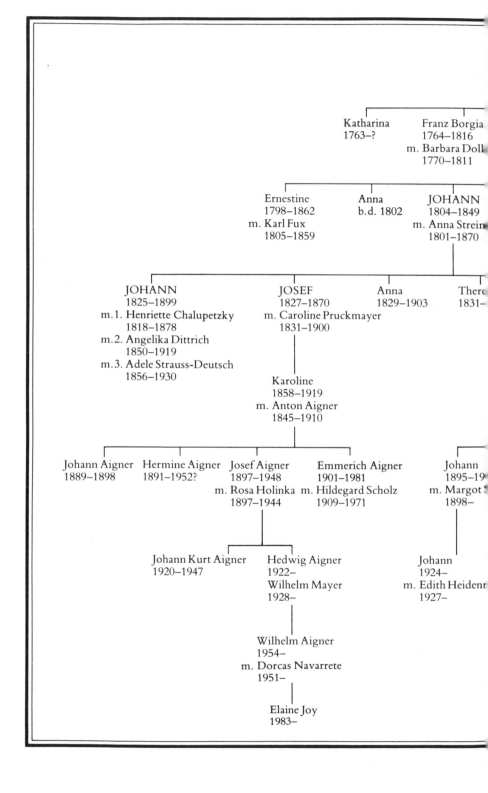

Katharina
1763–?

Franz Borgia
1764–1816
m. Barbara Doll
1770–1811

Ernestine
1798–1862
m. Karl Fux
1805–1859

Anna
b.d. 1802

JOHANN
1804–1849
m. Anna Strein
1801–1870

JOHANN
1825–1899
m.1. Henriette Chalupetzky
1818–1878
m.2. Angelika Dittrich
1850–1919
m.3. Adele Strauss-Deutsch
1856–1930

JOSEF
1827–1870
m. Caroline Pruckmayer
1831–1900

Anna
1829–1903

There
1831–

Karoline
1858–1919
m. Anton Aigner
1845–1910

Johann Aigner
1889–1898

Hermine Aigner
1891–1952?

Josef Aigner
1897–1948
m. Rosa Holinka
1897–1944

Emmerich Aigner
1901–1981
m. Hildegard Scholz
1909–1971

Johann
1895–19
m. Margot
1898–

Johann Kurt Aigner
1920–1947

Hedwig Aigner
1922–
Wilhelm Mayer
1928–

Johann
1924–
m. Edith Heiden
1927–

Wilhelm Aigner
1954–
m. Dorcas Navarrete
1951–

Elaine Joy
1983–

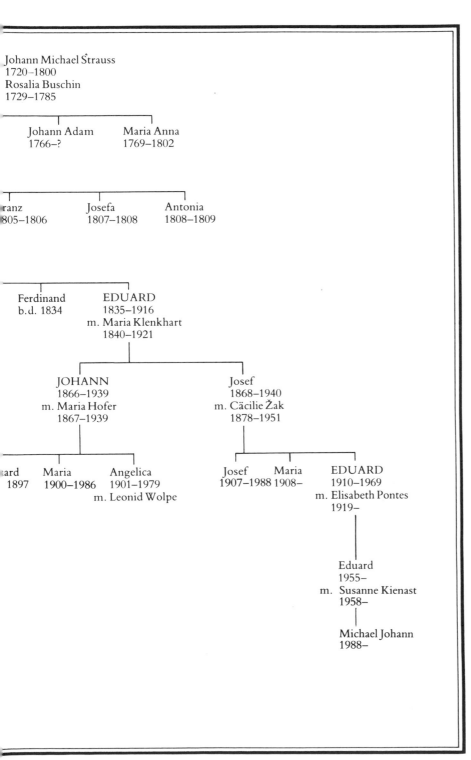

Johann Michael Strauss
1720–1800
Rosalia Buschin
1729–1785

Johann Adam   Maria Anna
1766–?   1769–1802

ranz   Josefa   Antonia
805–1806   1807–1808   1808–1809

Ferdinand   EDUARD
b.d. 1834   1835–1916
                m. Maria Klenkhart
                1840–1921

JOHANN   Josef
1866–1939   1868–1940
m. Maria Hofer   m. Cäcilie Žak
1867–1939   1878–1951

ard   Maria   Angelica   Josef   Maria   EDUARD
1897   1900–1986   1901–1979   1907–1988   1908–   1910–1969
                    m. Leonid Wolpe   m. Elisabeth Pontes
                                                                 1919–

                                                                 Eduard
                                                                 1955–
                                                                 m. Susanne Kienast
                                                                 1958–

                                                                 Michael Johann
                                                                 1988–

INTRODUCTION

THE SERIOUS Strauss student wishing to undertake original research in Great Britain is beset by a number of problems, not the least of which is the general dearth of such vital nineteenth-century source material as Austrian newspapers and periodicals. Regular research trips to Vienna have been financially impracticable, and for this reason I am indebted especially to the Austrian cultural historian and Strauss feuilletonist, Professor Franz Mailer, for unsparingly placing at my disposal much invaluable material.

I should also like to express my heartfelt thanks to Professor Dr Max Schönherr; Professor Dr Hanns Jäger-Sunstenau; Dr Otto Biba of the Gesellschaft der Musikfreunde in Vienna; Herr Franz Feldkirchner; Dr John Whitten; Mrs Dana Kacperczyk; Richard Macnutt; Miss Hannelore Schmidt of the Austrian Institute, London; Frank Andrews and George L. Frow of the City of London Phonograph and Gramophone Society; Robert Dockerill of EMI Records (UK); the Bank of England; Philip G. Povey, Vice-Chairman of the Johann Strauss Society of Great Britain; and Hofrat Magister Dr Franz Patzer, Director of the Wiener Stadt- und Landesbibliothek, and his indefatigable team. The quotation from Eduard Strauss I's letter of 20 May 1895 is reproduced by gracious permission of her Majesty the Queen.

Sincere gratitude is extended worldwide to those kind individuals, particularly Frau Elisabeth and Dr Eduard Strauss and other present-day Strauss family members, who allowed me access to their private collections of letters and other documents, which have proved such a rich source of primary information, much of it hitherto unpublished. This wealth of detail has not only demanded editing, it has also required translation. In this I am truly indebted to my good friends Robert Nicholls and Peter Eustace, for accurately transcribing innumerable passages of nineteenth-century German prose into English, thereby enabling me to draw upon much original material which I should not otherwise have had time to consider.

My editor, Candida Hunt, has provided enthusiastic and expert guidance throughout the writing of this book. To her and to Sian Prior, who undertook the painstaking preparation of the index, I offer my warmest thanks. I am also most grateful to Diane Davies for typing out the final draft of my manuscript, and remind her that it was she who volunteered for the task!

Finally, I should like to thank my wife, Marilyn, for her unfailing patience, encouragement and assistance, despite her own hectic schedule of work.

It will be clear that any attempt to compress almost 175 years of artistic achievement into a mere 272 pages must be at the expense of detail. Notwithstanding, I hope that this book will clear aside much of the fanciful debris that has been allowed to accumulate for more than a century, and that what remains will be deemed no less compelling a story than that which the moguls of Hollywood would have us all believe.

PETER KEMP
Marlow Bottom, Buckinghamshire
October 1984

1

My father was a musician by the grace of God
. . . guided by an inner, irresistible impulse.

(Johann Strauss II, 30 November 1887)

The whole world knows Johann Strauss, the Waltz King, with his incomparable melodies. There is hardly any other type of music which is so German and so close to the people as that of the great Waltz King. Johann Strauss is long since dead. He has become immortal. Jewish legacy-hunters have seen to it that some of his earthly descendants are today living in abject distress . . . Shocking factual reports about the ways and doings of these Jewish liars and swindlers . . . Read *Stürmer* No.23, and the continuations in Numbers 24 and 25!

WHEN THIS advertisement for the anti-Semitic Nazi newspaper, *Der Stürmer*, appeared on innumerable hoardings in early June 1939, few people, least of all the Nazi propagandists themselves, could have foreseen that it was to prompt one of the most bizarre acts of Second World War documentary falsification perpetrated by the Third Reich.

Between 1935 and 1937 a group of Viennese genealogists tracing the Strauss family tree brought to light an entry in a register at St Stephen's Cathedral, Vienna, which recorded, on 11 February 1762, a marriage between

Johann Michael Strauss, a respectable man, servant . . . a baptised Jew, single, born in Ofen★, son of Wolf Strauss and his wife Theresia, both Jewish . . . And the respectable and virtuous Rosalia Buschin, born in Gföll [Gföhl], in Lower Austria, daughter of Johann Georg Buschin, a former huntsman, and his wife Eva Rosina . . .

In the wake of Austria's forcible annexation to the German Reich in 1938, public knowledge of the Waltz King's Jewish ancestry would have discredited *Der Stürmer*. The paper's proclamation was patently inaccurate as, his Semitic origins aside, Johann Strauss II died without issue, bequeathing part of his valuable estate to his Jewish-born widow, Adèle. Moreover, a suppression of Strauss family music, which was an important element in radio and concert repertoire in the Reich, would have been calamitous. Despite their attempts at concealment, the Nazi authorities failed to prevent leakage of the

---

★The old German name for the Hungarian town of Buda.

15

genealogists' findings, and they determined to adopt a more radical solution. Accordingly, the Cathedral marriage register was confiscated and passed to the Reich Office of Genealogy in Berlin, later being replaced by a skilfully forged copy from which the offending entries had been removed.

★   ★   ★

The 'servant', Johann Michael Strauss, had left his Hungarian native town of Ofen in about 1750 in the company of his master, Count Franz von Roggendorff. Their destination was Vienna, seat of the Habsburg monarchy. Later, when von Roggendorff (by then a field-marshal lieutenant) moved on, Johann Michael remained, settling in the music-filled Danube quarter of the city as a 'journeyman upholsterer', and converting from Judaism to Catholicism. He died from consumption, in a poor-house, in 1800.

The second of his four children, Franz Borgias, was thirty-three when, on 23 October 1797, he married Barbara Dollmann, the 27-year-old daughter of a Viennese coachman. She was to bear her husband six children, of whom only two, a girl and a boy, survived childhood. At first, Franz Borgias Strauss – described by a contemporary as having 'a somewhat grotesque appearance, with a bald head set on an exceedingly thick neck, thick ears, a copious stomach and broad, inward turned feet . . . He never wore a neckerchief, and his buffskin boots were never polished' – earned a living as an itinerant waiter around Vienna, but records show that from 1803 to 1808 he was the tenant of a small tavern and dwelling within the house 'Zum heiligen Florian' (Holy Florian) at No.7 Flossgasse, a back street in the Viennese suburb of Leopoldstadt. It was here*, on 14 March 1804, that the couple's first son was born: baptized Johann Baptist, the infant was destined to become the founder of the Strauss musical dynasty.

In 1808 Franz Borgias moved his family to the nearby Weintraubengasse where, in the house 'Zum guten Hirten' (The Good Shepherd), he managed another tavern until 1811. Here, as in the Flossgasse premises, the young Johann Strauss grew up amid the sounds of the wandering 'Beer-fiddlers' and the various folk-dances they brought with them from their travels along the Danube, such as the Ländler, Deutscher and Tanz – the immediate progenitors of the Viennese waltz. Their music evidently fascinated him:

When musicians played in the larger of the two rooms in the tavern, the boy crouched under a table, unseen by his father, in order to be able to hear the players.

(Eduard Strauss I: Erinnerungen, 1906)

When Johann was only seven his mother died, a victim of 'creeping fever'. Two years later, in 1813, his father remarried, his bride the

---

*Not in 'Zum guten Hirten', as often claimed.

16

Linz-born Katharina Theresia Feldberger. By now the family had returned to No.7 Flossgasse, but tragedy struck again when, on 5 April 1816, Franz Borgias was discovered drowned in one of the Danube waterways. He left a debt-ridden estate, and the young Johann and his 17-year-old sister, Ernestine, were placed under the guardianship of Anton Müller, a tailor, though they continued to live with their stepmother. Determined that his ward should learn a middle-class profession, in 1817 Müller apprenticed the reluctant 13-year-old Johann to a Viennese bookbinder, Johann Lichtscheidl, for a period of five years. We may be sure that the youngster was equally determined to pursue a different career, for as Eduard Strauss relates:

What [my father] had to deny himself during the daytime he devoted himself to at night with redoubled fervour; in a tiny attic he practised and played on an extremely primitive violin, to his heart's content.

Stories of the cruelty Johann suffered during his apprenticeship, of his running away and of his early musical tuition with one Polischansky, remain unsubstantiated. Indeed, the Guild Book of Viennese Bookbinders shows clearly that 'Herr Lichtscheidl released his apprentice, Johann Strauss, from his articles' on 13 January 1822, his apprenticeship duly completed.

In 1825 Müller certified to his ward's 'skilled musical instruction', though the identity of Johann's first tutor(s) has never been established. In later years he studied thorough-bass and instrumentation with the famous Ignaz Ritter von Seyfried, and violin with the violin virtuoso and theorist Leopold Jansa. Johann's level of technical competence, however, even during his bookbinder's apprenticeship, was sufficient to gain him a place as a string player in the dance orchestra of the popular, if eccentric, Michael Pamer, where he acquired valuable practical experience. Strauss left Pamer's orchestra in 1819 to join a trio which had already made its successful début in Vienna that spring. Comprising two violins and a guitar, the trio had been formed by Joseph Lanner and the brothers Karl and Johann Drahanek, and with the addition of the 15-year-old Strauss, as viola player, the ensemble grew to a quartet. Lanner, the son of a Viennese glovemaker and three years older than Strauss, had also served his time in Pamer's dance band before seeking his independence. 'Blond Peppi' (Lanner) and 'Black Schani' (Strauss) became firm friends, and for a while shared lodgings.

The music which the ensemble played at this time included dance pieces and popular melodies from contemporary operatic works, but the greatest acclaim was reserved for Lanner's own compositions. At first these took the form of rustic Ländlers, usually made up of six unrelated dances with coda in rhythmic three-quarter-time. Lanner soon adopted the practice of giving specific names to his dances — instead of compositions designated merely as *Four German Dances*

17

(Mozart) or *Six Contredanses* (Beethoven), Lanner chose titles like, for example, *Neue Wiener Ländler* (op.1) and *Tyroler-Ländler* (op.6). Whilst Lanner himself did not originate this titling system, it was an important commercial step, subsequently taken up by almost all other dance-music composers with the positive encouragement of their publishers and enabled the sheet-music buying public more readily to recall individual works.

The origins of the waltz itself are both complex and comparatively obscure. The German verb 'walzen' (to waltz), referring to the gyrating movement of a dancing couple, was certainly current in Austria in 1754 since there is a reference to it in Joseph Kurz's comedy *Der auf das neue begeisterte und belebte Bernardon*, but until the last decade of the eighteenth century the various dances in three-quarter-time from Austria, southern Germany, Bohemia and elsewhere were commonly known generically as 'Deutscher' (German Dances). By 1792, however, the *Journal des Luxus und der Moden* could already report the overwhelming success of the waltz in Berlin. Later, the chronicler Count de la Garde wrote of one of the festivities accompanying the Congress of Vienna of 1814–15:

After the departure of the sovereigns the orchestra began to play waltzes. At once, an electrical stimulus seemed to be communicated to the entire assembled multitude . . . One can scarcely conceive of the power which the waltz exercises. As soon as the first bars are heard, countenances brighten, eyes come alive, a tremor of delight runs through everyone. The graceful spinning-tops take shape, start to move, interweave, overtake. One has to have seen the ravishingly beautiful women, aglow with flowers and diamonds, drawn along like bright meteors by this irresistible music . . .

Against such a backcloth, and much influenced by Carl Maria von Weber's concert-rondo for piano (1819), *Aufforderung zum Tanz* (Invitation to the Dance), in which the sequence of waltzes is framed by a well-defined Introduction and a final section recapitulating the principal themes, Lanner and Strauss, with their contrasting styles, began to develop, expand and formalize the Viennese waltz. Thus, they laid the foundations upon which others, and particularly Strauss's sons, would build. Through these later exponents the waltz was elevated to its classic form, reigning supreme across all social strata of nineteenth-century Europe.

The increasing popularity of the Lanner Quartet fostered its expansion until, on 1 May 1824, Lanner appeared for the first time at the head of a small string orchestra. This proved so great an attraction, especially during the busy annual Vienna Fasching* (Carnival) – in 1832, for example, some 772 balls were held in the city – that a second orchestra was formed, with 'vice-conductor' Strauss at its head.

*Until 1868 the Vienna Fasching began on 6 January and continued until midnight on Shrove Tuesday. The latter date, governed by Easter, could thus fall between the first week of February and the first week of March. From 1869 the restriction was officially abolished, permitting balls to take place also during Lent. Subsequently, the precise dates of the Fasching have become still more flexible.

The strain of conducting, composing, arranging, rehearsing and organizing began to take its toll of Lanner. Johann Strauss II later recounted that one morning Lanner felt too unwell to compose a set of waltzes promised for an event that same evening, and instead delegated the task to his companion, with the simple message: 'Strauss – see to it you come up with something'. The resulting piece – announced as Lanner's composition – 'was received with extra-ordinary favour'.

The realization of his own abilities as composer and conductor must surely have signalled to Strauss an escape from the financial problems that forced him to give lessons in order to supplement his income. In any case, events which were to follow served only to hasten this inevitable course of action.

In 1825 Lanner and Strauss began giving concerts at 'Zum roten Hahn' (The Red Rooster), a tavern in the Liechtenthal suburb of Vienna managed by Josef Streim and his wife Maria (*née* Rober). The couple's eldest daughter, Maria Anna, was a pretty girl of twenty-three when, during the Fasching of that year, she 'found herself in the arms, and soon in the bed, of the somewhat reckless young musician' (Franz Mailer: *Joseph Strauss. Genie wider Willen,* 1977). On 14 March 1825, his twenty-first birthday, Strauss applied to the authorities for a one-year passport to go on tour 'to Graz and the Imperial lands, to seek earnings', but was dissuaded from going by Anna, who knew herself to be expecting his child. On 11 July 1825 the couple were married, 'according to Catholic custom' in the parish church of Liechtenthal. Less than four months later, on 25 October, in their home at No. 76 Rofranogasse (later renumbered No. 15 Lerchenfelderstrasse) in the suburb of St Ulrich, Anna gave birth to a son.

He was christened Johann Baptist, after his father.

2

*Anyone in Vienna who has not seen
St Stephen's spire, the Sperl and Strauss,
does not know Vienna!*

(Popular adage in nineteenth-century Vienna)

O N 1 SEPTEMBER 1825, some eight weeks before the birth of
his child, Johann Strauss I parted company from Joseph Lanner
after a concert in the Viennese establishment 'Zum schwarzen Bock'
(The Black Ram). Much has been written of a bitter quarrel that
evening between the two men, of scuffles among the members of the
orchestra and audience, and of Strauss's departure with several of
Lanner's musicians. These accounts all stem from later writings; there
are no eyewitness reports, and the journals of 1825 mention nothing.
We know that in March 1825 Strauss had already applied for a one-
year passport, clearly planning to quit Lanner's orchestra. Whether
Lanner knew in advance of his colleague's intentions remains a matter
for conjecture. Certainly he commemorated Strauss's departure with
his *Trennungs-Walzer* op.19 (Separation Waltz) and, although the
precise date of first performance is open to question, some sources
believe that Lanner played it on 1 September, suggesting that he did
have prior knowledge.

Although the two men now pursued separate careers, neither
harboured the lasting resentment so often reported; in fact, Strauss and
Lanner worked together on a number of subsequent occasions,
including a benefit concert at 'Zum schwarzen Bock' on 19 October
1826 for the ailing Michael Pamer, their former employer. When
Lanner married Franziska Jahns on 24 November 1828, Strauss was
present to offer his congratulations, and in 1836 the two Musik-
Direktors jointly took the Citizen's Oath upon being granted the
Freedom of the City of Vienna.

Strauss had long since recognized the importance of establishing his
own orchestra to interpret his musical ideas exactly as he had
conceived them. Within a few weeks of parting from Lanner he had
founded the Strauss Orchestra, and began to receive various
engagements in Vienna's suburbs. Even for a musician as talented as
Strauss, competition with the firmly established Lanner Orchestra
could not have been easy, but Johann's fast-growing reputation
secured him regular work. On 7 May 1827, for instance, the

21

proprietor of the tavern 'Zu den zwey Tauben' (The Two Doves) announced in the *Wiener Zeitung* Wednesday and Saturday performances by Strauss with 'full orchestra, comprising twelve persons with wind and stringed instruments'. It was for a programme at this establishment that Johann wrote his appropriately titled *Täuberln-Walzer* op.1 (Little Doves Waltz), a chain of eight two–part waltzes without introduction or coda.

Over the years, influenced primarily by Strauss and Lanner, the structure of the Viennese waltz changed: the brief fanfare-like introductions became longer and frequently more descriptive, so to balance this the coda was extended, recapitulating the principal themes of the waltz. The waltz-chain, formerly a set of seven or eight unrelated waltz tunes, gradually became more of a self-contained unit, with each new theme seeming to grow naturally out of the preceding one, a development even reflected in the German language itself: the plural *Die* Walzer (the *waltzes*) eventually giving way to the singular *Der* Walzer (the *waltz*).

The extrovert Strauss lost no time in attracting an enthusiastic public to the 'Zwey Tauben', and when he began performances at 'Zur Kettenbrücke' (The Suspension Bridge) in Leopoldstadt in November 1827, his admirers went with him. It was here, during the 1828 Fasching, that Johann emerged as Lanner's greatest rival when he played for the first time his *Kettenbrücke-Walzer* op.4. The piece was Johann's first major success, and from that time the dance-loving Viennese divided themselves into two parties, the 'Lannerianer' and the 'Straussianer', each of which championed its idol with equal ardour:

By his very nature Lanner is superior to Strauss in his technical handling of the instrument and in the versatility of his performance . . . The music flows from the strings of his violin, now sweetly and softly, and now swelling up to stormy passion with a penetrating power which dominates the whole orchestra, suddenly shouting out with joy and immediately afterwards sounding melancholy again. As the Athenians said of Pericles that he knew how to create lightning and thunder with his speeches, so Lanner made the Viennese laugh and cry alternately.

In [Strauss's] waltzes a profusion of melodies effervesce and bubble, fizz and froth, dash and sweep like the five hundred thousand devils in the champagne, slipping their bonds and flinging one cork after another into the air. Yet each one of these corks of melody is a burning rocket . . . Each of Strauss's works can be likened to a firework display of colourful cascades, harmonious whirlwinds and rhythmical crackers. Everything explodes, nothing fizzles out, everything catches alight.

Strauss and Lanner and their respective publishers, Tobias Haslinger and Anton Diabelli, each responded to this rivalry and sought to capitalize from the competitive situation by producing new works of ever-increasing originality and quality. The friendly 'feud' was to end only with Lanner's death in 1843. The harmless rivalry between Straussianer and Lannerianer was surreptitiously encouraged from within the Austrian government, which was anxious to distract the populace from the potentially inflammatory subject of politics, thereby strengthening Metternich's policies of obscurantism and oppression.

In 1829 Joseph Lanner was appointed to the post of Musik-Direktor of the Redoutensäle in the Imperial Hofburg – two magnificent rooms in the Imperial Palace, Vienna, often given over to the concerts and balls of the nobility. But if that year was of importance to Lanner, it was to prove of even greater significance to Strauss when Johann Georg Scherzer, owner of the fashionable 'Zum Sperlbauer' premises in Leopoldstadt, signed a six-year fee-paying contract with him and his continually expanding orchestra. Opened in 1807, the 'Sperl', together with the competing Apollo-Saal in the Mariahilf suburb, had long since become the best-known and most popular of Viennese entertainment establishments. But by 1829 the Apollo-Saal, with its swan-lake, waterfalls, labyrinths, grottoes and five enormous ballrooms, accommodating up to 8000 visitors in an evening, was in decline and had been all but supplanted by the Sperl. For the 25-year-old conductor/composer, the elegant interior of the Sperl was to become almost a second home; indeed, over a quarter of his more than 250 compositions were to receive their first performances there. The shrewd Strauss also arranged for a fixed entrance fee to be levied on patrons attending his performances, rather than relying upon the then widespread, degrading and often unremunerative practice of passing around a collection plate. For his début here, on 4 October 1829, Johann Strauss composed his *Sperls Fest-Walzer* op.30 (Sperl's Festival Waltz). With its several halls bedecked with flowers and palms, and 'more than a thousand lamps burning in the high and mighty chandeliers', the ornate Sperl was the regular venue of the splendid 'Representation Balls' of organizations such as the Gesellschaft der Musikfreunde (The Society of the Friends of Music) and the legal and medical professions.

The years 1830 to 1836, during which my father presided over the music at the 'Sperl', will always remain memorable in Viennese musical history. The audiences were immense, their enthusiasm unbounded, and as my father was persuaded to accept engagements at other places of entertainment too, he had at his disposal during the Fasching an army of musicians, some 200 strong. From this he selected a corps of élite – his Stammorchester – which, by unceasing and scrupulous rehearsal, he succeeded in bringing to a point of perfection such as no other private orchestra had ever reached.

(Johann Strauss II, in the Foreword to the Complete
Edition of his father's works, 30 November 1887)*

As yet, neither Lanner nor Strauss had ventured outside the

*Although this widely quoted Foreword infers authorship by Johann Strauss II, evidence suggests that it was in fact ghostwritten by the revered music critic, Eduard Hanslick.

confines of Vienna, but for the many visitors to the Austrian capital during the early 1830s they proved a major attraction not only with their waltzes, upon which both men now concentrated, but also with their many galops, potpourris and other compositions. Accounts of their triumphs spread swiftly to other parts of the world. The 21-year-old Chopin noted, in 1831, that 'Lanner, Strauss and their waltzes obscure everything', while Richard Wagner, recalling his stay in Vienna during mid-summer 1832, wrote:

I shall never forget the extraordinary playing of Johann Strauss, who put equal enthusiasm into everything he played, and very often made the audience almost frantic with delight. At the beginning of a new waltz this demon of the Viennese musical spirit shook like a Pythian priestess on the tripod, and veritable groans of ecstasy which, without doubt, were more due to his music than to the drinks in which the audience had indulged, raised their worship for the magic violinist to almost bewildering heights of frenzy.

Wagner's observations about Strauss's 'extraordinary playing' highlighted one of the vital elements of a Strauss concert, the success of which evidently owed much to the visual aspect of the performance.

During the 1830s Lanner and Strauss consolidated their position as the foremost dance-music composer/conductors of their day, finding themselves increasingly in demand as dance halls and other entertainment establishments proliferated in and around Vienna. Increasingly, too, both men sought to dedicate their newest compositions to persons of status, a practice which added greatly to a composer's prestige.

In autumn 1833 Johann accepted the first of many invitations that were to take him beyond the boundaries of his native city. Together with his orchestra he journeyed down the Danube to the Hungarian town of Pest – in 1872 united with the town of Buda on the opposite bank to form the municipality of Budapest. His impact was immediate: 'The great ball festivity in the Redoutensaal, Pest, which took place on 7 November . . . was extraordinarily well attended and a most sparkling affair', reported a Pest newspaper. 'The highly gifted composer was received with rejoicing, and his achievements were accompanied by such a storm of applause that the room resounded.' In Vienna, the *Theaterzeitung* (16 November 1833) summarized simply: 'Herr Strauss . . . triumphed with the first stroke of his bow.' Johann's waltz *Emlék Pestre – Erinnerung an Pesth* op. 66 (Memory of Pest), dedicated 'to the noble Hungarian Nation', recalls the visit. Returning to Vienna, the composer wrote to his physician, Dr Carus, on 29 December:'. . . my left arm is much strained which I attribute to my playing the violin, which has hurt me . . . Cure me, noble man, and I will compose a "Health Waltz" which will inspire you to dance a galop on your golden wedding anniversary.'

After nine hectic months of concerts and balls in Vienna, Strauss decided in 1834 to embark upon a longer tour, and accordingly, on 10 November, left for Berlin with his orchestra of thirty men. There followed a rapid succession of engagements, including performances before the King, the Prussian Princes Carl and Wilhelm, the Russian Ambassador and the visiting Tsar and Empress of Russia. Rewarding both financially and artistically for Strauss, his appearance brought him a large sum of money from the King and the present of a golden snuffbox from the Tsar. From Berlin, Johann made the journey home via concert stops in Leipzig, Dresden and Prague, arriving in Vienna on 14 December. As with the earlier visit to Pest, Strauss commemorated his Berlin sojourn with a waltz – *Erinnerung an Berlin* op.78 (Memory of Berlin).

In 1835 Strauss and his orchestra undertook a three-month trip through southern Germany, with a total of forty concerts in nineteen different towns. The following year saw his most extensive tour to date; lasting almost four months, it took him via Prague, Leipzig and Hanover to Hamburg, thence to Amsterdam, Rotterdam, Düsseldorf, Cologne and Brussels, and eventually back to Vienna on 30 December that year. As before, he was greeted everywhere with fervour.

By now, Anna Strauss had borne her husband a further five children, and the family had several times moved home in Vienna – 'It had to be comfortable, but not cost much'. Josef, their second son, was born on 20 August 1827 in 'Civic Dwelling House' No. 39 in the suburb of Mariahilf; Anna at No. 31 Leopoldstadt, in the Donaustrasse; and Therese at No. 255 Leopoldstadt, on the corner of Josefigasse (today called Karmelitergasse). In 1833★ the family moved to the spacious and imposing house 'Zum goldenen Hirschen' (The Golden Stag), No. 314 Leopoldstadt, on the Taborstrasse. Here, on 4 January 1834, the couple's third son, the frail Ferdinand, was born, destined to live only ten months. This address was also the birthplace of the sixth and last child, Eduard, born on 15 March 1835.

The 'Hirschenhaus', as it was known, was large enough for Strauss father to have his own private quarters, where he could work undisturbed on his compositions and hold orchestral rehearsals for his concerts. Performing into the early hours of the morning, Johann was left with little time for composing the constant stream of new material demanded of him, and he was obliged to develop rapid working methods. He was often assisted in this by Philipp Fahrbach senior, for some ten years a flautist in the Strauss Orchestra and himself one of the most prominent members of another Austrian musical dynasty. Strauss and Fahrbach adopted the following system: after Johann had sketched his ideas for a new work, and had effected any necessary improvements, he would then prepare a fair copy of the first violin part in which (as was usual with nineteenth-century Viennese

★This date is given by Eduard Strauss I in a plan he made of the Hirschenhaus interior. While the majority of Strauss biographers identify the year as 1834, this seems unlikely since Ferdinand was born on 4 January 1834 in the Hirschenhaus.

conductors who led from the violin) the principal melody was to be found. The two men then entered upon a work-sharing programme. Fahrbach would study the first violin part and prepare the flute part based upon it. Strauss then wrote out the double-bass line, and from it Fahrbach would prepare the trombone part. This process continued until the composition was completed. At other times Strauss might write a full score which he then sliced up into strips, enabling several copyists simultaneously to prepare the individual instrumental parts for the players, a task occupying only a few hours. Thus orchestration, rehearsal and performance could all be accomplished within the same day. A remark by the conductor/composer Adolf Müller senior, on the autograph score of Johann's *Cachucha-Galopp* (op.97) of 1837, records an even swifter genesis: 'This galop was composed by Johann Strauss one hour before the opening of the ball, written out by the copyists, performed without rehearsal, accorded exceptional applause and repeated three times.'

The constant pressures upon the somewhat irascible Strauss led to a gradual alienation from his wife and family, which became increasingly marked during the mid-1830s with his arduous and prolonged orchestral tours away from home. Anna knew Johann to have had several brief affairs, but from the altered tone of his letters dating from this time she may well have suspected the existence of a serious rival for his affections. She was surely unprepared, however, for the news which greeted her just two months after the birth of her son Eduard, that her husband was openly admitting paternity of a daughter by his mistress, Emilie Sophia Anna Trambusch*. Emilie, daughter of a military surgeon, was about nineteen years of age when she met the elder Johann in about 1833. An attractive Austrian milliner, born in 1814 in the small Moravian town of Saar (now Zdár) of mixed Czech and German parentage, she was to bear Strauss a total of seven illegitimate children between 1835 and 1844. The second of these love-children was born in 1836, and Anna Strauss's humiliation was made complete by the announcement that the boy was to be named Johann, like her own first-born. Nevertheless, principally for financial reasons, she tolerated the situation until 1844, when she sued for divorce. Until this was granted in 1846, the estranged Johann lived in a separate apartment within the Hirschenhaus, afterwards leaving to set up home with Emilie.

On 4 October 1837, Strauss father set off on a tour that was to prove the most ambitious and lengthy of his career. The outward journey from Vienna took him through southern Germany, where he gave a number of concerts, and on to Strasbourg. On 27 October he and his orchestra of some twenty-six men reached Paris where, with only brief excursions to Rouen and Le Havre, they remained until the end of February 1838. The visit is commemorated in two works – the

* Alternative forms of this name – Trampusch and Tramposch – exist in a number of documents.

26

spectacular galop *Der Carneval in Paris* (op.100) and the *Paris Walzer* (op.101), the Coda of which features a quotation from *La Marseillaise* in waltz-time. Johann's reception in the French capital was phenomenal. In an article for the *Journal des Débats* (10 November 1837), Hector Berlioz wrote:

We knew the name of Strauss, thanks to the music publishers . . . that was all; of the technical perfection, of the fire, the intelligence and the rhythmic feeling which his orchestra displays, we had no notion.

Strauss played before the French royal family in the Tuileries, and his public concerts were attended by such prominent musicians as Adam, Auber, Berlioz, Cherubini, Halévy, Meyerbeer and Paganini, as well as by the French 'Quadrille King' Philippe Musard, with whom Strauss also gave joint performances. Moreover, Johann even played first violin in the orchestras of Musard and Jean-Louis Dufresne in order to gain a thorough understanding of the 'quadrille française', which was largely unknown to the Viennese until Strauss introduced it, with enormous success, during the Fasching of 1840. In all, Strauss wrote some thirty-nine pieces in this genre, many on original themes, and others based on operatic and non-operatic works by other composers.

From Paris the tour continued through principal towns in Belgium and the Netherlands, where the existence of an extensive railway system afforded temporary relief from exhausting journeys by horse-drawn mail-coach and carriage. With few of the conveniences of modern travel, the drain upon the band's physical reserves must have been enormous, but a letter written home in March by one of the musicians is illuminating:

Strauss always rents the most elegant hotels with the best tables d'hôte, where frequently there are so many and various courses that several of us do not know whether the meal should be eaten or drunk. For every comfort is attended to, so that rich travellers could scarcely find better. In Paris we occupied an entire hotel for a full four months, where on average, including their salary, every individual costed 11 francs a day, and moreover, in the extremely severe, terribly cold winter, Strauss had to have all the rooms heated, and for the wood alone on many days paid 60-80 francs. In short, Strauss won much honour in Paris, but damned little money; and yet he acted for us all with the greatest readiness, and never was any payment delayed, indeed, as far as our salary is concerned, several of us even drew payments in advance. In short, Strauss cares for his men just as a fond father cares for his children.

A fresh challenge now beckoned Strauss from across the North Sea – England. He and his orchestra had already been away from Vienna for some twenty-seven weeks, and as one of his players, Ludwig Scheyrer, noted: 'Within the company, parties had formed, which were of the opinion that they would be parted from Europe for ever if they once set foot on board a ship.' One mutinous member, jealous of

Strauss's success, even attempted to persuade his colleagues to renege against their leader. Strauss, learning of this plan,

pointed out to them in very injured terms the sacrifice which he constantly made for them, reminded them strongly and earnestly of their contracts, sincerely praised the devotion with which they had formerly treated him and drew their attention to the offers, the guarantees and the letters of recommendation to the most distinguished inhabitants of London which he had in his pocket.

Thus the misgivings were overcome, the troublemaker ousted, and on the night of 11 April 1838 'a good-humoured and hopeful band of artists' crossed from Vlissingen to England in the steamship *Princess Victoria*.

3

*So perfect a band was never before heard on
this side of the Channel. Orchestras we may
boast, the individuals composing which are
equal in talent to these, but the perfection of
such an ensemble we have never yet reached.*

(*The Morning Post*, London, 18 April 1838)

STRAUSS'S trip to England could not have been better timed, for
the nation was preparing for the forthcoming coronation of the
18-year-old Queen Victoria, and the accompanying celebrations
promised the Viennese Kapellmeister* rich rewards. Understandably,
therefore, he might well have been alarmed by suggestions that the
coronation, planned for June, might have to be postponed until the
following year, or at least until later in 1838. Government ministers
feared the ruination of tradespeople by a coronation occurring in the
middle of the 'London season', as the capital would become deserted
immediately afterwards. Despite these fears, Coronation Day was
announced for 28 June.

Strauss made his first appearance with a 'Grand Concert' on
Tuesday, 17 April at the Queen's Concert Rooms, Hanover Square.
The Times (18 April 1838) reported:

The pieces performed were chiefly his own waltzes, but they are done in a
manner most extraordinary and altogether novel in this country. He has so
completely trained his band to work with him, that all separate individuality
is lost, and an effect is produced like that of an accurately constructed
machine; the most eccentric instruments, such as bells, castanets, and
cracking whips, are occasionally introduced, and the construction of many
pieces is highly fantastic, yet never is the mechanical precision lost for an
instant.

An enthusiastic review in *The Morning Post* (18 April 1838) echoed
the earlier observation of Wagner:

We had almost forgotten to notice the superior talent of STRAUSS himself
on the violin; he performs with peculiar energy, and imparts much of his own
spirit to his band . . .

*Term referring to a conductor in charge of his own orchestra.

29

This first concert, nevertheless, was poorly attended, a circumstance resulting from the combined effects of inclement weather, inadequate advertising, a competing attraction at the Opera and the high entrance fee of 10s. 6d, deemed to be 'ridiculous' (and subsequently reduced).

Further concerts took place daily, not only at Hanover Square but also at Willis's Rooms in St James's and at two establishments in Bishopsgate Street – the London Tavern and the City of London Tavern. The performances were now attracting packed houses comprising 'the nobility, gentry and public'. The programmes varied little in their actual content; there was always a selection of Strauss's own waltzes, potpourris and galops, alongside overtures and other operatic pieces by composers such as Auber, Bellini, Hérold and Meyerbeer. From its earliest days the Strauss Orchestra had performed an important cultural rôle, that of introducing works by the classical masters to a public which would not otherwise have troubled to hear them.

A call by *The Morning Post* (30 April 1838) for Strauss 'to gratify the love of dancing inherent in humanity' was answered by his engagement for a series of Almack's Subscription Balls at Willis's Rooms, for which he received a total fee of 600 guineas. At Almack's he encountered some criticism on the grounds of 'being too noisy for the room, and too quick for English dancing' (*Court Journal*, 19 May 1838).

Between 17 April and 28 July Strauss and his band gave a total of seventy-nine London performances, not all of them noted in the diary of Johann Thyam, a clarinettist in Strauss's orchestra, whose records have provided the basis for past biographers. An analysis of these appearances reveals 8 State Balls and dinner parties at Buckingham Palace attended by Queen Victoria; 6 Almack's Subscription Balls at Willis's Rooms; 19 private balls and concerts hosted by members of the nobility, including the Dukes of Wellington, Devonshire, Cambridge, Buccleuch and Sutherland, the Ambassadors Extraordinary of Austria and France, the Countess of Cadogan and Mrs Lionel de Rothschild; 2 public balls; 2 charity concerts at the Royal Beaulah Spa, Norwood; 39 public concerts of his own and 3 major concerts shared with such eminent artists as the singers Grisi, Persiani, Albertazzi, Rubini, Tamburini and Lablache, and the conductor Michael Costa. On 23 May an audience attending a concert by the pianist Ignaz Moscheles witnessed a performance of Beethoven's *Choral Symphony*, with musicians from the Philharmonic, Italian Opera and Royal Academy Orchestras, assisted, according to *The Morning Post* (19 May 1838), 'by Strauss's celebrated brass instruments and a chorus of sixty voices'.

For Strauss, the highlight of his stay in London must surely have been the occasions on which he and his band played before the young Victoria at the new Buckingham Palace. It was at the first of these, the opening State Ball of the season, on 10 May, that Johann introduced his waltz novelty, entitled *Hommage à la Reine d'Angleterre* (Homage to the Queen of England)★, which he dedicated to the as yet uncrowned monarch. The composition features Arne's *Rule Britannia* in its march-like Introduction and concludes with a quotation from *God Save the Queen* in waltz tempo. *The Times* (12 May 1838) reported that 'this new set of waltzes . . . were much admired by Her Majesty', and thereafter Strauss featured the piece both at the Palace and elsewhere.

Johann had not been long in London before he found himself the defendant in a court case brought by one George Street, the keeper of a lodging house and hotel in Ryder's Court, Leicester Square. Unable to offer sufficient accommodation for Strauss and his twenty-seven musicians, Street arranged alternative lodgings for some of them. Dissatisfied with the uncleanliness, bad food and the high price, Strauss and his band departed without due notice. The jury found in favour of the plaintiff, and Strauss was ordered to pay, on top of £27 16s to Street, court costs amounting to £140. Strauss was unable to find this sum, having already been robbed of £97 by a thieving London hotel servant, and only the ready surety offered by the London music publisher Robert Cocks – in return for the right to publish Strauss's waltzes in Britain – removed the burden of debt from his shoulders.

During his residence in London, Strauss made a five-day visit to Cheltenham and Bath, a precursor of the six-week provincial tour of Britain he was to begin on 30 July, taking him as far afield as Dublin ('I have received a very remunerative invitation') and Ryde, Isle of Wight. On 13 September he left London to fulfil engagements in France, proposing also to travel on to Milan for the coronation of the Austrian Emperor, Ferdinand I, as King of Lombardy. The latter plan was not realized; in the event, it was not Strauss but Joseph Lanner, making one of his rare journeys outside Austria, who secured the honour of conducting at the various attendant functions.

Strauss had been well satisfied with his tour of Britain, and wrote of it on 15 September from Boulogne, in a letter to Adolf Müller senior:

. . . I found myself in a different town almost daily, as one may travel here exceedingly quickly by virtue of the good horses and excellent roads. In particular, of great advantage to the traveller are the railways, which mode of transport I have used extensively, e.g. in Liverpool, Manchester, Birmingham, etc . . . The cost of travelling with 28 persons in England, largely by express coach, to lodge in hotels and to fulfil all possible requirements in a respectable manner, reaches the unbelievable . . .

So outstanding was the success of this tour that, hardly having landed in France, Johann received an invitation to return once again to England. This he accepted, and on 26 September arrived in Southampton to continue his concert tour of Britain for a further nine weeks. During the course of his time in England, Ireland and Scotland

*Published by Haslinger in Vienna (1838) as *Huldigung der Königin Victoria von Grossbritannien, Walzer* op.103.

he gave performances in thirty-one separate towns, making return visits to several venues.

In November, Strauss was reported to be suffering from 'illness of a serious character' – severe shivering fits, dry cough and chest pains – and this forced him to postpone concerts in Derby and Leicester. His indisposition was not helped by a Derbyshire doctor, who prescribed an exceedingly strong dose of opium, as a result of which Johann 'was almost relieved of all earthly sufferings'. When the rescheduled concerts eventually took place in Derby and Leicester (28 and 30 November respectively), Strauss was too unwell to complete more than half of each programme and relinquished his leadership to an assistant. An invalid, he left England on 2 December with his orchestra and crossed to Calais on the homeward journey to Vienna. In Calais he felt his strength sufficiently restored to give a farewell concert in the rooms of the Philharmonic Society, but he collapsed and was carried from the platform. Between bouts of delirium he was brought via Paris, Strasbourg, Stuttgart, Ulm, Munich and Linz to Vienna, which he reached only three days before Christmas 1838 – almost fifteen months after his departure. The *Theaterzeitung* reported: 'Strauss has at last arrived in Vienna, but suffering so much that it will be a considerable time before he is fully recovered . . . ' Two weeks later, on 13 January 1839, though still ailing, Johann made his reappearance before the Viennese public at a ball in the Sperl with a new waltz, given the heartfelt title: *Freuden-Grüsse (Motto: Überall gut – in der Heimath am besten)* op.105 – Joyful Greetings (Motto: Good everywhere – best at home).

For most of 1839 Strauss contented himself with the round of balls and concerts in Vienna, only leaving his native city for a lightning visit to Brünn (Brno). He remained in Vienna throughout 1840. In contrast to the grand tours of 1834–8, the years 1841 to 1847 were characterized by a number of much shorter guest appearances in Austria, Hungary, Austrian Silesia, Saxony, Prussia and Germany, the greater part of each year being devoted to engagements in his native Vienna.

In 1843, at the height of his career, Strauss's former friend and rival, Joseph Lanner, succumbed to a typhus infection and died on Good Friday, 14 April. At his funeral two days later, with Strauss at the head of the 1st Citizens' Regiment band, 20,000 Viennese paid their last respects to 'the Father of the Viennese Waltz'. Now unopposed, Strauss asserted his position as undisputed 'Waltz King' with the first performance of his masterly waltz *Loreley-Rhein-Klänge* op.154 (Echoes of the Rhine Lorelei), written for a children's charity promenade festival on the Wasserglacis on 19 August that year, and attended by an audience of 3500.

But the elder Johann was quite unaware that, from within the Hirschenhaus, a new and unexpected rival was soon to emerge – a rival who was not just to challenge but eventually to eclipse him.

Lithograph of Joseph Lanner, by Gutsch and Rupp.

Johann Strauss I in 1829, at the age of twenty-five. The portrait, by Josef
Kriehuber, adorns the title page of the composer's *Des Verfassers beste Laune.*
Charmant-Walzer op.31, published by Tobias Haslinger.

Map of Vienna in 1833, showing the inner city surrounded by a solid ring of bastions and defensive city walls. Beyond the broad green belt of the Glacis can be seen the suburbs of Vienna. Published by Baldwin & Cradock, London.

DER OBERE

PRATER

SCALES

English

Wien

French

VIENNA
(WIEN)

Published under the Superintendence of the Society for the
Diffusion of Useful Knowledge

NOTE

Br Brucke	Bridge	Hof	Belonging to the Court
Eng Englische	English	K K Königlich Samm	Royal Imperial
Font Fontaine	Fountain	Mkt Market	Market
Gas Gasse	Street	Neu Neuer	New
Gart Garten	Garden or Park	Pl Platz	Place or Square
Gr Grosse	Great	St Strasse	Street or Road
H Haus	House	Thor	Tower

The City
has 11 Gates Thorn and 1317 Houses
The Suburbs
are divided into 34 Gemeinde with
38 Barriers Linienthore containing
6557 Houses Total population 350000

Matzleinsdorfer
Linie

Published by Baldwin & Cradock, 47 Paternoster Row 1833.

Engraved & Printed by J. Cleghorn

The tavern 'Zum heiligen Florian' at No.7 Flossgasse, Leopoldstadt, birthplace of Johann Strauss I.

Page from the full score of an unpublished work by Joseph Lanner, in the composer's hand. Like Haydn, Lanner began each new composition by writing the words *Mit Gott* (With God) in the top right corner of the first page.

Strauss father and Lanner vied with each other to present spectacular and lavishly lit open-air musical entertainments, such as that pictured above. Presented by Strauss on 21 July 1834, with gas lighting displays by Carl F. Hirsch, it was entitled 'Eine Nacht in Venedig' (A Night in Venice).

Title page from a pianoforte anthology published by Tobias Haslinger. Vienna, in 1830. The lithograph depicts the newly opened Tivoli amusement park on the Grüner Berg, in the Viennese suburb of Meidling, where Johann Strauss father and son both performed. Clearly shown is the primitive 'roller-coaster' – an attraction which lives on in the title of the elder Strauss's waltz, *Tivoli-Rutsch* op.39 (Tivoli-Slide).

Lithograph from the outer cover of Joseph Lanner's *Paradies-Soirée-Walzer* op.52 (1831). The Paradise Garden, shown here with Corti's Coffee Salon, adjoined the Vienna Volksgarten and was a popular rendezvous for the aristocracy and middle-classes in the early 1800s. Joseph Lanner performed here frequently from 1834 onwards. In 1874 the new Hof–Burgtheater was erected on the site.

One of the lavish ballrooms in the 'Sperl'. The orchestra is located at the far end of the room. Watercolour by Gustav Zafourek.

The Africa Room – one of several halls devoted to different parts of the world in the 'Neue Elysium'. This innovative and popular Viennese establishment was constructed in 1840 in the underground wine cellars of a former Jesuit monastery.

Woodcut of a ball in the Sofienbad–Saal, Vienna, after a drawing by Franz Kollarz, circa 1855. All the professional musicians in the Strauss family, from Johann I to Eduard II, conducted in this resplendent ballroom. The Sofienbad-Saal is one of several rooms in the Sofiensäle building, which is used today for balls, conferences and recording sessions.

WIEN,

Eigenthum und Verlag der k.k.Hof-u.priv.Kunst-u.Musikalienhandlung
des Carl Haslinger, q.m Tobias.

Pen and ink drawing by Berndt of Johann Strauss I, showing the composer's
facsimile autograph as k. k. Hofball-Musikdirektor.

Advertisement for a concert by Strauss father at the Hanover Square Rooms, London, during his visit to Britain in 1838.

Title page of the original pianoforte edition of Johann Strauss I's *Radetzky-Marsch* op.228, published by Haslinger, Vienna, in 1848.

Autograph musical quotation by Johann Strauss I from his *Fortuna-Polka* op.219 (1848).

The 'Hirschenhaus', home of the Strausses from 1833 to 1886.

Mother Anna Strauss, photographed in 1869.

The original gravestones of Joseph Lanner and Johann Strauss father in the Strauss-Lanner Park, Döbling, formerly the old Döbling Cemetery. In 1904 the composers' remains were transferred to graves of honour in Vienna's Central Cemetery (Zentralfriedhof).

Birthplace of Johann Strauss II at No. 15 Lerchenfelderstrasse, demolished in 1890. Pen and ink sketch by Ludwig Wegmann.

'Am Dreimarkstein No. 13', Salmannsdorf, on the edge of the Vienna Woods. Here, in the summer home of his maternal grandparents, the 6-year-old Johann Strauss II composed his first waltz.

Johann II's sketch (1898) for his nephew, Hans Simon, of his first waltz, published in 1881 as *Erster Gedanke* (First Thought). According to Strauss's second wife, Lili, the piece was originally notated by mother Anna Strauss in August 1831, but some musicologists now suggest the date August 1832. (Courtesy of Hedi and Peter Stadlen, London)

Interior of Dommayer's Casino in Hietzing, venue of the younger Johann's début in 1844. On the right of the photograph is the area occupied by the orchestra. The building was demolished in 1907.

The Polka. Viennese lithograph circa 1860.

Page from the younger Johann's sketchbook from the 1870s and 1880s. Throughout his life Strauss often called upon ideas jotted in such books, the earliest dating from August 1843. (Courtesy of the Wiener Stadt- und Landesbibliothek)

4

Now the brat Johann also intends to write waltzes, although he has not got a clue about them – and even for me, being the first in my field, it is terribly difficult to create something new . . .

(Remark attributed to Johann Strauss father)

JOHANN Strauss the Elder was adamant that his sons should not pursue musical careers, a view at first shared by mother Anna. There is no evidence to suggest that he feared family competition; rather his standpoint reflected the experience of a man who knew intimately the hardship and insecurity of his profession. Accordingly, in autumn 1841, after successfully graduating from the respected Vienna Schottengymnasium (where, as choristers of St Leopold's Church, they were exempted from school fees during their last two years), the younger Johann and Josef were entered as students in the Commercial Studies Department of the Polytechnic Institute of Vienna (then still called the Technische Hochschule). Contrary to reports, Johann junior took his studies seriously and was awarded First Class with Distinction in his bookkeeping examination. Nevertheless, he refused private tuition to prepare him for the career in banking which his father had planned for him. While Josef remained until 1846 to complete his studies in technical drawing, mathematics and mechanical engineering, Johann left after the 1841-2 academic year, having resolved to devote himself to music. He recognized that a period of intensive musical study lay ahead of him, a prerequisite for the licence required before he could perform publicly as a music-director. In later years, the younger Johann recalled that Strauss father had happily allowed his two eldest sons to learn the piano but,

he thought that we were just tinkling at the keys in an amateurish fashion. We alone worked passionately at it, and I can honestly say that we were both accomplished pianists. Of this he had no inkling. The rehearsals for his concerts were held at our home. We boys paid close attention to every note, we familiarized ourselves with his style and then played what we had heard straight off, exactly in his spirited manner. He was our ideal. We often received invitations to visit families . . . and would play from memory, and to great applause, our father's compositions.

33

One fine day, an acquaintance congratulated him – it was the publisher Haslinger – on our success. He was not a little astonished. 'The boys will come here!' he decreed abruptly. We crept with foreboding into our father's room. In a few brief words he informed us of what he had heard, and ordered us to play for him. He had an upright piano, which was common at that time. Pepi [Josef] explained that we could not possibly play on such an instrument. 'What?' he exclaimed. 'You can't play on that? All right then! We'll have the grand piano from the apartment here!' The grand piano was brought in, and we played with style; we brought out all the instrumentation. Smiling, our father heard us through, and one could perceive the pleasure and emotion in his face. 'Boys, you play as well as anyone!' That was all he said, but as a reward both of us received a beautiful burnouse.

Johann father's affair with Emilie seriously reduced the flow of income to his legitimate dependants. Even while he was abroad, Johann, using his friend Adolf Müller as intermediary, clandestinely sent substantial sums of money to his common-law family. Moreover, in his will (10 October 1847) Strauss bequeathed his estate to Emilie and their five surviving children, stipulating that 'My children from my marriage with Anna Strauss, neé Streim, are to be restricted to their legal portion'. Despite Anna's attempts (in the name of her sons) to contest the will, it was upheld, leaving Johann II, Josef, Anna, Therese and Eduard Strauss to share a meagre 1549 gulden (about £130 sterling, today equivalent to £3325). By the time the estate was eventually divided in 1852, Emilie and her children fared even worse.

During the period of her husband's infidelity, Anna, with commendable foresight, strove to ensure that her eldest son should be fully prepared for his rôle as the family breadwinner. To the best of her ability she fostered his love of music and secretly made arrangements for him to receive violin lessons from Franz Amon, first violinist in her husband's own orchestra. Johann II recollected:

In order to be able to pay my teacher, I gave piano lessons to the son of a master-tailor in the Leopoldstadt, and to a young girl aged between 13 and 14 – Csihak was her name; she lived with her parents in the Hirschenhaus . . . I received sixty kreuzer an hour, with which I paid for my violin tuition. Now, my teacher said to me . . . I ought to practise in front of a mirror in order to grow accustomed to an elegant bearing and beautiful bowing technique, since for one who is going to be on show elegance of appearance is essential. Now, I followed these teachings faithfully. One fine day I was again standing in front of the mirror fiddling away when the door opened, and in walked my father. 'What?' he shouted, 'you play the violin?' – He had no idea of this. By chance he had come upon the fact that I wanted to become a professional musician. There was a violent and unpleasant scene. My father wanted to know nothing of my plans.

Supported by his mother, the younger Johann began his instruction in harmony and counterpoint, initially with the theorist Professor

Joachim Hoffmann, owner of a private music school. Thereafter, Johann continued these studies under the respected composer Joseph Drechsler, at that time organist and Regenschori at the church 'Am Hof' and professor at the k.k. (Imperial-Royal) Normal Hauptschule. An exercise in harmony for four voices by the young Strauss (the oldest extant notes in his own hand) and a magnificent gradual, *Tu qui regis totum orbem*, for four vocal parts and wind accompaniment, date from this time.

The youngster also received lessons in his chosen instrument from the violin teacher Anton Kohlmann, ballet *répétiteur* at the Vienna Court Opera. With excellent testimonials from both Drechsler and Kohlmann, the 'modest, unpretentious, truly respectably educated young man' approached the Viennese authorities on 3 August 1844:

I intend to play with an orchestra of twelve to fifteen players in restaurants and, indeed, at Dommayer's in Hietzing who has already assured me that I can hold musical entertainments there as soon as my orchestra is in order. I have not yet determined the remaining venues, but I believe that I will receive sufficient occupation and income . . . I would mention that apart from dance-music items I will also perform opera pieces and concert works, as and when they are demanded.

The municipal council granted the request on 5 September, and the young Strauss immediately set about forming his orchestra from the work-hungry musicians who frequented the Viennese tavern 'Zur Stadt Belgrad'. On 8 October 1844 'Herr Kapellmeister Johann Strauss' drew up a carefully worded one-year contract with twenty-four musicians, detailing the rights and obligations of the parties under eight separate sections, including punctuality and discipline at rehearsals and performances, careful handling of instruments and music, illness, prohibition of substitutes and settlement of disputes.

Only a week after Johann had submitted his application to the authorities, Anna Strauss instituted proceedings for divorce from her husband. Distressed by his parents' deteriorating relationship, the 18-year-old Kapellmeister poured out his own feelings in a heartfelt letter to his 'dearly beloved father', whom he still idolized:

Realizing that the loving son would lack the strength and determination to face up to his dear father in this tug-of-war of the heart . . ., after I had exerted all the strength of my heart and mind regarding the step which is so important and so decisive for the future of my mother, and since the development of my meagre talents is due, next to Mother Nature, to my own Mother who, in view of the present unhappy situation, which could only be improved by you, would otherwise be left without protection and assistance . . . I have decided to let my poor ability in my chosen profession demonstrate my small thanks to her. Neither you, dear father, nor the world, if they consider it carefully, will disapprove of this, my immutable resolve, to remain at the side of my mother.

35

On 10 October 1844 the *Wiener Zeitung*, confirming earlier press reports, carried the following historic announcement:

[14161] **Einladung**
zur
Soirée dansante
welche Dinstag am **15. October 1844**,
selbst bey ungünstiger Witterung in
Dommayer's Casino
in Hietzing Statt finden wird.
Johann Strauss
(S o h n),
wird die Ehre haben, zum ersten Mahle sein eigenes Orchester-Personale zu dirigiren, und nebst verschiedenen Ouverturen und Opern-Piecen, auch mehrere seiner eigenen Compositionen vorzutragen. — Der Gunst und Huld des hochverehrten Publicums empfiehlt sich ergebenst
Johann Strauß jun.
Eintrittskarten zu 20 kr. CM. sind in der k. k. Hof-Musikalienhandlung des Pietro Mechetti und Comp, in Stierböck's Kaffehhaus in der Jägerzeil, in Säbesam's und in Puth's Kaffehhäusern in Mariahilf zu bekommen. Eintrittspreis an der Cassa 30 kr. CM. Anfang um 6 Uhr.

On the day before this début, the newspaper *Der Humorist* commented prophetically:

If it is true that the apple never falls far from the tree, then the friends of dance and the manufacturers of shoe leather can have great hopes for this heir presumptive to the waltz-throne. May the bow of the father hover protectively over the violin of the son!

Although the event was advertised as a 'Soirée dansante', such was the overwhelming demand for tickets that the attendance precluded any possibility of dancing. Indeed, the journalist Dr Franz Wiest reported in *Der Wanderer* (19 October) that 'to get a seat at 7 o'clock was almost as difficult as getting a seat in the Upper House of the English Parliament'. Johann Nepomuk Vogl, in the *Österreichische Morgenblatt* (19 October) concluded that 'it was possible only for a fanatical enthusiast to put up with the scuffling, the pushing and being trodden upon in this heat for several hours'.

An exact record of the pieces played at Johann's début may never be fully ascertained; no newspaper carried the full programme, and a souvenir copy of the original, presented to Strauss on his 50th Jubilee in 1894, has since disappeared. Nevertheless, a study of press coverage, considered alongside the usual format of such entertainments, makes it possible to reconstruct the order of music with a fair degree of certainty.

1. Overture: *La Muette de Portici* (Auber)

Translation of the *Wiener Zeitung* (10 October 1844) advertisement for
Johann Strauss II's public début at Dommayer's Casino, Hietzing. (See
opposite page)

2. Cavatina: *Robert le Diable* (Meyerbeer)
3. *Gunstwerber Walzer* (op.4) (Wooers of Favour)
   (Johann Strauss II)
4. Overture: *La Sirène* (Auber)
5. *Loreley-Rhein-Klänge, Walzer*, op.154 (Johann Strauss I)
6. ?
7. *Herzenslust Polka* (op.3) (Heart's Content) (Johann Strauss II)

INTERVAL

8. Overture: *Ein Sommernachtstraum* (Franz von Suppé)
9. *Debut – Quadrille* (op.2) (Johann Strauss II)
10. (Possibly an operatic piece, or a Strauss father work, though
    not a waltz)
11. *Sinngedichte Walzer* (op.1) (Epigrams) (Johann Strauss II)

ENCORES

Of that most persistent of stories concerning the attempted
disruption of the début by supporters of Strauss father, there is no
substantiating evidence. Indeed, not one journalist noted any disturbance – but reporting on a concert by the conductor/composer Joseph

A. Adam in the Casino Zögernitz the previous Sunday (13 October), at which Herr Adam performed his latest waltz, entitled *Gunstbewerber*, *Der Wanderer* condemned the presence of a hired claque. One can only suggest that the marked similarity of waltz title and proximity of performance dates led to confusion of the events, and thence to the legend.

Press reports were unanimous, both in their praise of 'Strauss junior' and in their conviction that they had witnessed a truly historic musical event at Dommayer's:

The young leader . . . was greeted on his appearance with thunderous signs of kindness and encouragement, and his [own] compositions were all encored several times, an honour which was given to '*Sinngedichte*' perhaps five times. All the compositions are written in that characteristic style which makes Strauss dance-tunes so irresistible and popular, and also with regard to the impressive instrumentation the influence of his father is not to be overlooked . . . A very favourable effect was created when the son played the very popular *Lurley Walzer* [sic] by his father, by which he gave expression not only to his filial admiration but also to his strivings to take his father's long-preserved mastery as his example. This waltz also had to be repeated three times.

(*Wiener Allgemeine Theaterzeitung*, 17 October 1844)

Der Wanderer (17 October) considered that 'Strauss's own compositions achieved the greatest success . . . he ought to be well known, even abroad, in a short time', while in the same paper two days later Dr Franz Wiest noted in a lengthy report the effect of Strauss's music as it 'flashes through us electrically from head to little toe . . . he is working up there, spraying sparks like a galvanic battery'. He continued:

It is seldom that gifts and talents of the father are passed on to the sons, but of Strauss son one can really say: *He is a waltz incarnate!* Not that the two waltz pieces which Strauss son performed before us today, '*Gunstwerber*' and '*Sinngedichte*', distinguished themselves by their brilliant originality of thought, but they vibrate with that rhythmical flourish, and glow with that characteristic Viennese lightheartedness which, with the exception of Strauss father, no living waltz composer can create . . . Strauss son, at the age of twenty-one [sic] has learned more as a composer and conductor than Strauss father could have gained in twenty-one years in his field. But this should not, and cannot, be a reproach – this is nothing more than a blessing of progress . . . Triumph, my Strauss son, to be only twenty-one years old, and already to have done so much for eternity in waltz and quadrille! Triumph, my Vienna, which now has a Strauss father and a Strauss son in its midst . . . Good night *Lanner*! Good Evening *Strauss father*! Good Morning *Strauss son*!

And what of Strauss father's reaction to his son's début? Although not known to have been performing elsewhere that evening, the elder Johann seems not to have attended Dommayer's, since his presence there would surely have been reported. Doubtless, however, either he or his publisher, Haslinger, would have secured the services of their own eyewitness, probably Carl Friedrich 'Lamperl' Hirsch, lighting specialist of innumerable Strauss and Lanner outdoor festivals. Strauss father was justifiably angered by his son's blatant defiance of paternal authority and, perhaps as a direct result of Ferdinand Dommayer's willing participation in the début, was himself never again to play at the Hietzing establishment – scene of so many of his own early triumphs.

During the remainder of 1844 Johann junior continued his engagements at Dommayer's as well as performing at such venues as Lindenbauer's Casino in Simmering and the Sträussel-Säle in the Theater in der Josefstadt. The young composer's gift for orchestration, already noted in the début night reviews, also drew comment from the visiting pianist Ignaz Moscheles:

I heard him perform at Domeyers [sic] . . . and his Waltzes, Quadrilles and Polkas delighted me no less for their effective instrumentation as well as for their spririted performance. They perform also Overtures of Cherubini, Weber, Mozart in the very best style.

(Letter, dated 27 December 1844)

Yet if Johann II had placed undue confidence in the pronouncement by *Der Humorist* (21 October) that 'He has made his name', this was to be dispelled with the coming of the 1845 Carnival. Strauss father's popularity continued undiminished, despite the success of his son and public knowledge of Anna's divorce action. Since Vienna's major entertainment establishments already had contracts with the elder Johann, the younger was unable to consolidate the whirlwind success of his début in his native city – a situation which was to persist until after his father's untimely death in 1849, when the various managements gradually transferred their contracts from father to son. In the meantime, with the most prestigious engagements, including those at Court, securely in the hands of Johann senior and certain of his contemporaries, only the smaller venues offered the newcomer promise of employment. Indeed, for a time there remained the threat that Strauss son's bold venture might still fail. Aware that his greatest support was to be found in youthful Viennese society, especially that of the minority communities – the Bohemians, Serbians and Slavs – the younger Johann set about wooing this sector with appropriately titled compositions such as the waltzes *Die jungen Wiener* op.7 (The young Viennese) and *Jugend-Träume* op.12 (Youthful Dreams), the *Czechen-Polka* op.13 and the *Serben-Quadrille* op.14.

The first evidence of 'official' recognition for the young Strauss came in 1845 when he was called upon to accept the honorary position of Kapellmeister* of the 2nd Vienna Citizens' Regiment, a post which had remained vacant since the death of Joseph Lanner two years earlier. The function of the regiment, more social than military, was to appear at numerous parades and festive occasions held in the city,

*The title here means 'Bandmaster'.

and since Strauss father had been appointed Kapellmeister of the 1st Vienna Citizens' Regiment (in 1832) the honour can only have served to heighten the rivalry between father and son.

Since 1831 both Strauss father and Joseph Lanner had been entrusted with conducting ball-music at Court; with Lanner's death in 1843 the privilege passed to Strauss alone. For a number of years the latter had endeavoured to obtain a closer commitment at Court, and on 7 January 1846 had written requesting the Austrian Emperor, Ferdinand, to confer upon him 'the highest honour of being allowed to carry the title of "k.k. Hofball-Musik-Direktor"' (Director of Music for the Imperial-Royal Court Balls). On 24 January this request was granted, 'with the condition that there is no salary or emolument connected with this title, nor does it confer exclusive right to the assumption and leadership of the music for the Court- or Chamber-Balls'. This purely honorary title, specifically created for Strauss father, was to remain exclusively within the Strauss family until relinquished by Eduard Strauss in 1901 on the grounds of 'advanced years and his state of health', whereupon it passed to the last of the great k.k. Hofballmusik-Direktors, the Viennese conductor/composer Carl Michael Ziehrer.

The Carnival of 1846 offered little encouragement to the younger Johann, and he was forced to seek orchestral engagements outside Vienna in order to earn a living. His first excursion took him to Graz, Ungarisch-Altenberg and Pest-Ofen,* while in 1847–8 he undertook a six-month tour with his orchestra through Hungary and Siebenbürgenland to Bucharest and Wallachia. Ambitious plans to proceed to Constantinople were later abandoned. His success was considerable, and the folk-music of these other nations left their impressions in such pieces as the waltz *Klänge aus der Walachei* op.50 (1848). During the same period, Strauss father was also touring with his own orchestra: in 1846 he visited Brünn, Breslau and Ratibor, and in 1847 Hamburg, Hanover and Berlin.

1847 was an important year for Johann II, marking the beginning of his long and fruitful affiliation with the influential Wiener Männergesang-Verein (Vienna Men's Choral Association), for whom he was to create a total of nine choral compositions – six waltzes, two polkas and a march, including such evergreens as the waltzes *An der schönen blauen Donau* (By the beautiful blue Danube) and *Wein, Weib und Gesang!* (Wine, Woman and Song!). It was the purely orchestral waltz *Sängerfahrten* op. 41, however, which Johann dedicated to the Wiener Männergesang-Verein in 1847 – the 'Singers' Journeys' of the title being the Association's name for its artistic tours. To the dedicatees of his graceful waltz, Strauss wrote on 9 June 1847:

If the outcome of my meagre talent gives you only a part of the pleasure that your immense vigour has given to me, then it will find its most handsome reward therein.

*From 1872 known as Budapest.

40

5

The carnival is over, the fast has begun, the violins are silent and the time of severity is plainly upon us.

(*Der Humorist*, 9 March 1848, concluding its
report on the 1848 Vienna Carnival)

ON 24 FEBRUARY 1848 the beginnings of the European bourgeois revolution broke out in Paris and spread swiftly to Hungary and Prague. On 13 March they flared in Vienna as a spontaneous revolt against the despised police state of the Austrian Chancellor, Prince Clemens von Metternich. Students and workers joined forces in the streets, and soldiers were deployed against the crowds. Metternich resigned, and fled the capital. The Vienna Citizens' Regiments were disbanded and in their place appeared the National Guard and the revolutionary students' Academic Legion. Emperor Ferdinand I granted the abolition of censorship and the freedom of the press, and promised a formal constitution.

In May, however, a fresh revolutionary upsurge in Vienna led to further street battles, the erection of barricades and the flight of the Emperor and his family. There followed the bloody October revolution: on the 31st of that month, after a full-scale bombardment, Vienna finally surrendered unconditionally to the Imperial forces commanded by Windischgrätz, Jellačić and Radetzky. The Revolutionary leaders were imprisoned and executed, and in late autumn the National Guard was prohibited.

Johann II wrote that this era of revolution 'had an alarming effect upon my father's spirit: this artistic soul did not feel at ease amid the noise of these days . . . He held himself distant from the questions of the day, and hoped that the future would bring a return to an epoch which was more favourable to his art'.

During the Carnival of 1848, immediately prior to the March revolution, Johann senior's creativity had reached a pinnacle, and waltzes like *Die Adepten* op. 216, *Amphion-Klänge* op. 224 and *Aether-Träume* op. 225 won him recognition from even the most hard-line opponents of his musical style. Yet despite wishing to hold himself 'distant', Strauss father could not ignore the changing times, and produced a *Marsch der Studenten-Legion* op. 223 (March of the Student-

41

Legion), a *Freiheits-Marsch* op.226 (Freedom March) and a *Marsch des einigen Deutschlands* op.227 (March of a unified Germany), the last commemorating the May meeting of the German National Congress. It was in August 1848 that he composed the march which was to bring him immortality – a work which, at one and the same time, branded him inextricably as a proponent of the established monarchy while alienating him from pro–Revolutionary sympathizers. Led by the 82-year-old Commander-in-Chief of the Austrian Army, Field-Marshal Johann Josef Wenzel, Count Radetzky von Radetz, the Imperial Habsburg troops routed the Italian forces at Custozza in July 1848. To mark this decisive conquest, a 'Grand Impressive Victory Festival, with Allegorical and Symbolic Representation and Exceptional Illumination, in Honour of our Courageous Army in Italy, and for the Benefit of the Wounded Soldiers' was organized for 31 August on the Vienna Wasserglacis.★ Strauss father was commissioned to provide a new composition for the festivities and, aided by Philipp Fahrbach senior, obliged with the *Radetzky-Marsch* (op.228). The piece, which incorporates two Viennese folk-songs, was reportedly completed in just two hours, and was resoundingly acclaimed.

In contrast to his father, Johann II supported with youthful conviction the revolutionary elements in Vienna. Returning from his orchestral tour in May 1848 he became Kapellmeister of the recently formed National Guard in the Leopoldstadt suburb of the city, and for 'the Gospel of Liberty' wrote such pieces as the *Revolutions-Marsch* op.54 and the waltzes *Freiheits-Lieder* op.52 (Songs of Freedom) – originally entitled *Barrikaden-Lieder* (Songs of the Barricades) – and *Burschen-Lieder* op.55 (Students' Songs). He acceded to the wishes of the students to set to music J. H. Hirschfeld's poem *Freiheitslied*, 'because, since my return to my liberated country, which is now twice as dear to me, I have been thinking of expressing my admiration and respect for the students, our champions of liberty . . .', and assigned the resulting *Studenten-Marsch* op.56 to the Academic Legion. His humorous 'joke polka', *Liguorianer-Seufzer* op.57 (Liguorian Sighs) – its caterwauling Trio mocking the hated pro-Metternich religious order of Liguorians (Redemptorists), who had been temporarily expelled from Vienna with the onset of revolution – caused such a sensation in the city that the censor immediately confiscated its printed edition.

On 15 August Johann junior travelled with his orchestra to Brünn to take part in a large festival, for which he wrote his *Brünner Nationalgarde-Marsch* op.58. On 6 December 1848 he was interrogated by the police in Vienna for having played the French revolutionary song *La Marseillaise* at 'Zum grünen Tor' three days earlier.

★Today occupied by the gardens of the Stadtpark (opened in 1862), the Wasserglacis was part of the broad tract of open land (the Glacis) once encircling the inner city of Vienna.

In his defence, the young Kapellmeister stated that,

with regard to political or nationalistic interests I am indifferent which pieces I am called upon to play. Nevertheless, my political tact tells me that in these highly charged times . . . any piece is to be avoided which could provoke any kind of political upset, or could touch national sympathies . . . However, there are places where it is not possible to side-step sufficiently in this respect, and if one did not satisfy the demands of the audience, it is to be feared that one might provoke a riot.

He added that he had only bowed to pressure to play *La Marseillaise* when his refusal threatened a disturbance, and that 'if a ban on these cases is to be applied strictly, then as music-directors we must be protected by a guard from insults and outrages, because of our refusal to play this or that piece . . .'

The case against Strauss was apparently dismissed. That month, Austria welcomed a new ruler. In the shadow of the October revolution Emperor Ferdinand had abdicated and, on 2 December 1848 at Olmütz, his 18-year-old nephew, Franz Joseph I, began a reign which was to span almost sixty-eight years.

The Vienna Fasching of 1849 was lacklustre, and the people restless. During January, Strauss father made a tour of Prague and Olmütz with his orchestra before returning to his native city to fulfil engagements at the Sperl and in the Volksgarten. He yearned to embark upon another extensive tour – his new waltz, performed in the Sofiensaal on 13 February, foretold as much: *Des Wanderers Lebewohl* op.237 (The Wanderer's Farewell). On 6 March he left Vienna and travelled first to Germany. Journeying by steamship and coach he gave concerts in Munich, Ulm, Augsburg, Stuttgart, Heidelberg, Heilbronn, Mannheim, Frankfurt-am-Main, Mainz, Koblenz, Bonn, Cologne and Aachen. With his orchestra of thirty-two men, he was obliged 'for reasons of cost, to avoid any lengthy stay without performances' (Letter, 20 March 1849). In many towns, where news of his imperialistic *Radetzky-Marsch* had preceded him, there were unpleasant scenes as rebellious students decried him as a 'black and yellow' (the Habsburg colours) reactionary. In Brussels his reception was considerably more enthusiastic. From here he travelled to Antwerp and Ostend. As on previous tours, Strauss contacted music publishers and dealers, musicians and booksellers, shortly in advance of his arrival, with regard to arranging accommodation, concert venues and advertising. From Louvain he wrote on 16 April to the London music publisher Robert Cocks, requesting him to procure 'decent lodgings'; on the night of 21 April Strauss and his band crossed to England, where eleven years earlier they had experienced such triumphant acclaim. Here, as before, he hurled himself into a hectic round of engagements. Reporting on Johann's second concert at the Hanover Square Rooms, *The Morning Post* (26 April) observed:

If the revolutionary mania of Austria has unsettled Germany, at least England has no reason to lament the political mischief; for no doubt to this circumstance are we indebted for [Strauss's] presence amongst us . . . Time has dealt kindly with him, for his broad, honest Teutonic face is still full of intelligence, and his fire and energy have not a jot abated.

Strauss brought his English audiences a number of new compositions, and it was at a State Ball at Buckingham Palace on 30 April, before 1600 guests, that he introduced his *Alice-Polka* op.238, written in honour of Queen Victoria's six-year-old daughter. On 14 May Strauss gave the first of two 'Grand vocal and instrumental concerts' at London's Exeter Hall (for which he wrote his *Exeter-Polka* op.249) and for the first time shared the spotlight with a fellow Viennese, making her first visit to England, Jetty Treffz. 'A handsome woman, with a ripe mezzo-soprano voice, a charming style, and great dramatic feeling' (*The Morning Post*, 3 May), Jetty also had the honour of performing before Victoria and Albert at Buckingham Palace, and her reception in London was tremendous. Her singing of *Trab, trab, trab* (Kücken), *I'm a merry Zingara* (Balfe), *Home, Sweet Home* (Bishop) and *Comin' thro' the rye* won the solid admiration of her audiences. *The Morning Post* (29 June) even published a five-verse poem in her honour, incorporating the titles of some of her most popular numbers. Little did Strauss know then that his fellow artiste was one day to become the wife of his own eldest son!

Besides fulfilling engagements in and around London – at the homes of the nobility, in Buckingham Palace, at Almack's Subscription Balls (for which Johann composed the *Almacks-Quadrille* op.243) and at public concerts – the Strauss Orchestra journeyed further afield to Reading, Oxford and Cheltenham during their two-and-a-half month stay in England, and gave a total of forty-six performances. Such was the immensely high regard in which Strauss was held that several members of the royal family and aristocracy arranged a touching 'Farewell Matinée Musicale' for his benefit, 'as proof of their satisfaction of the admirable manner in which he has conducted the music at their balls and soirées this season'. This farewell public performance took place on 6 July at the Riding School of the Knightsbridge Barracks, and for this occasion Johann wrote his *March of the Royal Horse Guards*.★ At midnight on 10 July, Strauss and his 'celebrated band' departed from Dover for Ostend, arriving back in Vienna on 14 July.

On 22 September 1849 the Vienna City Council honoured Field-Marshal Radetzky with a grand afternoon banquet in the Redoutensaal of the Imperial Hofburg. 250 guests were present; the Strauss Orchestra had been engaged for the event and was to perform a specially commissioned *Radetzky-Bankett-Marsch* by Strauss father. The 'Herr k.k. Hofballmusikdirektor', however, failed to appear, and

★The work was later published in Vienna as the *Wiener Stadt-Garde-Marsch* op.246, but with the positions of the main section and trio reversed.

44

the march remained unfinished. At his apartment in the Kumpfgasse, which he shared with Emilie and their children, Strauss lay ill with scarlet fever, contracted from one of his illegitimate offspring. Anna Strauss's enquiries simply brought the assurance that Johann was recovering.

Early on the morning of 25 September the occupants of the Hirschenhaus received the news that Strauss father had died during the night. Eduard Strauss later wrote that Emilie had stripped the apartment in the Kumpfgasse of 'whatever could not be riveted or nailed firmly down', leaving 'the poor deceased on wooden slats which had been taken from the bed and laid on the floor'. This version of events has persisted, despite the fact that the lengthy official inventory of personal effects entirely refutes all such claims.

On 27 September the funeral procession, with the coffin borne by members of the Strauss Orchestra, left the Kumpfgasse for a service of benediction at St Stephen's Cathedral, and thence to Döbling Cemetery where Strauss was laid to rest next to his former friend Joseph Lanner. Two military bands, a civilian band led by the elder Philipp Fahrbach and a delegation from the Wiener Männergesang-Verein, paid their last respects. 100,000 Viennese followed the procession and lined the route.

In England, *The Illustrated London News* (13 October 1849) concluded its lengthy obituary of Strauss with the words:

If there had been no Strauss, we should not have had Musard or Jullien. Hosts of imitators have sprung up since Strauss, but to him will remain the glory of originality, fancy, feeling and invention.

In his own tribute in the *Gazette Musicale* (Paris, 3 October), Berlioz echoed the sentiments of a Viennese correspondent:

Vienna without Strauss is like Austria without the Danube.

*Strauss's name will be worthily continued in
his son; children and children's children can
look forward to the future, and three-quarter
time will find a strong footing in him . . .*

(*Der Wanderer*, Vienna, 17 October 1844, reviewing
Johann II's début at Dommayer's Casino)

THE YOUNGER Johann's revolutionary sympathies during
1848 brought him under continued attack from the Viennese
press, especially *Die Geissel* (The Whip) in its column *Kleine
Geisselhiebe* (Little Whiplashes). Strauss retaliated, 'using the means of
expression most familiar to me: music'. His cheerful polka *Geisselhiebe*
op.60, first played after his police interrogation that December,
featured cracking whips, mocking laughter and snatches from the
Revolutionary songs *La Marseillaise* and *Das Fuchslied*. After his
father's death fresh criticism erupted, and Johann felt moved to
publish an extensive address in the *Wiener Zeitung* (3 October 1849). In
this 'Sincere thanks and earnest entreaty to the esteemed Viennese
public', he wrote:

Any son is to be pitied who weeps at the grave of his prematurely departed
father; even more to be pitied, however, is the one whose fate is directed by
the hostile elements of shattered family circumstances, and who, having been
abandoned to the often partisan judgement of the public, has to listen to the
judgement on himself and on those who have remained faithful to him from
the strongly condemnatory mouths of his opponents, while no weapon is at
his disposal in defence of his actions other than to point to a deserted mother,
and brothers and sisters who are not yet of age. In order to support and feed
the latter, I dared to use my modest talent! . . . It was not a case, as hostile
opponents have suggested, of entering into a prize-fight with the proven far
superior powers of the most skilful master of the craft, who was, at the same
time, always my beloved father . . . I chose the art for which I felt a vocation
and an inclination to become a weak disciple . . . I only wish to earn the
smallest part of that favour which my deserving father so richly reaped! . . .
and thus, at the same time, to fulfil my duty to my mother and my brothers
and sisters.

In consequence of this appeal, and because 'The Orchestra of the
late Strauss' had elected the younger man its new leader, public
opinion became markedly more conciliatory. On 7 October 1849, in

the Kolonadensaal of the Volksgarten, Johann stood for the first time at the Orchestra's head, for a concert of works by his father.

During the 1850 Vienna Carnival, Strauss son was kept busy with regular engagements at those venues previously the exclusive preserve of Strauss father. Yet his petitions to be allowed to conduct the ball-music at the Imperial Court met with continued opposition, as there was official resentment towards his siding with the insurgents during 1848. After the elder Strauss's death, Archduke Franz Carl and his wife Sophie (the parents of Emperor Franz Joseph I) recommended Philipp Fahrbach senior to conduct the music at Court, despite Johann II's zealous attempts to secure the post for himself. In August/September 1849, at the very latest, the younger Johann had realized that his declared support for the 'Revolutionaries' Circle' was proving prejudicial to his career. Nevertheless, he was loathe to announce publicly his change of allegiance, and thus discreetly introduced his patriotic march *Kaiser Franz Joseph* (op.67) with a noticeable absence of publicity.

Johann seized every possible opportunity to advance his career, and eagerly sought invitations to perform at the homes of the nobility and aristocracy. For a birthday celebration at Maxing, the Swiss-style home of Archduke Ferdinand Maximilian (younger brother of Emperor Franz Joseph I), he composed his waltz *Maxing-Tänze* op.79 (1850), and when the British Ambassador, the Earl of Westmorland (formerly Lord Burghersh), took up residence at the Palais Coburg in Vienna, Strauss provided the music for the house-balls there. The waltz *Windsor-Klänge* op.104 (Echoes of Windsor) and the *Albion-Polka* op.102 – dedicated respectively to 'Her Majesty Queen Victoria of Great Britain and Ireland' and 'His Royal Highness Prince Albert of Saxe-Coburg-Gotha' – both owe their origins to Westmorland's presence in Vienna. The Earl and Countess of Westmorland were both accomplished musicians – the Earl's compositions include several Italian operas and a Grand Mass – and Johann performed a number of their works, such as the *Julianische-Quadrille* and *Katharine-Quadrille*.

When, in 1850, a meeting was planned between Emperor Franz Joseph and the Russian Tsar, Nikolai I, during an autumn festival in Warsaw, Strauss contrived to secure an invitation to perform there with his orchestra before the assembled guests. Thus Johann, denied the position of Musikdirektor at the Court of his own Emperor, appeared before his sovereign as Musikdirektor for the Tsar!

Gradually, opposition to Strauss within the Vienna Hofburg began to crumble. During the 1851 Carnival Johann was engaged to conduct at a charity ball in the Redoutensaal (for this he composed his *Maskenfest-Quadrille* op.92), and the following year was at last summoned to conduct the music at Court- and Chamber-Balls, initially sharing this post with the elder Fahrbach. However, his aspirations to the title of k.k. Hofballmusik-Direktor, as successor to his father, were to remain unfulfilled for a further eleven years.

For grand Court functions the young Johann and his orchestra were attired in high-necked red tail-coats over white trousers, duty-dress adopted after complaints in 1843 that the black civilian dress of Johann father's orchestra was unsuitable in surroundings where all other gentlemen wore uniform.

Like his father before him, Johann II paid for his relentless exertions with repeated breakdowns in health. Following a collapse at the end of February 1851, he was reported during early March to be 'dangerously ill' from typhoid and 'nervous fever', and the press even rumoured his death. His health improved temporarily, but recurrent bouts of sickness forced him to cancel engagements later that year. In the autumn, Strauss felt sufficiently recovered to embark on a concert trip to Germany, taking his leave of Vienna with the waltz *Mephisto's Höllenrufe* op.101 (Mephistopheles's Summons from Hell), first heard on 12 October in the Volksgarten at a scenic festival portraying 'The Journey into the Lake of Fire'. In this composition there are clear signs of Johann's attempts to expand the waltz-form of his late father.

1852, the year of his first appearance as conductor at the Imperial Court Balls (7 February), also saw one of the earliest of Johann's 'masterworks', the waltz *Liebes-Lieder* op.114 (originally announced in the press as *Liebes-Gedichte* and actually performed as *Liebes-Ständchen*), and the delightful *Annen-Polka* op.117. He must surely have been encouraged by an article in the *Theaterzeitung* (27 May 1852):

His talent is constantly being revealed in a striking and outstanding manner. It manifests itself on all sides, and pushes its way through all obstacles. It now turns out for certain that Strauss Father has been fully replaced by Strauss Son.

The unceasing demands upon the 26-year-old Kapellmeister to organize engagements, compose, arrange, rehearse and, frequently, to conduct at several different venues on the same day, eventually proved too much for him. At the beginning of December 1852, after an exhausting concert tour through Prague, Leipzig, Berlin, Hamburg and Dresden, he was again taken ill. His return to public life was repeatedly announced and postponed, and not until 16 January 1853, in the Volksgarten, did he actually reappear with his orchestra. The following day he played at the Sofienbad-Saal, and introduced two new works, the *Freuden-Gruss-Polka* op.127 (Cheerful Greeting) and a waltz, dedicated to the pianist (and later conductor) Hans Guido von Bülow, *Phönix-Schwingen* op.125 (Wings of the Phoenix) – the latter referring to Strauss himself having risen, like the mythological bird, 'from the ashes'. The title also alluded to 'Phoenix', an unsuccessful contemporary transport enterprise, rival to the traditional Viennese Fiaker, which had promised faster and cheaper travel. Strauss's waltz, with its soaring motif, is especially brisk and stylish!

On 18 February 1853 there was an abortive attempt upon the life of the Austrian Emperor. Johann, ever eager to ingratiate himself further in the eyes of the Court, was swift to respond with his specially composed *Kaiser Franz Joseph I Rettungs-Jubel-Marsch* op.126 (March of Rejoicing at the Deliverance of Emperor Franz Joseph I).

Johann was tireless in his artistic endeavours. He recognized that 'the public attends a Strauss concert expecting to be put into a *happy* mood', as he later wrote to his brother Eduard, and he was aware of the importance of presenting novelties. Over the years, Johann, Josef and Eduard Strauss, above all other musicians, helped to pave the way for acceptance of Wagner's 'progressive' musical style in Vienna, by introducing to the public there orchestral selections from his operas *Tannhäuser*, *Lohengrin*, *Tristan und Isolde* and *Die Meistersinger von Nürnberg*, years before their first Viennese stage productions, and, in the case of *Tristan* and *Die Meistersinger*, even before their respective world premières. Wagner, for his part, admired the work of his 'champion' and called Johann 'the most musical brain of the age'. He later wrote in his essay, *Das Wiener Hof-Operntheater* (1863): 'A single Strauss waltz, so far as gracefulness, refinement and musical content is concerned, towers above the majority of the often laboriously procured foreign-produced creations . . . '

Johann's already weakened constitution was unable to withstand such sustained activity, and he suffered a nervous breakdown. His doctors urged a prolonged rest-cure in Bad Gastein, near Salzburg, and Bad Neuhaus bei Cilli. Mother Anna despairingly viewed this enforced removal of her eldest son and head of the Strauss Orchestra, fearing the certain ruination of the family. Together, Johann and his mother determined that, at least in the short term, brother Josef would have to deputize as conductor. The latter at first resisted, then characteristically resigned himself to the situation. To his future bride, Caroline Josefa Pruckmayer, Josef wrote on 23 July 1853:

The unavoidable has happened; today I play for the first time at the Sperl . . . I wholeheartedly regret that this has happened so suddenly . . .

For his début, Josef was forced to conduct with a baton, rather than from the violin in customary 'Strauss style', since he had not yet mastered the instrument.

At this stage he fully intended to resume his chosen profession upon Johann's return. For Josef Strauss, however, Fate had other plans.

7

*Pepi is the more gifted of us two; I am merely
the more popular . . .*

(Johann Strauss II, about his brother, Josef)

JOSEF STRAUSS – 'Pepi' to his family and friends – was born in
'Civic Dwelling House No. 39' in the Viennese Mariahilf suburb
(on the site of present-day No.65 Mariahilferstrasse) on 20 August
1827, the second of Strauss father's children. An excellent student
from the outset, he completed his courses in technical drawing and
mathematics at the Polytechnic Institute in Vienna, for six years
complementing his studies with private tuition in figure-, landscape-
and ornamental drawing at the Academy of Fine Arts. Josef's
diligence was rewarded in 1850 by a testimonial asserting that 'he
deserves to be recommended with merit to anyone in his chosen field
as architect'. His drawings, miniatures, silhouettes, watercolours and
family caricatures, all executed with the utmost finesse, reveal the
artist's sharp eye for detail, which in the years ahead would manifest
itself again and again in his music, particularly in descriptive polkas
like *Moulinet* op.57 (Little Mill), *Die Schwätzerin* op.144 (The Gossip),
Die Spinnerin op.192 (The Spinner) and *Die Libelle* op.204 (The
Dragonfly).

The polka originated in Bohemia as a dance in 2/4 time, and in
Vienna during the 1840s it largely replaced the galop which had been
so popular there for two decades. By the late 1850s Viennese concert
and dance repertoires featured variants such as the slower and more
feminine 'polka française' (French polka), the hectic 'polka schnell'
(quick polka) and the 'polka-mazurka'. The last of these, combining
polka steps with the 3/4 time of the mazurka, perhaps found its most
perfect expression through the pen of Josef Strauss, who exploited this
dance form to the full by alternating between major and minor keys,
creating subtle changes in mood. His use of the minor key,
particularly in the polka-mazurka and waltz, imparted a wistful,
tender quality that was so much a part of Josef's nature.

Between 1843 and 1845 Josef wrote an anthology of poems, and his
ambitious five-act drama, *Rober* – for which he wrote the text,
visualized the settings, and provided numerous sketches of the
characters, costumes and scenery – probably dates from this period. In

the academic year 1845-6 he studied mechanical engineering at the Polytechnic. 'Less than frequent' attendances notwithstanding, he achieved a First Class assessment in his final examination. After completing a bricklaying and stonemasonry apprenticeship, Josef was employed from August 1846 to August 1847 as an architectural draughtsman for the Vienna City Architect, Anton Übel, who later attested to the young man's excellence.

In contrast to his somewhat reserved and peaceable nature, Pepi took up arms during the 1848 uprising and, as Eduard Strauss later recalled, 'marched on 26 October* with the Academic Legion to the Tabor, where he saw action in the firing line of the Nassau Regiment'. Only by the greatest good fortune did he escape with his life when Jellačić's dreaded Seressaner troops traced him to the Hirschenhaus. Just two months later, on 23 December, however, he reacted vehemently against his father's ruling that he should enter upon a military career:

Leave me where I am; leave me what I am; don't snatch me away from a life that can bring me manifold joys, a life full of expectation, a social position, from which one can gain respect. Do not cast me into that rough, inconsistant world which destroys all feeling for humanity, a world for which I am not fitted, to which I was not born . . . I do not want to learn to *kill* people . . . I want to serve mankind as a *human being* and the State as a citizen. If I can do this I will be inwardly thankful, and will live out my days in peace and happiness . . .

Johann senior seems not to have challenged the obvious devotion of his second son to his 'civilian' aspirations; at any rate he was not in a position to enforce his own will upon Josef, for he spent much of the following year touring with the Strauss Orchestra and died shortly after his return.

For the next few years Josef's technical career flourished:

1851 – Architectural foreman, supervising building of stone dam and sluice on Danube tributary at Triestingbach-bei-Trumau, Lower Austria.
1852 – Draughtsman in technical office of Viennese machinery building factory.
Publishes *A Collection of Examples, Formulae, Tests and Tables in Mathematics, Mechanics, Geometry and Physics*, successor to book of logarithmic tables prepared while still a student.
1853 – Offered job collaborating on supervision of two large buildings in Vienna. Scheme abandoned. Attends courses on hydraulic engineering and water-works construction, with intention of gaining engineering diploma.
In May, presents Vienna Municipal Council with detailed plans for street-cleaning machine (designed with fellow engineer), utilizing moving vehicle to operate rotating

*In his book *Erinnerungen* Eduard Strauss I mistakenly links this event to 6 October 1848. The recent researches of Professor Franz Mailer, however, identify the correct date as 26 October.

brushes – forerunner of present-day system. Initially rejected as 'impracticable', but later adopted. Announces intention to present designs for snow-clearing machine – plan never realized.

And yet this 'genius against his will', as the writer Hans Weigel best described him, was forced into a position of the greatest responsibility at the head of a family 'music business' which he had no desire to join, and for which he had received no formal training.

Just one month after his successful début as conductor of the Strauss Orchestra, Josef was obliged to deputize for his brother as composer. By Johann's own admission, both he and Pepi were 'accomplished pianists', and Josef had written a number of unpublished virtuoso piano pieces. Moreover, as the possessor of a fine bass voice, he had also composed a few unpublished songs for bass voice and piano – some to his own texts. But it was now to the demands of the dance that he was required to apply his talents. For the Parish Festival Ball in the Viennese suburb of Hernals, on 29 August 1853, Josef apprehensively set about the task of providing the customary new piece, and entitled the resulting waltz *Die Ersten und Letzten* (The First and Last), clearly considering his function to be of a purely temporary nature. *Bäuerle's Theaterzeitung* (31 August) did not share this viewpoint, noting that Josef's opus 1 had to be repeated six times. It continued:

This latest flowering of the dance is positive proof of the brilliant talent of Herr Strauss, and we allow ourselves the agreeable hope that this composition will not be the last, but that Josef Strauss . . . will soon produce a sequel.

In the event, the critic's request for a 'sequel' was more than fully met in over 300 original dance compositions and 500 orchestral arrangements of other composers' music, all written within the astonishingly brief space of seventeen years – surely an unparalleled feat for such a reluctant musical disciple.

With Johann's health continuing to cause anxiety, there seemed to be no sign of an early resumption of Josef's previously ordered life. Furthermore, martial law, in force throughout Austria since 1848, was lifted on 1 September 1853, giving rise to a proliferation of entertainment establishments which promised only to increase demand for the Strauss Orchestra – a demand which Johann, alone, could not meet. With his customary assiduity, Josef applied to the music-school proprietor and Professor of Harmony, Franz Dolleschall, to study 'the principles of thorough-bass and composition', and on 16 March 1857 received an examination certificate testifying to his 'most excellent results' and 'greatest competence in the practice of music'. Josef took violin lessons from Franz Amon, principal violinist with the Strauss Orchestra and Johann II's own teacher; not until 23 April 1856, however, did he feel sufficiently confident to appear before the public directing the orchestra from the violin, in the distinctive manner of a 'Vorgeiger'. Appropriately, the new waltz he brought to this occasion was entitled *Die Vorgeiger* (op. 16).

On 18 September 1853, 'completely restored after his illness', Johann Strauss made his reappearance before an audience of three thousand at Unger's Casino in Hernals with his specially composed *Wiedersehen-Polka* op. 142 (Reunion-Polka). Josef slipped into the background, and conducted neither during the nine-week Carnival 'campaign' of 1854 nor during that spring, a period when his own health was causing him problems. For Johann, however, this was a time for consolidation. With a keen sense for the topical and commercial, he commemorated the marriage, on 24 April, of Emperor Franz Joseph and the Bavarian Princess Elisabeth with his aptly titled dedication waltz *Elisabethsklänge*, later renamed *Myrthen-Kränze* op. 154 (Myrtle Wreaths).

Only when Johann left for a further rest-cure in Gastein did Josef resume direction of the orchestra. The first of his new works presented in July 1854, *Die Ersten nach den Letzten Walzer* op. 12 (The First after the Last Waltz), hints at his resignation to an extended, if reluctant, stay in the world of music. Nevertheless, it was with relief that Josef relinquished the baton upon Johann's return at the end of July, for persistent headaches plagued his waking hours – a manifestation of suspected congenital brain damage that was to cloud his days.

Josef was the first of the three Strauss brothers to marry when, on 8 June 1857, he took his childhood sweetheart, Caroline Josefa Pruckmayer, to the altar of the parish church of St Johann Nepomuk in the Praterstrasse. Upon their marriage Caroline moved into the Hirschenhaus with her husband and, on 27 March 1858, the couple's only child, Karoline Anna, was born. It was Josef's dream to emancipate his wife and daughter from the confines of the Strauss family home, but this dream was to remain unfulfilled.

8

*One lives only in Russia! There is money
here, and because this is available life exists,
nothing but life!*

(Johann Strauss II, in a letter to his
publisher Carl Haslinger, August 1857)

IN SEEKING to attract passenger traffic to their nineteen-mile
stretch of line from St Petersburg to Pavlovsk, the Tsarskoye-Selo
Railway Company of St Petersburg constructed an elegant music
pavilion and entertainment centre at the terminus, in the spacious
public grounds of Pavlovsk Park, near the palace of Grand Duke
Constantin Nikolaievich. The Vauxhall Pavilion, as the complex was
called (after the famous pleasure-gardens in London), had been opened
in May 1838 and many international musicians had since performed
there. Plans to engage Strauss father in 1839 had come to nothing,
Josef Labitzky appearing in his place. The Hungarian Johann Gung'l
regularly played there during the summer months between 1845 and
1848, and his uncle, Josef Gung'l, from 1850 to 1855. Since the latter's
popularity was waning, the railway management determined to
replace him: their obvious choice was Johann Strauss II. Accordingly,
in 1854 a delegation made the lengthy journey to Gastein, where
Johann was recuperating, and an agreement was reached for him to
conduct the summer concerts at Pavlovsk in 1856. A second contract,
dated 23 November 1856 and binding Johann to two further concert
seasons in 1857 and 1858, stipulated that he was to give daily concerts
from 2 May to 2 October with an orchestra of not less than thirty
musicians, 'some of whom may be chosen from his orchestra existing
in Vienna'. He was given free rein in 'the choice of classical operas,
garden- and dance-music', but 'in this he is to follow the taste of the
local audience, and apart from his own compositions is also to perform
the most popular and latest compositions of other famous masters,
with a full orchestra and under his personal direction'. In return,
Strauss received free accommodation and travelling facilities, four
benefit concerts and, for the five-month engagement of each year
'18,000 silver roubles★ . . . inclusive of his own and his orchestra's
wages and travel costs' – payments that laid the foundations of his
later, considerable, fortune. In 1856 he was provided with an orchestra

★Today worth approximately £63,600 sterling.

of selected Russian musicians, but in subsequent years he was required, by contract, to organize his own orchestra. In order to reduce travelling expenses Strauss only employed a nucleus of Viennese players, relying mainly upon hand-picked musicians from Berlin, a prudent choice, for in May 1857 he wrote from Pavlovsk to Haslinger:

My orchestra is causing a sensation, and they deserve it, too, for would to God I had such a band in Vienna. I cannot speak *too highly* of this one . . .

So successful were Strauss's concerts at Pavlovsk that he appeared there each summer from 1856 to 1865, with visits also in 1869 and 1886. These 'Russian summers' were not only personally prestigious for Jean (as Johann now liked to be called); many of his best-loved compositions originate from this period and, indeed, were first performed in Russia, such as *Tritsch-Tratsch-Polka* op.214 (named after a contemporary Viennese satirical weekly publication, which in turn took its name from a play by Johann Nestroy), *Pizzicato-Polka* (written jointly with his brother Josef, in 1869) and the *Egyptischer Marsch* op.335 (celebrating the opening of the Suez Canal in 1869). Other well-known compositions appeared with titles later altered for Viennese audiences: *Champagner-Polka* op.211 (originally *Ball-Champagner-Polka*), *Persischer-Marsch* op.289 (originally *Persischer-Armee-Marsch*), the polka *Im Krapfenwald'l* op.336 (originally *Im Pawlowsk-Walde*) and *Russischer Marsch* op.426 (dedicated to Tsar Alexander III, and originally entitled *Marche des gardes à cheval*). From Strauss's twelve Russian visits date many delightful, though less familiar, pieces, some incorporating Russian folk-melodies; the list includes the waltzes *Grossfürstin Alexandra* op.181 (dedicated to Grand Duchess Alexandra Jossiphovna); *Souvenir de Nizza* op.200 (dedicated to Maria Alexandrovna, Empress of Russia, and originally entitled *Souvenir an Riga*); *Abschied von St Petersburg* op.210 (originally *Mes adieux à St Petersbourgh*); the *Newa-Polka* op.288; the *St Petersburg-Quadrille* op.255; the *Krönungs-Marsch* op.183 (dedicated to Tsar Alexander II on his coronation in Moscow, for the celebrations of which Strauss was invited to play); the fantasies *Russische-Marsch* op.353 and *Im russischen Dorfe* op.355, and a potpourri on melodies by Glinka called *Hommage au public russe*. Johann's *Bauern-Polka* op.276 (Peasants-Polka), with its vocal refrain, 'brought a storm of applause such as no Beethoven symphony movement could yet have received', and was so frequently demanded that its bewildered composer was driven almost to distraction.

Before his initial departure for Pavlovsk, however, Johann appears to have harboured serious reservations about entrusting the direction of the Vienna-based Strauss Orchestra to brother Josef. In 1855 the youngest brother, Eduard, had made his début in the Strauss Orchestra as a harpist, and it is conceivable that Johann already regarded 'Edi' as his natural successor as interpreter of the family's music. Interpretation aside, Johann was not alone in recognizing the artistic value of Josef's compositions. The latter had been approached by C. A. Spina – a rival of Johann's own publisher, Haslinger – with a proposal to publish some of his works, and Johann may well have feared that, during his absence from Vienna, Pepi's compositions could detract from his own hard-won success. His hesitation in finalizing arrangements for his departure annoyed Josef, who reminded his elder brother that he had not become a musician of his own volition, adding frankly:

To have done with appearing before the public would be no threat to me, at least no calamity. My love of music does not show itself in ¾ time, neither do I feel a penchant for it. – I am therefore quite prepared to lay down the baton . . .

Johann recanted and prepared for Russia, leaving Josef to develop his own musical career – a career which, in about 1864, was to flourish into a fascinating artistic contest with his elder brother, and stimulate both men to some of their finest compositions. Josef also considered it his duty to extend the repertoire of the Strauss Orchestra to include more of the 'futuristic' music of composers such as Wagner, Berlioz and Liszt; in turn this 'new music' left its impression on a number of Josef's works, including his magnificent concert-waltz *Perlen der Liebe* op.39 ('Pearls of Love', written as a wedding gift for his wife Caroline in 1857) and two highly praised pieces from 1858 (both now lost), the concert-waltz *Ideale* and an ode for male chorus and orchestra, *An die Nacht* (To the Night). Similarly, Johann was inspired to attempt 'symphonies in three-quarter time', like the waltz *Gedankenflug* op.215 and the concert-waltz dedicated to the pianist Anton Rubinstein, *Schwärmereien* op.253. When Vienna's 'music pope', the critic Eduard Hanslick, heard the daring Wagnerian-style instrumentation of Johann's waltz *Schallwellen* op.148 (Sound Waves), he complained in the *Neue Freie Presse* (6 October 1854):

The wretched chord sequence blasted out by the trombones, which forms the second section of [Waltz] No.1 . . . could certainly be used in the finales of those operas which end in a particularly bloodthirsty way . . . If Strauss continues writing waltzes in the style of 'Schallwellen', what will then remain for Meyerbeer to put in his next operas?

The Strauss waltzes *Schallwellen*, *Wellen und Wogen* (op.141), *Schnee-Glöckchen* (op.143) and *Novellen* (op.146) Hanslick deprecatingly termed 'new waltz-requiems'.

On 18 May 1856 (6 May by the Russian calendar), after the customary *Russian Hymn*, Johann began his first concert in Pavlovsk with the overture to Balfe's opera *The Devil's in It*, presenting also works by himself, Strauss father, Verdi and Meyerbeer. With numerous repeats and encores the evening concert lasted until 1 a.m. Strauss, the idol of Vienna, was soon the idol of Russia – some cigarette packets even bore his portrait and facsimile autograph. Among his audiences were members of the Russian Court and aristocracy, at whose private functions he performed, and occasionally the Tsar himself and other members of the royal family. The Grand Dukes Michael and Constantin even appeared from time to time as cellists in Strauss's orchestra.

Johann was besieged by the Russian women, whom he later immortalized in his waltz *Les dames de St Petersbourgh*, prudently rechristened *Wiener Frauen* op.423 (Viennese Ladies) for his Austrian admirers! In 1858 he began a deep romantic involvement with one Olga Smirnitzky, the musically gifted young daughter of aristocratic Russian parents. His passionate letters to Olga, whom he nicknamed 'L'Espiègle' (The Mischievous One) show him to have seriously contemplated marriage, but the liaison, conducted secretly because of parental disapproval of the Viennese Kapellmeister, ended abruptly in spring 1860 when Olga wrote to her 'dearest Jean' in Vienna:

Do not condemn me when you read these lines. I will be brief and omit explanation. I have been engaged for two weeks . . . Forget your unfaithful imp . . .

Johann set aside all hopes of a future with Olga, but memories of her live on in his polka-mazurka *Der Kobold* op.226 (The Imp), originally entitled *L'Espiègle*. It should be mentioned that Strauss's *Olga-Polka* op. 196 (1856) refers not to Olga Smirnitzky, but to the Grand Duchess Olga, formerly Princess Caecilie of Baden, wife of Grand Duke Michael.

Strauss's preparations for his fifth 'Russian summer' were preceded by the busy 1860 Vienna Carnival. Johann was by now the undisputed 'Carnival King', and, together with his brother Josef, dominated Vienna's ballrooms. For every Carnival they were expected to produce a constant stream of new dance–dedications for the festivities of the numerous associations, student faculties and other groups. With each set of waltzes, at that time usually comprising five sections, each section being made up of two melodies, Eduard Hanslick warned of 'inartistic wastefulness, which must soon exhaust even the most gifted powers of creation', since 'the narrow, strictly compact form of the waltz does not permit of even the slightest development of a melody'. Throughout, the Strausses maintained a supremely high standard of invention, displaying also considerable resourcefulness and humour in the titles they gave to many of their dedication pieces: among those for the medical students at Vienna University are Johann's waltzes *Erhöhte Pulse* op.175 (Raised Pulses), *Paroxysmen* op.189 and *Die ersten Curen* op.261 (The First Course of Treatments); for the engineering students his *Elektro-magnetische Polka* op.110, *Motor-Quadrille* op.129 and waltzes *Schallwellen* op.148 (Sound Waves), *Libellen* op.180 (Spirit Levels) and *Cycloiden* op.207 (Cycloids); for the law students Johann's waltz *Sentenzen* op.233 (Sentences), polka schnell *Process* op.294 (Lawsuit) and Josef's waltz *Petitionen* op.153, while for his benefit ball in the Sofienbad-Saal in 1848, Johann proffered the waltz–title *Sofienbad-Schweistropfen* (Sofienbad Sweat-Drops)! For the Vienna Artists' Association, 'Hesperus', of which all three brothers were members, Johann wrote his waltz *Künstler-Leben* op.316 (Artist's Life), Josef the waltz *Aquarellen* op.258 (Watercolours) and Eduard the polka française *In Künstlerkreisen* op.47 (In Artistic Circles). The many dances for the Vienna Authors' and Journalists' Association, 'Concordia', include Johann's polka *Durch's Telephon* op.439 (Over the Telephone), Josef's polka schnell *Eingesendet* op.240 (Letter to the Editor) and Eduard's polkas *Stempelfrei* op.56 (Free from Stamp Duty), *Mit der Feder* op.69 (With the Pen) and *Probe-Nummer* op.199 (Specimen Copy). Additionally, several waltzes featured Introductions (and occasionally Codas) of an appropriately descriptive nature, evocative of their titles, like Johann's *Lava-Ströme* op.74 (Streams of Lava), with its splendid volcanic eruptions; *Telegraphische Depeschen* op.195 (Telegraphic Despatches), portraying the tapping of the telegraph keys and flashing message along the wires; the musical seascapes *Wellen und Wogen* op.141 (Waves and Billows) and *Nordseebilder* op.390 (North Sea Pictures); and Josef's *Delirien* op.212, which brilliantly conjures up the frenzy of delirium.

Often compositions were only written at the very last moment, the titles of the promised works having been announced in advance. Thus it was with Johann's aptly named waltz *Accellerationen* op.234 (Accelerations), composed for the Engineering Students' Ball in the Sofienbad-Saal on 14 February 1860. That such feats were possible speaks as much for the self-confidence of the Strausses as for their enviable musicianship. In principle, the three Strauss brothers personally orchestrated all their own dance-compositions, unlike their father, and, even when pressed for time, they would add to the completed melody-line chord symbols and their own coded instructions for the copyists, thereby ensuring that the resultant orchestrations were *precisely* as they required. A full score was always written exactly to the composer's directions, to enable the publisher to prepare sets of orchestral parts, and also piano and other arrangements. According to Eduard, Johann was the quickest at orchestration, completing the Introduction, all five two-part waltz sections and Coda of his waltz *Wiener Pun[s]ch-Lieder* op.131 (1853) in just nine hours.

In March 1860 Johann attended a production by Johann Nestroy of Jacques Offenbach's 'Opéra bouffon', *Orphée aux Enfers* (Orpheus in the Underworld), at the Carl-Theater, and in accordance with the popular practice of constructing quadrilles on themes from contemporary stageworks, wrote his *Orpheus-Quadrille* op.236, recalling Offenbach's melodies.

During the following year's Carnival, Johann decided to introduce his brother Eduard as a ballroom conductor, and announced for 5 February 1861: 'For the first time in Vienna. THREE BALLS IN ONE EVENING . . . Three large orchestras' – each to be under the direction of a different Strauss brother. At the 1859 Carnival there had already been great excitement when, on 28 February, Johann and Josef had alternated in the conducting of *two* Strauss Orchestras for an uninterrupted programme of dance-music at the Sofienbad-Saal – for which they jointly composed their *Hinter den Coulissen Quadrille* (Behind the Scenes). But the emergence of a third Strauss, leading a third orchestra, was nothing short of sensational. 300 musicians played their way through 50 dances, including 14 waltzes, 10 quadrilles, 9 French polkas, 8 polka-mazurkas, 8 quick polkas and a schottisch. The name given to this latest Sofienbad-Saal spectacle – *Carnevals Perpetuum mobile, oder: Tanz ohne Ende* (Carnival's Perpetual Motion, or Non-Stop Dancing) – inspired Johann to another of his popular novelties, the 'musical jest' *Perpetuum mobile* op.257, first performed that April at his farewell concert prior to leaving for Russia. Also in 1861, on 29 December, Johann and Josef combined to present another novelty – *Jupiter and Pluto: A Musical Posse in 40 Scenes*, during the course of which the Strauss Orchestra (as 'Jupiter') and the Music-Corps of Tsar Alexander of Russia's Infantry Regiment (as 'Pluto') conducted a musical question and answer exchange, leaving the public to guess the identity of pieces indicated only by question-marks on the printed programme.

On 6 April 1862, in the Wintergarten of the Dianabad-Saal in Leopoldstadt, Johann allowed Eduard to make his début as a conductor of concerts with the Strauss Orchestra. It was soon to become apparent why he wanted Eduard to gain this experience. Declining an offer to appear in Paris with his orchestra for a fee of 100,000 francs annually for three years, and with the family orchestra now securely in his brothers' charge, Johann left for his seventh season in Pavlovsk. Once there, intermittent and undiagnosed 'illness' frequently led Johann to relinquish conductorship to a deputy until, in July, he telegraphed home for the now competent Eduard to replace him. Mother Anna intervened, however, and insisted that Josef be sent instead, the latter being much annoyed at having to tear himself away from work and family responsibilities at short notice. (In an attempt to placate his irate brother, Johann promised to arrange Russian engagements for Josef in 1863 and 1864, though duped him by later signing the contracts for himself.)

Josef made his début in Pavlovsk on 2 August (21 July in the Russian calendar), jointly conducting with his brother, before an audience of 8000, a programme of works by W. V. Wallace, Wagner, Mendelssohn, Glinka, Schubert, Offenbach, Erkel and Bulakhov, as well as some of their own compositions. Josef wrote to Haslinger: 'My début on Saturday was splendid. Almost every piece had to be repeated . . .' As to Johann's 'illness', Josef clearly suspected his brother of malingering in order to break his contract. He notified his wife, Caroline, on 6 August (25 July in the Russian calendar) that Johann had departed Russia early that morning 'fresh and healthy – (never before was he thus)', adding: 'This time he has fooled physicians, doctors, everybody.' Josef continued: 'Jean is as if changed?! Everything is unimportant to him except money . . . How I have been disappointed in my hopes and expectations. I wept tears alone when I thought of you, of my good child, of home . . . Jean said to me when I asked him how much of the money would come to me – "What is it that you want? You are in Petersburg. Do you want more?" . . . So revolting, miserly, filthy has this person become that it disgusts me to speak of him.'

Whether or not guilty of deception, upon his return to Vienna Johann wrote his publisher a hasty note, dated 26 August:

Dear friend Haslinger, shamefully cheated soul of a printer! Will you come along to my house tomorrow at 7.00 in the morning – to be my supporter at the wedding to take place one hour later? Reply at once, you inky-fingered dealer in notes! Jean.

On 27 August 1862, in St Stephen's Cathedral, Vienna, 'Herr Johann Baptist Strauss, Kapellmeister and Musikdirektor' was married. His bride was 'Henriette Carolina Josepha Chalupetzky, of single status' – known to the musical world as Jetty Treffz.

9

*I feel so completely happy and joyful to
belong to my Jean, whom I love with all the
strength of my soul and heart . . .*

(Jetty, in a letter to Josef Strauss. Vienna, 28 August 1862)

BORN IN Vienna on 1 July 1818, the only child of a Viennese
goldsmith, Henriette Chalupetzky studied music in her native
city, adopting her mother's maiden name, Treffz, for professional
purposes. Noted for her 'mezzo-soprano voice of beautiful quality,
remarkable for freshness and equality of tone throughout the register'
(*The Musical World*, London, 5 May 1849), she gained wide acclaim
throughout Austria, Germany and France, but her greatest triumphs
were realized in England where, in 1849, her engagements included
appearances alongside Johann Strauss father. Upon her return to
Vienna she retired from the stage, a wealthy woman. Between 1841
and 1852 she bore seven illegitimate children, in about 1843 becoming
the mistress of the banker Moritz Todesco, with whom she remained
for the next eighteen years. Todesco often hosted private soirées in the
salon of his Viennese home, to which the most eminent personalities
in the world of music, art and literature were invited. It was at one of
these functions, probably during the winter of 1861–2, that Johann
Strauss and Jetty renewed an acquaintance that had begun some
sixteen years earlier at one of the theatre–balls held in the Sträussel-Säle
in Josefstadt, and which had been fostered later in the home of Moritz
Greiner, brother-in-law of the conductor Johann Herbeck. Johann and
Jetty's relationship deepened. Upon their marriage, Jetty did not sever
all links with her past, as has been previously thought: recently
discovered letters in her hand prove that she at least maintained a
correspondence with her children. As 'Frau Strauss' Jetty concentrated
her remarkable talents upon becoming the complete companion for
her husband – wife, lover, artistic adviser, private secretary,
organizer, music-copyist, and even nurse. She also brought to the
marriage considerable personal wealth, and this, together with the
savings that Johann's mother and Aunt Pepi had accumulated from his
earnings over the years, assured Johann's financial security.

Considering Jetty's dubious former lifestyle, and the fact that, at
forty-four, she was Johann's senior by seven years – Josef considered

her 'very well preserved' – it is perhaps not surprising that the Strauss family (indeed, many Viennese) expressed astonishment and concern over the match. Sensing disapproval, Jetty astutely penned a number of warm-hearted letters to her new relatives. To the pessimistic Josef, in far-away Pavlovsk, she wrote on the day after her wedding:

Give me your dear hand, and support me in the fine task of winning the love and affection of your family.

Soon Josef revised his unfavourable opinion of his sister-in-law and her hastily contracted marriage to Johann. When, in 1869, Jetty accompanied the two brothers to Pavlovsk, Josef wrote to Caroline:

Jetty is indispensable. She writes up all the accounts, copies out orchestral parts, sees to everything in the kitchen, and looks after everything with an efficiency and kindness that is admirable.

(Letter dated 2 May 1869)

Just as mother Anna Strauss had managed the family 'concert agency' within the Hirschenhaus after her husband's desertion, so now Johann was perfectly happy to leave to Jetty not only the organization of his concert tours and, subsequently, theatre contracts, but also much of the associated correspondence. Her excellent business mind made her an ideal partner for the financially somewhat naïve Johann, who had formerly entrusted responsibility for monetary matters to his mother, and, during some of his Russian engagements, to his mother's widowed sister, Josefine Waber, known to the family as 'Aunt Pepi'. Jetty understood fully the nature and creative potential of the man she had married. To her, above all others, is due the credit for having guided Johann towards the composition of operetta. For biographers to attribute this significant step to an alleged remark by Jacques Offenbach ('You ought to write operettas!') is to do Jetty a grave injustice. Strauss and Offenbach certainly did not meet before 1864, if indeed they met at all. Moreover, on the very day in January 1864 that *Der Zwischenakt* noted Offenbach's arrival in Vienna, Strauss was reported to be already at work on an operetta.

From the beginning, Jetty intended that Johann should gradually withdraw from his strenuous year-round conducting activities, now that the Strauss Orchestra was in the capable hands of Josef and Eduard, and allow himself more time for composition. Anxiously she observed how the hectic pace of Johann's life was mentally and physically exhausting him, and determined that their honeymoon in Venice should be 'a complete rest' for him. This resolve notwithstanding, Venice saw the creation of the waltz *Carnavals-Botschafter* op.270 (Carnival's Ambassador), one of Strauss's very few post-Carnival works dating from that year. Another, dedicated especially to Jetty, was the *Bluette, Polka française* op.271. Upon their

Johann Strauss II, photographed in the 1850s by Ludwig Schrank, Vienna.

The Vauxhall Pavilion at Pavlovsk, Russia. Lithograph by C. Schultz after a drawing by J. Meyer, printed by Lemercier of Paris.
(Courtesy of the Historisches Museum der Stadt Wien)

Josef Strauss (1827–70), whose 'dual nature' the journalist Siegmund Schlesinger described as 'so audaciously "stylish", so high-spiritedly Viennese, when in cheerful company, and so artistically dreamy in the realm of your music . . .'

Josef Strauss's wife, Caroline, with their daughter Karoline Anna.
(Courtesy of the Österreichische Nationalbibliothek)

Johann II with his first wife, Jetty, photographed in 1867.

Angelika ('Lili') Dittrich, second wife of Johann Strauss II.
(Courtesy of the Österreichische Nationalbibliothek)

Johann Strauss II with his third wife Adèle, and her daughter Alice,
photographed by L. Grillich, Vienna, circa 1890.
(Courtesy of the Historisches Museum der Stadt Wien)

Eduard Strauss I with his wife Maria, and their sons, Johann (*left*) and Josef, photographed in the 1870s. (Courtesy of the Österreichische Nationalbibliothek)

Anna ('Netti') Strauss (1829–1903), elder daughter of Johann I.

Therese Strauss (1831–1915), younger daughter of Johann I.

The 'Strauss–Palais' in Igelgasse, before and after being almost totally destroyed by wartime bombing in autumn 1944.
(Courtesy of Franz Feldkirchner, Salzburg)

Title page of the pianoforte first edition of Johann II's *Tritsch-Tratsch-Polka* op. 214, published in 1858 by Carl Haslinger. The 'Prittle–Prattle' of the title is delightfully portrayed by the artist.

Johann Strauss II in characteristic pose, conducting his orchestra at a Court Ball. Painting by Theo Zasche.

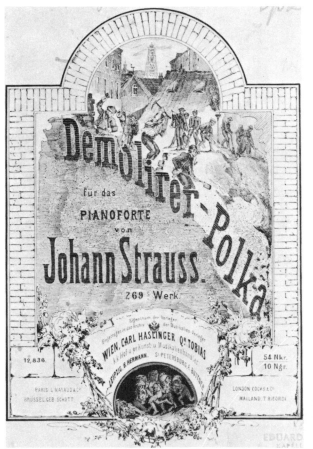

A fine example of the imaginative artwork adorning many nineteenth–century first editions. Haslinger's publication of the *Demolirer-Polka* op.269 by Johann II shows the demolition of the ancient bastions encircling the inner city of Vienna.

Carl Michael Ziehrer photographed in 1863, the year of his début as composer and conductor.

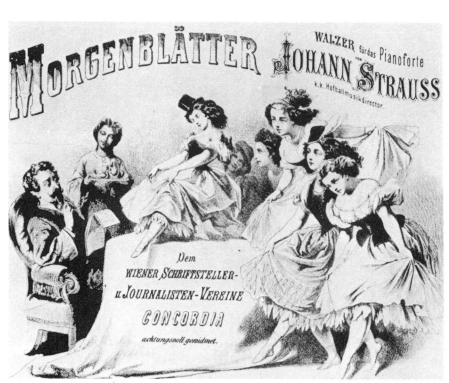

Title pages from C. A. Spina's original pianoforte editions of Johann II's *Morgenblätter* and Offenbach's *Abendblätter* waltzes.

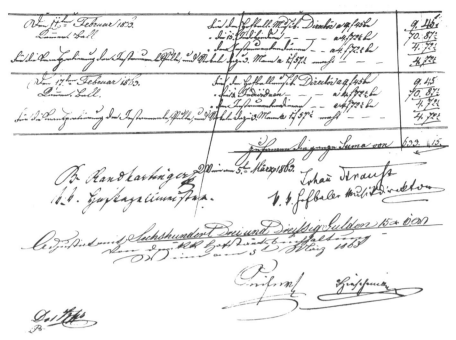

Johann Strauss II's signature as 'k. k. Hofball-Musikdirektor', as it appeared for the first time on a statement of account for performances at Court- and Chamber-Balls during the 1863 Vienna Carnival.

return from honeymoon, the newlyweds moved into an apartment at No. 21 Singerstrasse. Jetty recognized the importance of living near the Strauss family, yet remaining free from its smothering influence. In 1863 the couple took up residence at No. 43 Praterstrasse, but moved again the following year to a home in the Weihburggasse.

In January 1863 doctors actually banned Johann from composing, to give him time to overcome his exhaustion and depression. He broke the ban but once, for a 'Patriotic Festival' in March organized by Carl Haslinger and himself, leaving the ever-obliging Josef to compose all the Carnival dance-dedications to which Johann had previously committed himself.

Jetty now urged her husband to reapply for the coveted title of k. k. Hofball-Musik-Direktor, already twice (1856 and 1859) refused him on the grounds of his being 'a reckless, improper and profligate person', as a confidential police report for the Court noted in May 1856. In his obsequious petition of 20 February 1863, recording his career, achievements and 'happy marriage', he stated his intention

to restrict his own personal musical endeavours from this time onwards only to the balls at the all-highest Court, the noble households and the closed Corporations, and otherwise, at the very most, to the concerts in the k. k. Volksgarten, since it is the Court locale . . .

65

adding that he would entrust all remaining public engagements to his brothers. On 25 February 1863 he was awarded the honorary title by decree, all previous objections to his 'civil and moral' behaviour having been mitigated by his many artistic, patriotic and charitable accomplishments. The first of Johann's published compositions to display his new title was the waltz *Leitartikel* op.273 (Leading Article), written for the 'Concordia' ball in the Sofienbad-Saal on 19 January 1863. It was also the first of the Strauss family's compositions dedicated to this influential association.

In the spring Johann left for his annual journey to Pavlovsk, this time accompanied by Jetty, who gave a number of lieder performances there, including recitals at the Imperial Court at Tsarskoye. Writing home, Jetty, 'the happiest of wives', talks of her 'idyllic life' with her 'Jeany-boy . . . who has made life seem desirable to me again after it had become loathesome and a torment to me'.

While harmony reigned in this 'God-blessed marriage', as Johann termed it, the composer's correspondence with his Viennese publisher, intimate and family adviser, Carl Haslinger, began to betray marked signs of a deteriorating relationship. Good-natured badinage in the highly entertaining letters between the two men was replaced by recriminations concerning a serious disagreement over fees involving Haslinger's Russian publishing partner, A. Büttner. The once close friendship between composer and publisher became irreparably severed and they parted company, professionally and privately. Haslinger somehow persuaded the other Viennese publishers against signing contracts with the Strauss brothers, whereupon Johann, intent on sidestepping the boycott, applied to the authorities, and received permission for a licence to run his own publishing house and music business from which to issue his own and his brothers' compositions. In November 1863 Haslinger promoted a rival composer, the 20-year-old Carl Michael Ziehrer. Only after Josef Strauss's untimely death, however, did the newcomer begin to assert himself as the greatest challenger to the domination of the Strausses. Indeed, as late as October 1868, Jetty wrote disparagingly of Ziehrer, that 'in spite of all Haslinger's machinations . . . he really has no talent, and what his teacher, Hasel, works on he then publishes as *his own* compositions . . .'

Recognizing the futility of the publishing boycott, the firm of C. A. Spina subsequently broke it and, by the end of January 1864, had offered contracts to all three Strauss brothers. Spina continued as the Strausses' Viennese publisher until 1872, when the company's assets were acquired by the firm of F. Schreiber. In 1879 Schreiber, in its turn, was taken over by the Hamburg-based company of A. Cranz.

In May 1863 Spina had published Johann's quadrille (op.272) on themes from Verdi's opera *Un ballo in maschera*, but the first of Strauss's works to appear under the new contract was the waltz

Morgenblätter op.279, written as his obligatory dedication piece for the 'Concordia' Ball in the Sofienbad-Saal on 12 January 1864. Learning that the visiting Jacques Offenbach also planned to submit a waltz for this ball, Strauss wrote in December 1863 to Dr Eduard Hanslick, requesting him, as intermediary ('since I do not have the pleasure of knowing M. Offenbach personally'), to inform the visitor of his desire to issue both waltzes from his own publishing house, 'which is shortly to be opened'. Upon his contract with Spina, however, Johann abandoned his publishing project and the two waltzes appeared simultaneously from Spina. Probably at the suggestion of the 'Concordia', Offenbach's waltz was entitled *Abendblätter* (Evening Papers), and the festivity assumed an element of friendly rivalry when the 'Concordia' committee named Strauss's hitherto untitled offering *Morgenblätter* (Morning Papers). Contrary to most biographers' accounts, however, Offenbach was not present at the ball (though he was in Vienna, supervising rehearsals of his opera *Die Rheinnixen* at the Court Opera), and both waltzes were conducted by Johann Strauss at the head of the Strauss Orchestra. The suggestion that Johann's waltz was less favourably received than Offenbach's also seems unfounded, for while first-night press reviews neither support nor refute such a claim, subsequent performances of *Abendblätter* engendered little enthusiasm, and the *Wiener Zeitung* (1 March 1864) commented retrospectively:

And strangely enough, Herr Offenbach's 'Abendblätter'* withered even on the first night when he threw them into the lap of the audience alongside Strauss. Nobody had ears for it.

Posterity has pronounced firmly in favour of *Morgenblätter*, while sadly, the compelling *Abendblätter* is seldom heard today.

Like the rest of his family, Johann II maximized the potential of advertising and knew instinctively how to exploit current trends in order to enhance the popularity and sales of his music. The titles which the Strausses gave their compositions read like a social, cultural, technological and political guide-book of the times. When, early in 1864, Austria and Prussia united against Denmark over the issue of Schleswig-Holstein, Strauss glorified the alliance in his marches *Deutscher Krieger* op.284 (German Soldiers) and *Verbrüderungs* op.287 (Brotherhood), the latter written for a charity concert in Berlin in aid of wounded soldiers and dedicated to King Wilhelm I of Prussia. This 'brotherhood' between the two nations, however, was to be short lived; two years later they were at war.

While Johann and Jetty were in Pavlovsk for the 1864 concert season, Josef and Eduard continued to hold sway over the Viennese dance scene. Moreover, Josef was reaching new heights as a composer. On 6 September he introduced his waltz *Dorfschwalben aus*

*A German pun! *Abendblätter* can mean both 'Evening *Papers*' and 'Evening *Leaves*'.

Österreich op.164 (Village Swallows from Austria) and the polka-mazurka *Frauenherz* op.166 (Woman's Heart) at a concert in the Volksgarten. Josef's aspirations to break free from the Hirschenhaus and establish independence with his wife and daughter were encouraged when he signed a contract to give concerts in Breslau from October 1864. His letters home, however, reveal the venture to have been unsuccessful both financially and artistically, and plans for his family's 'emancipation' were baulked. Furthermore, partly through Johann's interference, his attempts to secure concert engagements in London and Paris were frustrated. Meanwhile, in Russia, recurrent illness forced Johann to relinquish his leadership, and already he was insisting that Eduard, rather than Josef, should replace him for the first half of the following year's Pavlovsk engagement.

Faced with this further display of fraternal rejection, Josef applied himself with even more than customary vigour to the 1865 Vienna Carnival. A succession of outstanding compositions was crowned by his sublime waltz *Geheime Anziehungskräfte* op. 173 (Mysterious Powers of Magnetism) – better known by its alternative title, *Dynamiden* – which in its conception, power and sensitivity surpassed anything yet created by his elder brother. When, in 1925, the German composer Richard Strauss acknowledged in the *Wiener Tagblatt*:

And with the waltzes from 'Rosenkavalier' . . . how should I not have thought of the laughing genius of Vienna?

he was referring to Johann II, yet it is the opening melody of Josef's *Dynamiden* that the Act 2 *Rosenkavalier* Waltz so strikingly resembles:

Josef Strauss: *Geheime Anziehungskräfte* (Dynamiden), Waltz 1A

Richard Strauss: Baron Ochs's waltz, *Der Rosenkavalier* Act 2

Josef's unremitting mental and physical activity during this period was not without cost to his delicate health. Violent headaches preceded a sudden collapse into unconsciousness at his work desk, and his doctors urged him to take a holiday; this he deferred for several weeks until Eduard returned from Russia to relieve him. In the interim, his work pattern was relentless, and when, in August, he and Caroline left for the country, he allowed himself just six weeks' respite before resuming a pace of life that was anathema to his constitution.

Eduard had not been a success in Russia in 1865, despite his popularity with 'the women and youngsters', but Johann partially redressed the situation when he took over in mid-July. His penchant for novelty led him to give the first-ever public performance of music by the young Russian composer Peter Ilyich Tchaikovsky when, on 11 September (30 August, Russian calendar), he performed the latter's *Characteristic Dances*, later revised and incorporated into Tchaikovsky's opera *The Voyevode* op.3. By the close of this tenth Pavlovsk season, Johann had resolved not to renew his own contract for 1866. Mindful of Eduard's poor reception, he attempted to obtain the engagement for Josef, but this plan was thwarted by the railway management, who instead chose the German conductor Heinrich Fürstenow.

Increasing tension between Austria and Prussia, as the two powers struggled to extend their territories, led inevitably to the outbreak of war in the spring of 1866. Once again Johann's patriotism flared: he and Jetty offered one of their homes as an officers' hospital, and all three brothers donated the proceeds of their concerts for 'humanitarian purposes'. On 3 July, after a campaign of only seven weeks, the Danube monarchy met sudden and bitter defeat at Königgrätz (Sadowa). In its wake an intense depression spread across all classes of the Austrian populace.

The spectre of Königgrätz even shrouded the Carnival festivities of 1867. Only a few of the great Representation Balls took place, and most of these were poorly patronized. The *Wiener Zeitung* distilled the general mood:

Nowadays, nobody steps on to the smoothly polished parquet of the dance hall in a bright, witty or jocular frame of mind; everyone merely hopes to find the like there.

Reflecting the serious spirit of the times, the Court replaced its own sparkling annual ball with a Court concert. Other institutions followed this example, including the Wiener Männergesang-Verein, who presented, in place of its traditional rollicking 'Fools' Evening' a more sedate carnival song-programme. Scheduled for 15 February 1867 in the Dianabad-Saal, this event provided the venue for the first performance of what has become the most celebrated waltz of all time.

As early as 1865 Johann Strauss had been requested by the Wiener Männergesang-Verein to compose a choral work especially for them. He had declined this 'honourable and flattering invitation' because of preoccupation with possible legal action involving the Pavlovsk management, but pledged:

I hereby commit myself next year, if I am still alive, to make up for what I am now hindered from doing, and I offer the esteemed Association a new composition – written especially for the purpose – with pleasure.

This promise was not fulfilled, but during 1866 Strauss certainly began sketching some of the themes for the choral waltz, his first, which he was eventually to present to the Association for its 1867 song-programme – *An der schönen blauen Donau* op.314 (By the beautiful blue Danube). Johann originally submitted a four-part unaccompanied chorus to the Männergesang-Verein, shortly afterwards sending a hastily written piano accompaniment which bore the apology: 'Please excuse the poor and untidy handwriting – I was obliged to get it finished within a few minutes. Johann Strauss.' At that time the composition comprised a set of just *four* waltz numbers, together with an Introduction and brief Coda. To these four waltzes and Coda the Association's poet, Josef Weyl, added the text. Then Strauss produced a *fifth* waltz section, which required Weyl to reword the fourth waltz, set words to the fifth and add a revised text to the Coda. Only shortly before the first performance was it decided to furnish the work with an orchestral accompaniment, which Johann duly provided. While there is general agreement that the title *An der schönen blauen Donau* stems from the poetry of Karl Isador Beck, it is apparent that Strauss's waltz only received its now familiar name at the very last moment. The Association's records and minutes, the various sets of musical parts and the newspaper announcements prior to 15 February refer merely to a 'Waltz for chorus and orchestra by Johann Strauss, k.k. Hofballmusikdirektor. Dedicated to the Wiener Männergesang-Verein (new)'. It is not known who was responsible for adding the title to the waltz, and the phrase 'An der schönen blauen Donau' does not actually appear in Weyl's text.

Because Johann and the Strauss Orchestra were performing at the Imperial Court on the night of the première, the Wiener Männergesang-Verein gave the first performance of Strauss's choral waltz under the baton of their chorus-master, Rudolf Weinwurm, accompanied by the orchestra of the 'König von Hannover' Infantry Regiment, which was temporarily stationed in Vienna. In contrast to the oft-repeated story of the work's initial failure, many of the Viennese newpapers recorded the extraordinary success of the première:

The lovely waltz, with its catchy rhythms, ought soon to belong among the most popular of the prolific dance-composer . . .

(*Die Presse*, 17 February 1867)

Hofballmusik-Direktor Strauss celebrated a great and deserved triumph with his waltz 'An der schönen blauen Donau . . .'

(*Die Debatte und Wiener Lloyd*, 17 February 1867)

The waltz was truly splendid . . . The composition was received with rejoicing, and had to be repeated by tempestuous general demand.

(*Fremdenblatt*, 17 February 1867)

This single encore perhaps disappointed the somewhat spoiled Waltz King: to Ignatz Schnitzer, later the librettist of Strauss's *Der Zigeunerbaron*, Johann philosophized:

The waltz was perhaps not striking enough. But when one has choral composition and vocal parts in mind, one cannot think solely of dancing! If the audience had expected anything different from me, then indeed *this* waltz cannot have pleased them much!

Yet an idea of the unique popularity achieved by *The Blue Danube* may be gauged from a comment by Hanslick seven years after its première:

Alongside the National Anthem by Father Haydn, which celebrates the Emperor and the Imperial Household, we have in Strauss's 'Beautiful blue Danube' another National Anthem, which sings of our land and people.

Weyl's satirical text (often amended), which 'left much to be desired', according to *Die Debatte und Wiener Lloyd*, urged peasants, landlords, artists and politicians to forget their sad lot by joining in the Carnival festivities. The Association's subsequent performances of the waltz in this version were numerous, but were mainly restricted to their smaller concerts. Eventually, in 1890, the Association's Franz von Gernerth provided the now generally adopted text in which, for the first time, the words 'Donau so blau . . .' ('Danube so blue . . .') appeared. On 10 March 1867 the first performance of the waltz for orchestra alone, featuring the extended Coda absent from the choral version, was heard in the Volksgarten during a *Revue of all the dance-pieces composed for this year's Carnival* by Johann, Josef and Eduard Strauss. A glance at the dances they wrote for that 1867 Carnival illustrates how admirably the brothers responded to the challenge of those depressed days in once carefree Vienna. In a list totalling twenty-five new works are to be found Johann's waltzes *Künstler-Leben* op.316 (Artist's Life) and *Telegramme* op.318, and his contrasting polkas *Leichtes Blut* op.319 (Light of Heart) and *Lob der Frauen* op.315 (In Praise of Women), as well as Josef's waltzes *Delirien* and *Marien-Klänge* op.214 and polkas *Arm in Arm* op.215 and *Die Windsbraut* op.221 (The Gale).

With the Fasching behind him, and encouraged by Jetty, Johann now focused his attention beyond Austria, on a city which his father had already taken by storm. Accordingly, the couple made preparations to depart for Paris and its International World Exhibition.

10

Splendid rejoicing as <u>at no time</u> *in my life!!!*
The most beautiful concert of my career!
*Vivat the English, from the bottom of my
heart!*

(Johann's diary entry for 26 October 1867,
ending his Covent Garden season)

MANY BIOGRAPHERS attribute Strauss's presence in Paris to
an invitation from the French composer and patron Comte
d'Osmond, but this assertion remains unsubstantiated. Certainly, from
early 1867 the Comte was concerned in the arrangements for certain of
the festivities involving Strauss, but it is apparent from correspondence
that Johann and Jetty financed the venture themselves, in the absence
of any definite invitation or engagement proposal.

In order to proceed, however, Johann's first priority was to find
himself an orchestra, as the Strauss Orchestra was committed to
appearances in Vienna under Josef and Eduard during the summer
months. After hopes of joining forces with Josef Gung'l were dashed,
Strauss reached agreement to share the conducting of concerts in Paris
with Benjamin Bilse, the 'Royal Prussian Director of Music', using
Bilse's excellent orchestra, some members of which later founded the
Berlin Philharmonic.

Writing from Paris on 15 June 1867 to Ludwig Eisenberg (Johann's
future biographer), Jetty confessed that 'the beginning was *very*
difficult', since her husband had decided against costly 'advertising
and trumpetings' to announce his arrival in Paris. Johann was
nonetheless eager to make his début in the French capital as
conspicuous as possible. A year earlier he had dedicated his waltz
Wiener Bonbons (op.307) to the wife of the Austrian Ambassador in
Paris, the influential Princess Pauline Metternich-Winneburg. Now,
upon his arrival in Paris, as the Princess recounted in her memoirs★,
Johann Strauss 'requested of us the privilege of directing the orchestra
at the Embassy Ball, to which we consented, of course, with the
greatest pleasure'. The ball took place on 28 May in the magnificent
ballroom of the Austrian Embassy, attended by a glittering élite
including Emperor Napoleon III and the Empress Eugénie, the King

---

★*Éclairs du passé* (1922).

and Queen of the Belgians, and Crown Prince Friedrich of Prussia. At the head of Bilse's fifty-strong orchestra, Strauss, initially apprehensive, celebrated a deserved triumph.

The following day Johann gave the first of two concerts with Bilse and his orchestra in the Théâtre Italien, one half of each programme comprising serious music under Bilse, and the other being devoted exclusively to dance-music under Strauss. Yet the Parisians did not take Johann to their hearts until the proprietor and editor-in-chief of *Le Figaro*, Henri Auguste de Villemessant, repeatedly championed the Viennese Waltz King in his newspaper, and the concert venue transferred to the Exhibition Club building, the 'Cercle International'. With this came a change of fortune, as Jetty reported to Eisenberg:

The receipts have increased *every* day . . . and the public is so frantically aflame for Jean that I cannot find words to depict *this* enthusiasm . . . they are simply crazy for this Viennese music.

Among Johann's repertoire for these concerts were the waltzes *An der schönen blauen Donau, Morgenblätter* and *Nachtfalter* (op.157), and the polkas *Tritsch-Tratsch, Par force!* (op.308) and *Maskenzug* (op.240), all works already popular in Vienna. A novelty was Johann's *Figaro-Polka* (op.320), written in gratitude to de Villemessant, and first played at the Cercle International on 30 July, on which day its piano edition appeared in *Le Figaro*.

By contrast, Bilse attracted little interest, and it was perhaps jealousy on his side that led the two men to part in discord. Jetty wrote: 'Offers are coming in – for Jean *alone*, without Bilse – which would guarantee him a fortune of half a million francs in 2 years.' While Bilse and his orchestra remained in Paris until mid-September, Strauss gave his final concert on 9 August, and the following day left with Jetty for England.

Johann's invitation to conduct at the new season of Covent Garden Concerts at the Royal Italian Opera House, London, from 15 August to 26 October, may have resulted from the enthusiastic recommendation of the Prince of Wales (later King Edward VII) whom Strauss had met at the Paris Exhibition. On 8 August 1867 the British press carried an announcement by the Director of the Covent Garden Concerts, John Russell:

The orchestra will be the most complete ever assembled in England. It will be chiefly selected from that of the Royal Italian Opera, but increased in strength, and, in respect to individual executants, improved where it has been thought possible to do so . . . The Director cannot refrain from expressing his satisfaction . . . that he has succeeded in making an engagement with that most celebrated conductor and composer of dance music, Herr JOHANN STRAUSS . . .

As in Paris, Johann undertook 'the entire superintendence of the musique de danse', leaving the direction of classical and operatic selections to the conductor, composer and double-bass virtuoso, Giovanni Bottesini. Apart from international instrumental and vocal soloists – including 'that favourite artiste, Mdlle. Jetty Treffz, who will sing some of the newest German Lieder' – the season also featured eight full military bands from Europe and Russia. Programmes were frequently arranged on a day-to-day basis, and often an advertised piece was replaced by one which had proved popular the previous evening. *The Times* (16 August) wrote of the first concert:

Each of the three pieces played by the orchestra under the direction of Herr Johann Strauss was received with genuine enthusiasm. This gentleman, who strongly resembles his father in manner, seems also to possess a large share of those qualities which led to his father's renown. He conducts the orchestra, like his father, fiddle in hand, and joins in the passages of most importance. This he does with wonderful animation, accompanied by a certain amount of characteristic gesticulation, which also has something to do with the general impression created . . . That Herr Strauss is a man of mark can hardly be doubted, and that the future success of the Covent-garden Concerts depends materially upon him is, we think, unquestionable.

The Prince of Wales was in the audience on the second evening, and afterwards conversed with Strauss for some fifteen minutes in the Royal Box.

Johann's personal diary shows that in London the most frequently performed of his compositions was the *Annen-Polka* which, with encores, was played a total of eighty-two times during the sixty-three concerts. *The Blue Danube*, which received its first British performance with orchestra and chorus of 150 male voices on Saturday 21 September, was one of the less frequently performed pieces. Also in his programmes were a number of works that Strauss had arranged or written especially for his English audiences: these included 'a new festival valse comique on popular melodies' (published in Vienna as *Erinnerung an Covent-Garden* op.329 – 'Memory of Covent Garden'), comprising such popular music-hall songs as 'Champagne Charlie', 'The Flying Trapeze', 'The Mousetrap Man' and 'Home Sweet Home'; the waltz *Londoners' Bouquets*, being a hybrid of Johann's published waltzes *Sängerfahrten* and *Controversen* (op.191); a *Potpourri-Quadrille*, interweaving French and German airs from Strauss's *Chansonnettes* and *Lieder-Quadrilles* (opp. 259 and 275) with 'Ye banks and braes o' Bonny Doon', 'There's nae luck about the house', and 'Wi' a hundred pipers an' a', an' a''; and an unpublished cornet solo, *Reverie*, written for (Jules?) Levy, acclaimed as 'the first cornet player in the world'.

At the close of the concert season *The Illustrated London News* (26 October) summarized: 'They have been, in all respects, the best promenade concerts ever given in this country'. Overjoyed, Johann and Jetty returned to Vienna, where Johann felt moved to organize 'Promenade Concerts' after the British style, with seating beside the orchestra for the serious listener and a 'promenade' area for casual visitors. The first of these concerts, in aid of charity, took place on 19 January 1868 in the spacious Blumen-Säle (Floral Halls) of the Wiener Gartenbaugesellschaft (Vienna Horticultural Society). Johann marked this event with the first performance of his polka-mazurka *Stadt und Land* op.322 (Town and Country), and introduced the Viennese to his *Figaro-Polka*.

With the Carnival and summer months of 1868 came fresh evidence of the artistic competition between Johann and Josef. Among the younger brother's successes were the waltzes *Sphären-Klänge* op.235 (Music of the Spheres) and *Wiener Fresken* op.249, and the polkas *Tanz-Regulator* op.238, *Eingesendet* op.240 and *Plappermäulchen* op.245. Convincingly, Johann met the challenge with his splendid waltz *Geschichten aus dem Wienerwald* op.325 (Tales from the Vienna Woods), and the polkas *Freikugeln* op.326 and *Unter Donner und Blitz* op.324 (Thunder and Lightning) – the latter being originally performed under the title *Sternschnuppe* (Shooting Star). In July Vienna's great pleasure park, the Prater, was the venue for the 3rd German Federal Shooting Contest, an event attracting some 10,000 international competitors. In celebration Johann, Josef and Eduard combined their talents to write the rousing *Schützen-Quadrille* (Shooting-Quadrille), to which each brother contributed two sections. Another novelty was heard on 12 October 1868 in the Sofienbad-Saal, when the Wiener Männergesang-Verein performed Johann's choral polka *Sängerslust* op.328 (Singers' Joy), accompanied by Johann and Josef on piano and the Association's own Adolf Lorenz on harmonium. That same year, marking the 25th Jubilee of the Association, Johann was granted the distinction of honorary membership to the Wiener Männergesang-Verein.

During 1868 Johann and Jetty left the city surroundings of No.54 Praterstrasse, their home since 1866, and took up residence in Hetzendorfer-Strasse (today, No.18 Maxinggasse) in the suburb of Hietzing. 'We have moved completely to the country', Jetty informed a friend on 19 October 1868. 'Johann has bought a small house here, so really nice and comfortable that we imagine we are living in dear Albion [England]. Opposite us is the Schönbrunn botanical garden, and the inside of our house is lovely . . . Johann found living and being in London so much to his liking that he could not rest until he had a little house to call his own.' For the next ten years the Hietzing villa was to bear witness to an astonishing burst of musical creativity, resulting in some of Johann's finest dance-pieces and at least five of his operettas.

After a break of four years, Johann accepted an invitation to give concerts again at Pavlovsk during the spring, summer and autumn of 1869, but only on condition that Josef accompanied him as understudy. Furthermore, the management undertook to engage

Josef in future years if he proved popular with the public, thereby ensuring him a degree of financial security. In fact Josef was now a very sick man, afflicted by renewed bouts of unconsciousness. Yet news of the Russian contract filled him with optimism and lifted him to the challenge of the 1869 Carnival: he presented ten new works, including the waltzes *Aquarellen* and *Mein Lebenslauf ist Lieb' und Lust* op.263 (The Course of my Life is Love and Laughter), the lighthearted quick polkas *Vélocipède* op.259 and *Eislauf* op.261 (Skating), and the rumbustious French polka *Feuerfest!* op.269 (Fireproof!) which was dedicated to the Viennese firm of F. Wertheim and Co. on completion of their 20,000th safe! Johann's contributions to the Carnival were limited to three, *Fata Morgana, Polka-Mazurka* op.330, and the waltzes *Illustrationen* op.331 and *Wein, Weib und Gesang!* op.333 (Wine, Woman and Song!). The last of these, a choral waltz written for the Wiener Männergesang-Verein's 'Fools' Evening' in the Dianabad-Saal on 2 February, bears a dedication to the Association's honorary chorus-master, Johann Herbeck. The full beauty of this work, with its magnificent 137-bar Introduction, led the critic of the *Neues Wiener Tagblatt* (4 February 1869) to predict:

The waltz will make its way in life, and will become just as popular as the piece 'An der schönen blauen Donau'.

Before departing for Pavlovsk the two brothers paid a brief visit to Pest for the Hungarian National Festival, and at a concert there on 16 March introduced two specially composed works – Josef's *Andrássy-Marsch* op.268 and Johann's quick polka 'dedicated to the noble Hungarian Nation!', *Éljen a Magyár!* op.332 (Long live the Magyar!).

This commitment fulfilled, Johann and Josef set off for Pavlovsk, leaving responsibility for the Strauss Orchestra in Vienna to Eduard.

11

Just as Josef had let himself be swayed, so
Johann was able to influence me, too, into
following his footsteps.

(Eduard Strauss I in his family biography, *Erinnerungen*, 1906)

WHEN THE 25-year-old Eduard made his conducting début in 1861, Johann II's musical achievements had all but eclipsed those of Strauss father. Josef, too, had gained a solid reputation as a composer and conductor. Thus Eduard from the outset found himself in the shadow of a legendary father and two supremely successful elder brothers: his many fine compositions failed to achieve the recognition they deserved because of the existing legacy of Strauss family masterpieces, and also because of increasing competition from the talented Carl Michael Ziehrer.

After primary school Eduard attended the Vienna Akademische Gymnasium from 1846 to 1852, and was an assiduous student. A gifted linguist, he mastered Latın and Greek at school, and through private study perfected French, Italian and Spanish. Convinced that his future lay in a career with the Austrian consular service, he applied for a place at the Oriental Academy, here intending also to become proficient at English. 'However, when my mother learned . . . that any person assigned to a consulate cannot expect any leave during the first ten years of his career, her mother's heart . . . raised emphatic objection to such plans.' In consequence Eduard abandoned his aspirations, and resigned himself to the inevitable.

Alongside studies in musical theory (under the esteemed Gottfried Preyer), violin (under Franz Amon) and piano, Eduard, on brother Johann's 'urgent recommendation', also received instruction in the harp (from the chamber virtuoso Antonio Zamara). Since there was a lack of proficient harpists at that time, Eduard considered he could secure 'a more than adequate income for the future' by mastering this 'extraordinarily sought after' instrument, and made his public début as harpist in the Strauss Orchestra on 11 February 1855. The occasion was Johann Strauss's own benefit concert in the Sofienbad-Saal, during which Eduard was featured as one of two harpists in the first public performance of Johann's *Glossen Walzer* op.163 (Marginal Notes, Waltz) written for the Law Students' Ball held twelve days earlier.

After six years of study Eduard applied for an appointment as harpist to a German court-theatre, but failed the audition as a result of self-confessed nervousness. Nevertheless he continued his musical studies 'with great diligence', and on 22 December 1863 Preyer was able to attest to Eduard's 'thorough knowledge in musical composition'. His first published work was the polka française for piano, *Mes sentiments*, which Haslinger published, without opus number, in early 1863 bearing the fraternal dedication 'À Jean Strauss'. Shortly afterwards Haslinger republished the piece as Eduard's opus 1, retitled *Ideal*.

While Eduard's earliest works, though tuneful, perhaps lack the inspiration found in his brothers' dances, many of his mature compositions (particularly those dating from the 1870s and 1880s) more than redress the balance, and are fully undeserving of the neglect that has befallen them. Especially noteworthy, among his output of over three hundred and fifty original compositions, are the polkas *Liebeszauber* (op.84), *Mädchenlaune* (op.99), *Augensprache* (op.119), and *Blauäuglein* (op.254), the *Kaiser Franz-Josef-Jubiläums-Marsch* (op.109), the Schubertian song 'Als ich dich sah' (op.261) and the waltzes *Fesche Geister* (op.75), *Doctrinen* (op.79), *Studentenball-Tänze* (op.101), *Die Abonnenten* (op.116), *Aus dem Rechtsleben* (op.126), *Das Leben ist doch schön!* (op.150), *Leuchtkäferln* (op.161) and *Schleier und Krone* (op.200). Eduard's waltzes are as individual as those of his brothers, Strauss father and Joseph Lanner, and from many there spills an optimism rarely heard in the works of his contemporaries. It was, however, on the schnell-polka that the stylish 'Edi' most markedly stamped his own peculiar genius, and seldom has his flair in this genre been excelled. Particularly impressive are *Bahn frei!* op.45 (Clear the track!), *Mit Dampf* op.70 (Steam up), *Auf und davon!* op.73 (Up and away!), *Knall und Fall* op.132 (Without warning), *Ausser Rand und Band* op.168 (Out of control), *Mit Chic* op.221 (With style) and *Ohne Bremse* op.238 (With the brake off). It is amusing to reflect that although several Strauss family compositions have titles relating to travel and means of transport (as above), none of the three brothers ever willingly undertook journeys. Johann II was reportedly filled with terror at the mere mention of the precipices on the mountain stretches over Semmering!

Despite the indisputable quality of his dance pieces, Eduard at times had difficulty finding publishers for his music. Johann remarked in 1892 that 'his compositions are not bad – but nobody wants to buy them'. Yet 'der schöne Edi' (handsome Edi), as he was known, was almost always acknowledged as an excellent conductor, and his ability, pertinacity and unremitting energy won worldwide acclaim. Writing of his début as concert conductor in 1862, the Viennese periodical *Der Zwischenakt* noted:

Herr Strauss . . . was enthusiastically greeted, and presented with rare feeling

DANCE MUSIC.

" He hops und schumps und marks der time,
Und shows such taste and *nous*,
Dot dere's to equal him no vun,
Mine clever Eduard Strauss ! "

Eduard Strauss I as caricatured in *Punch* (20 June 1885), during the composer's
first London visit. (Courtesy of the proprietors of *Punch*).

and accuracy all the waltzes composed by his brother Johann during this season. His conducting showed that in him we have a conductor of the same calibre. Long live the Strauss trinity!

As conductor of the Strauss Orchestra Eduard was a strict disciplinarian, demanding and receiving the very highest performance standards from his players. But his uncompromising manner led to frequent conflict with the musicians, as in spring 1878, when he dismissed forty-one of them for refusing to undertake a six-month concert tour of Germany and Sweden. When, under the title of 'Formerly the Eduard Strauss Orchestra', his players began giving concerts in Vienna under C. M. Ziehrer, Eduard successfully filed a court action against his rival for the improper and misleading use of his name. Later, responding to a 'perfectly impudent' letter (1884) from his cellist, Alexander Fimpel, Strauss unleashed a four-page tirade upbraiding the musician with every stroke of his pen:

. . . you dare to ask me for a salary increase? Must I recall to your memory that there are 23 cello pieces here that *you are unable* to play?

Eduard's wry wit concerning the vexed subject of musicians is also evident in a letter he wrote to a correspondent on 17 March 1874:

Would you be good enough to let me know whether you came across a 'Flutophone' at the Paris World Exhibition. This instrument is *supposed* to replace 2 flutes . . . O, my dear honoured friend! Did you not find at the Exhibition an instrument that would replace *all wind players* . . .

With Josef's untimely death in 1870 and Johann's increasing preoccupation with operetta composition, responsibility for the family orchestra passed to Eduard, in whose sole charge it was to remain until its disbandment in 1901. The 1880s saw the rapid upsurge in popularity of military orchestras, whose excellently trained musicians were able to offer their services to proprietors of Viennese entertainment establishments far more cheaply than their civilian counterparts. During the summer months from 1878 onwards Eduard and the Strauss Orchestra were forced to seek engagements outside Austria to ensure their income. Under Eduard the Orchestra embarked upon its most extensive concert tours to America (1890 and 1900-1), Russia (1894) and England (1885, 1895 and 1897), and Eduard estimated that during the twenty-three years of touring with his orchestra he visited '840 towns in two continents and gave concerts at 14 Exhibitions'. During the course of his summer concert seasons in London (for which he wrote works like *Old England for ever! Polka* op.239 and *Greeting Valse, on English airs*) he played before Queen Victoria both at Buckingham Palace and at Windsor Castle, and after a concert at the latter on 17 May 1895 the Queen presented him with a silver writing outfit, 'with the request that he should make use of it in penning his next composition'. In his letter of thanks (20 May) Eduard

Strauß D., Gemischtw. Verschl., IV. Allee
gasse 66, G. IV. Karolineng. 18.
— David, Gutspächter, IV. Alleeg. 66, [Trg.],
Milchdepot IV. Belvedereg. 24.
— David, Agent, II. Vereinsg. 28.
— Eduard, k.u.k. Hofballmusik-Dir., ⚜,Cmdr.
d. span. O.C.III., Offiz. d. braf. R.O., Bes. d.
ott.Medj.O.4., Cmdr.d.würt.Frdr.O., R.1.
d.fic.O.Frz.I., Bes.d.Ekrz.d.fächf.Albr.O.,
Mitgl.d.kön.philharm.Gef.zu Neapel,kaif.
braf.Ehren-Hof-Capellmeifter, Reichsraths-
ftraße 9.
— Eduard Wilhelm, Mufik-Dir.,VIII.Strozzi-
gaffe 32.
— Emil, k. k. Bmt., V. Ob. Amtshausg. 37.
— Emilie, Lehrerin, Ottak. Laudong. 21.
— Franz, Kanzlei-Diener d. NWBahn., IX
Badg. 12.
— Franz, Amtsdiener im LBerth.Minftm.,
Ottak. Hauptftr. 37.
— Frz.,Locomotivführer,Rdlfhm.Pereirag.9b.
— Franz, Schuhm., IIMeidl. Miesbachg. 32.
— Friedrich, Priv.Bmt., IX. Prechtlg. 3.
— Friedrich, Bartenfteing. 16, Gef. d. ⚐
Horicer mechan. Weberei v. Em. Feuerftein
& Cie., Helferftorferftr. 4.
— Guftav, Bmt. d. I. öft. Sparcaffe, VII.
Neubaug. 76.
— Heinrich, Bureau-Chef der Verfich.Gef.
„L'Urbaine", II. Praterftr. 16.
— Heinrich, II. Hermineng. 4, ⚐ Brüder
Strauß. Woll-u. Zwirnhdl..Fifcherftiege 2.
— Jakob Hermann, Hdl.-Agent, Realitäten-
Vermittl., VI. Mariahilferftr. 111.
— Johann, vorm. k.u.k.Hofballmufik-Dir., ⚜,
Offiz. d. it. KrO. u. d. perf. SLO., R. d. pr.
roth.AO.4., d. pr.KrO.4., d.fr.ELeg., d.it.
MLO., d. bad. ZLO. 1., d. span. If.O. u. d.
herz. fachf. Ern.HO. 1., Inh. d.r.Verd.M.a.
Al. N. Bande u. d. fachf. Ern.Verd.M., IV.
Igelg. 4.
— Johann, Gifelaftr. 6.
— Johann, Bmt., IV. Favoritenftr. 46.
— Johann, Caffier d. angl. öBank., Währing
Gürtelftr. 68.
— Johann, Fleifchfelcher, IX. Wiefeng. 12,
G. Franzistanerplaß 3.
— Johann, Nadler, Ottak. Hauptftr. 213.
— Johann Edmund, Bmt. d. Neufiedler Actien-
Gef. f. Papierfab., IV. Wohllebeng. 5.
— Jofef. III. Negelg. 2.
— Karoline, Capellmeifter-Wwe., II. Karme-
literg. 7.

Extract from Lehmann's 1891 residential directory of Vienna. The entries for
Eduard and Johann Strauss II list their numerous decorations and honours.

described the evening in Windsor Castle as 'one of the most beautiful
and memorable of my artistic career', continuing: 'I and my family
will always remember Her Majesty and the Royal Family with
undying veneration.'

Like his brother Johann, Eduard lost no time in amassing for himself a wide assortment of medals, decorations, brooches of honour and golden snuffboxes, most of them in return for musical dedications, and he seems to have been inordinately proud of his appointment as 'Honorary Imperial Brazilian Court Conductor' – much to Johann's amusement.

On 8 January 1863 Eduard married Maria Magdalena Klenkhart, the 22-year-old youngest daughter of Sebastian Klenkhart, one-time friend of Johann Strauss father and the owner of a coffee-house opposite the Sperl. (Eduard's own godfather had been the coffee-house proprietor Ferdinand Dommayer.) Upon his marriage Eduard brought his bride into the Hirschenhaus to join himself and the other eight members of his family, and in due course Maria presented her husband with two sons – Johann Maria Eduard (1866) and Josef Eduard Anna (1868), the first of whom (known as Johann III) was destined to carry the family musical tradition well into the present century. Eduard, who had himself been born in the Hirschenhaus, remained there until 1886 when he moved with Maria and their children to a newly built home at No. 9 Reichsrathsstrasse, close to the Rathaus (Town Hall) in the centre of Vienna.

It is apparent that relations between Eduard and Johann were frequently strained, and quite possibly Johann's unsolicited advice on aspects of musical interpretation, doubtless made in Eduard's best interests, may have been construed as criticism. At times Eduard was openly critical of his brother's actions, and in 1892 Johann admonished him in a letter:

You still see everything pessimistically – you always think that I want to work something across you. For goodness sake, stop these stupid remarks – how old do you have to become before you finally realize that in your brother you do not have an enemy? . . . Sometimes our relationship has been troubled through ambitious strivings on your part, but you should know that my brotherly feelings towards you have never altered.

Despite these assurances, it is clear from family correspondence that Johann did develop a deep mistrust of his youngest brother, especially in the period immediately following Josef's death. Eduard could surely have discerned little evidence of 'brotherly feelings' from Johann's will (30 March 1895), which omitted him 'for the reason that he finds himself in favourable circumstances'. Moreover, the codicil of 24 March 1897 can have given him even less comfort, being prepared at a time when Eduard, through no fault of his own, found himself in severely reduced financial circumstances:

Although the reasons for which I did not remember my dear brother Eduard in my will, to my knowledge, now no longer apply, I will not make any alteration on account of this. I hope that my brother's situation will improve.

Through his own dogged hard work and determination, Eduard ensured that it did.

12

*I have to put up with many disagreeable
things, but I endure them all, just to make
possible a happy and carefree life for* you.

(Letter from Josef Strauss to his wife, Caroline. Pavlovsk, 19 April 1869)

JOHANN and Josef's 1869 Pavlovsk season began inauspiciously.
In preparing for the trip, Johann had overlooked the twelve-day
time difference between the Russian and Western European calen-
dars, and incurred 'a grievous loss' through having to meet the
additional salaries of the orchestra, who had arrived two weeks early.
There were also problems with accommodation.

Josef's letters to Caroline, documenting his daily routine in
Pavlovsk, reveal the unshakeable love and yearning he felt for her.
Earlier differences and petty jealousies between the two brothers had
been subdued, but in view of Johann's extraordinary popularity Josef
was understandably apprehensive about his first Russian appearance
in seven years. 'My position here is no easy one', he wrote on
16 April (= 28 April), 'I have to fight against prejudices.' The relief
he felt at the 'really enthusiastic reception' of his début raised his
spirits, and helped to overcome his concern with financial problems
and his state of health. On 2 May (= 14 May) he spoke of living
'healthy and carefree'; furthermore, he was growing increasingly
confident of being engaged again in Pavlovsk the following year.
But by 29 August (= 10 September) his self-assurance had given way
to despair:

I don't look well, I have become paler, my cheeks hollower, I am losing my
hair, I am on the whole very run down. I've no impulse to work . . . The
uncertainty in which I live, not knowing whether I shall be engaged or not,
makes me all the more ill and dissatisfied.

In view of this 'uncertainty', he was embittered by disquieting
news from Vienna that Eduard, tired of being merely joint conductor
of the Strauss Orchestra, now planned to tour independently with it.
Josef's anger brought a sharp reproach from mother Anna Strauss,
who already foresaw the disintegration of the family business she had
so devotedly nurtured:

. . . [I] do not sleep, cannot eat, no rest, nothing but guile, strife and *envy*

85

among you – [I] won't have any more, you are concerned with nothing but *your own families*, and we are the whipping-boys . . . May God one day forgive you for it. *I have not deserved it, this ingratitude.*

(Letter, Vienna, 17 September 1869)

Despite its problems, the Pavlovsk season produced several new compositions, including Johann's *Egyptischer Marsch* (Egyptian March) and *Im Pavlovsk-Walde, Polka française* (later renamed *Im Krapfenwald'l*), Josef's *Aus der Ferne, Polka-Mazurka* op.270 (From far away), *Ohne Sorgen! Polka schnell* op.271 (Without a care!) and *Frohes Leben, Walzer* op.272 (Joyful life). The *Pizzicato-Polka*, also dating from this visit, was jointly composed by the brothers after Johann had failed to persuade Josef to write such a piece himself.

In September, Josef learned of the Pavlovsk management's decision to engage Benjamin Bilse, rather than himself, for the 1870 season. Forthwith, Josef determined to fill the post left vacant in Warsaw by his Prussian rival. The terms of the contract he hastily concluded with the Polish Schweizertal establishment to give concerts there between 15 May and 15 September 1870 were, however, anything but favourable. A now desperate desire to make himself 'free and independent' perhaps clouded his judgement.

The Pavlovsk season over, Josef, Johann and Jetty returned to Vienna. Amid continuing family disagreements, principally about Eduard, Josef suffered a mild stroke but, despite his mother's entreaties, remained resolute in his plans to proceed with the Schweizertal engagement. Meanwhile, that November (1869) Johann reached agreement with the Gesellschaft der Musikfreunde for regular Sunday Strauss Concerts to be held in the Society's as yet unopened concert hall, the Musikverein (venue of the present-day New Year's Day Concerts of the Vienna Philharmonic Orchestra), from the end of the following March. At the inaugural ball held in the new building on Saturday 15 January 1870, all three brothers were present to conduct their dedications to the august Society – Johann, the waltz *Freuet euch des Lebens* op.340 (Enjoy your life); Josef, the polka française *Künstlergruss* op.274 (Artist's Greeting); Eduard, the polka-mazurka *Eisblume* op.55 (Frost-flower).

The Vienna Carnival that year heralded more new compositions, among them a choral waltz for the Wiener Männergesang-Verein by Johann, *Neu-Wien* op.342 (New Vienna), whose witty text by Weyl drew upon contemporary issues like women's emancipation, inflation and the problems of Vienna's major reconstruction scheme. Decreed by Emperor Franz Joseph in December 1857, this far-reaching project scheduled a programme of modernization, beginning with the destruction of the ancient bastions which encircled the capital – already chronicled in Johann's *Demolirer-Polka* op.269 (Demolition-Men's Polka) of 1862 – thereby removing the division between the inner city limits and the surrounding suburbs.

At the height of the Carnival, the Strauss family was rocked by the first in a chain of personal tragedies when, on 23 February 1870, mother Anna died from 'suppuration of the lungs'. She was in her sixty-ninth year. The many obituaries and cancelled balls after her death bore testimony to the esteem in which she was held by the Viennese people. Her three sons, who owed so much to her sacrifices and sound good sense, mourned her greatly, yet Johann, betraying his obsessive dread of sickness and death, avoided the Hirschenhaus and did not attend his mother's funeral.

The Strauss brothers were again in evidence at the Musikverein on 13 March 1870, for the first of their Promenade Concerts to be held in its magnificent surroundings. There, too, on Easter Sunday 17 April, Josef made his last public appearance in Vienna with a farewell concert, before leaving for Warsaw in the company of the ailing Aunt Pepi.

The Polish venture was beset with problems from the outset: customs difficulties delayed both music and instruments, and the promised accommodation was unavailable. Above all, a number of the musicians (hired from various countries) failed to arrive, due to the negligence of the organizing agents. On 17 May, two days after the scheduled commencement of his concert season. Josef wrote to Johann:

I am disconsolate; no prospect of beginning. When this letter has reached your hands, the catastrophe will have reached its highest peak.

With Eduard's assistance, Josef at last succeeded in completing the orchestra of some thirty musicians, and enjoyed an encouraging reception at his first concert on 22 May. Although illness forced him to cancel his appearance five days later, a successful season seemed in prospect. But on 1 June the effects of anxiety and fatigue overtook him and, during his potpourri *Musikalisches Feuilleton* (unpublished and now lost), Josef suddenly collapsed on the conductor's rostrum. Still unconscious, he was taken back to his apartment. Caroline at once hastened to Warsaw where, as Eduard later wrote, she found her husband, 'his limbs paralysed, scarcely able to speak'. The Polish doctor attending Josef spoke of symptoms of 'cerebral apoplexy', possibly resulting from the bursting of a brain tumour. In Vienna, Johann acted swiftly. To protect at least a part of Josef's income from the Schweizertal season, he arranged for a 'provisional' replacement conductor, Gotthold Carlberg, to be rushed to Warsaw, promising to follow shortly himself. Johann and Jetty finally reached Warsaw at the end of June, but Johann, already ill with jaundice, had become so agitated on the journey that he required the services of a doctor. The *Kurier Warszawski*, initially critical of Johann's delay in travelling to Warsaw, and dubious of his ability to transform his brother's 'not too bad orchestra into an excellent one' (30 June 1870), reported ecstatically on the three concerts Johann gave in the Schweizertal on 4,

5 and 7 July. Johann then left with Jetty to fulfil an orchestral engagement in Baden-Baden, but this was unexpectedly cancelled owing to the outbreak of the Franco-Prussian War, and the couple returned home.

In mid-July, Caroline decided to move Josef back to the Hirschenhaus in Vienna – to the home he had striven for so long to escape. Here, on the afternoon of 22 July 1870, a month before his forty-third birthday, Josef died. Rumours that his demise resulted from injuries inflicted by drunken Russian soldiers are mere fabrication, but the true cause of his death may never be known, since his widow strictly forbade an autopsy, and the inquest merely reported death from 'decomposition of the blood'. On 25 July, Josef Strauss was laid to rest next to his mother in the family grave in the St Marx Cemetery. Before the year was out, the body of Aunt Pepi had also been buried alongside them.

Beyond all doubt, Josef's tragically early death denied the musical world a rich heritage. One can only wonder how his musical style might have developed had he, like his brothers, not been fettered by the commercial constraints of his time. The *Morgenpost*, in its obituary of Josef Strauss, noted that 'he died before he could realize the most precious ambition of his life – the composition of a grand opera'. Josef himself had said in 1869 that he was 'turning to other kinds of composition', and it is intriguing that his widow and daughter both write of an operetta which he supposedly wrote, but which mysteriously vanished immediately after his death. The fate of that operetta, if indeed it ever existed, has never been established.

In a centenary tribute to the composer in the *Illustriertes Wiener Extrablatt* (14 August 1927) Franz Chorherr, then the sole surviving member of the Strauss Orchestra to have played under Josef, wrote:

The young people of today, who enthuse about nothing but jazz, have simply no idea of his noble and heart-touching waltzes, or of how, when Josef Strauss played in the Volksgarten or the Musikverein . . . there were ovations that knew no end.

13

*If an operetta is to become popular, everyone
must find in it something to his liking . . .
The people in the gallery . . . rarely have
money to buy piano editions, even more
rarely a piano – One must therefore see to it
that something remains in their ears when
they've left the performance.*

(Johann Strauss II)

THE VIENNESE first sampled the delights of a stage work by
the Parisian operetta king, Jacques Offenbach, in 1856, when a
French touring company introduced them to his one-act bouffonnerie
musicale, *Les Deux Aveugles* (1855). On 16 October 1858, however,
the resident company at Vienna's Carl-Theater mounted Johann
Nestroy's production of Offenbach's *Hochzeit bei Laternenschein (Le
Mariage aux Lanternes*, 1857), and its enthusiastic reception by both
public and press opened the floodgates to a succession of works by the
composer. Viennese audiences, used to a staple of homespun musical
plays brimming with sentimentality and *Gemütlichkeit*, were
captivated by the satirical humour and sparkling music of Offenbach's
creations, and began to demand more from their own native theatre
composers. The first to accept the challenge was the Dalmatian-born
Franz von Suppé, at that time resident conductor/composer at
Vienna's Theater an der Wien. Until then he had written numerous
'Volksstücke' (folk-plays) and 'Possen' (farces), but his experimental
one-act *Das Pensionat* (1860) is generally regarded as the first true
Viennese operetta. Imitating Offenbach's style, Suppé repeated this
formula many more times with one-act works such as *Zehn Mädchen
und kein Mann* (1862), *Flotte Bursche* (1863), *Die schöne Galathée* (1865)
and *Banditenstreiche* (1867). The young Carl Millöcker, later the
composer of *Der Bettelstudent* (1882) and *Gasparone* (1884), also turned
his hand to writing operettas, such as the one-act *Diana* (1867) and the
full-length *Die Fraueninsel* (1868). But it was to Johann Strauss that
Vienna's theatre directors looked for an effective riposte to the
seemingly matchless Offenbach, whose financial demands they
viewed as exorbitant.

Almost from the time of their marriage, Jetty had sought to interest Johann in the composition of operetta; other considerations apart, she knew that stage works, unlike dance-music, attracted royalties. Johann resisted. Lacking an intuitive dramatic sense (a weakness that undoubtedly hindered him) he failed to recognize immediately how his sovereignty in the ballroom might be transferred to the stage. Eventually, Jetty's will prevailed. As early as January 1864, the Viennese press announced that Strauss's first stage work would appear 'shortly'. Amid persistent speculation Johann remained silent, familiarizing himself with the new genre. Two of his early attempts, a comic opera *Don Quichotte* and *Romulus*, an Offenbach-style bouffonnerie, were both still-born, although the *Fremdenblatt* stated in 1871 that Strauss had actually completed two acts of *Romulus*. Whatever the truth of this, its surviving score fragment and piano arrangement reveal only the hand of Johann's gifted stage mentor, the composer and conductor Richard Genée. In October 1868 Jetty disclosed a further attempt when she wrote that Johann had declined lucrative offers of appearances in Frankfurt, London and America, preferring to spend the winter 'working on an operetta for the Wiedner Theatre' (the old name for Vienna's famous Theater an der Wien). On 6 November 1868 *Die Presse* announced brisk progress with his operetta, *Die lustigen Weiber von Wien* (The Merry Wives of Vienna), whose text was by the successful librettist Josef Braun. The operetta appears to have been completed (it has since been lost), but Strauss had so completely adapted the lead to the individuality of the Theater an der Wien's popular soubrette, Josefine Gallmeyer, that when she unexpectedly signed a new contract with the rival Carl-Theater the project was dashed. Although Strauss composed with remarkable facility he was loathe to waste usable material, and almost certainly the *Merry Wives* score found new life in his later operettas.

Since 1869 the Theater an der Wien had been under the joint directorship of Maximilian Steiner and the celebrated singer and actress Marie Geistinger, creator of several Offenbach rôles in Vienna and future leading lady in the first four Strauss operettas. Steiner, grandfather of the Hollywood film music composer Max Steiner (1888-1971), concerned himself with administrative matters, leaving Geistinger responsible for the artistic side. In May 1870 Strauss, now more sure of his abilities as an operetta composer, signed an exclusive contract with the theatre for the seasons 1870–1 and 1871–2, guaranteeing him, among other benefits, a ten per cent share in the profits on the gross receipts of each performance.

Steiner was at pains to select suitable material for Johann's theatrical début, finally deciding upon a story from *The Arabian Nights*. Under the watchful eye of the technically experienced Genée, conductor at the Theater an der Wien, Strauss began work on *Ali Baba*. After substantial revision, at least two changes of name and several months' delay, the three–act operetta finally reached performance on 10 February 1871 as *Indigo und die vierzig Räuber* (Indigo and the Forty Thieves). Heading the cast were Marie Geistinger (Fantasca), Carl Matthias Rott (Indigo), Carl Adolf Friese (Romadour), Jani Szika (Ali-Baba) and Albin Swoboda (Janio). On the playbill, Steiner's credit for the stage adaptation masked the labours of several collaborators, and the operetta swiftly earned the sobriquet *Indigo and the Forty Librettists*. The long-awaited première attracted a capacity house, including prominent authors, journalists, musicians and composers, and Ludwig Speidel wrote in the *Fremdenblatt* (12 February) that the stock-jobbing for seats was so great that the Director of the Vienna Court Opera, Johann Herbeck, had to be satisfied with an improvised seat in the orchestra. The journalist Josef Wimmer described the evening:

When Johann Strauss appeared in the orchestra pit, he was greeted with a storm of applause. Just as, formerly, in the dance hall, he swung with bold verve onto the conductor's rostrum in the theatre; just as before, a darting fiery glance to the right, then a darting fiery glance to the left, and now the signal to begin . . . At the highlight of the evening, the waltz 'Ja, so singt man, ja, so singt man in der Stadt wo ich geboren', the whole house broke out into a jubilant shout, the occupants of the boxes and the stalls began to dance . . .

Despite the public's enthusiasm for *Indigo*, press reaction was mixed. While praising the 'charming dance motifs', Hanslick (*Neue Freie Presse*, 12 February) complained that the author of this 'dreadful libretto provides the composer with no characters . . . but with stuffed dolls which have neither point nor reason', and he criticized the 'pathetic action and offensively empty dialogue'. Hanslick continued: 'A man of Johann Strauss's reputation and talent would have done better not to have had anything to do with it . . . If, at least, it were over quickly! But this "operetta" lasts almost four hours!' the *Fremdenblatt* disagreed, considering 'the whole thing an estimable piece of work', promising 'the most splendid expectations for the future'.

Indigo achieved forty-six performances at the Theater an der Wien during 1871, besides many more in productions throughout Austro-Hungary and Germany. With a new book and various musical interpolations, the work reached Paris in 1875 as *La Reine Indigo*. Other revised versions followed, but the most durable remains *Tausend und eine Nacht* (Thousand and One Nights) of 1906, for which Ernst Reiterer reworked Strauss's score to suit an entirely new book, and in which arrangement the popular *Intermezzo* appears. The richly melodic score of *Indigo* afforded Strauss himself abundant scope for arranging several orchestral pieces from its themes, like the waltz *Tausend und eine Nacht* op.346, the polka schnell *Im Sturmschritt* op.348 (At the Double) and the swaggering *Indigo-Marsch* op.349. It is a measure of Johann's genius for melody that although *Indigo* and most of his subsequent operettas have long disappeared from theatre repertoire, much of their music continues to enjoy a life of its own, fashioned by the composer into orchestral dances and marches. Indeed, Hanslick said of *Indigo*: 'It is Strauss dance-music, with words added and rôles ascribed. Strauss cannot imagine a bright or even cosy text in any other form than that of the waltz or the polka.'

Just five weeks before the *Indigo* première, on 5 January 1871, Johann officially requested his release from the functional duties of k.k.Hofballmusik-Direktor, 'on the grounds of ill health'. Certainly Johann's health had been less than stable during the 1860s, but perhaps even more pressing was his determination now to devote himself wholeheartedly to stage composition. In his petition he referred to his manifold past achievements, to the demand he had created for Viennese music abroad (thereby assisting fellow Austrian musicians), and to the part he had played in popularizing the music of Richard Wagner ('when theatres and concert halls everywhere were closed to the great maestro'). Writing in the third person, Strauss added:

. . . he leaves it to the discretion of the high k.k.Obersthofmeister's Office to judge whether his long years of service, which materially brought in little, should for this reason recommend him for the granting of a distinction from the all-highest authority.

His release was granted by the Emperor himself on 12 January; besides the right to retain his title in name, Johann was awarded the Knight's Cross of the Order of Franz Joseph, 'in recognition of his merit as Conductor of Music at Court Balls, and as a composer'. On 18 February 1872 the honorary title and functional duties of k.k.Hofballmusik-Direktor were conferred upon Eduard Strauss, duties which he was to discharge for almost thirty years.

When Johann returned to Vienna in autumn 1871 from the Berlin première of *Indigo*, he received a visit from the Irish-born American composer and bandmaster Patrick Sarsfield Gilmore, who invited him to participate in a mammoth World's Peace Jubilee and International Musical Festival planned for the following summer in Boston, USA. Strauss had already agreed in principle to a short summer season in Pavlovsk in 1872, though he had not finalized the exact dates. The financial and artistic appeal of the American venture, however, outweighed the attractions of another Pavlovsk season, and Johann's acceptance of the Boston proposal cost him an expensive lawsuit brought by the Russian management.

Had it not been for Jetty, it is doubtful whether Strauss would have overcome his aversion to the lengthy sea voyage to America, irrespective of the tempting fee, which Eisenberg states was $100,000 (£20,000 sterling, today equivalent to £414,460), but Jetty says was $25,000. Notwithstanding, on 19 May 1872 Johann drafted his last will, naming Jetty as his sole heir and making provision for other family members. These beneficiaries included Jetty's stepfather, Josef

Ritter von Scherer, who at about this time unsuccessfully attempted to transfer his aristocratic title to Johann.

On 1 June Johann, Jetty and their two servants left Bremerhaven aboard the steamship *Rhein*, together with other celebrities bound for the Boston Jubilee – the acclaimed Viennese soprano Minna Peschka-Leutner, and from Germany the Band of the Kaiser Franz Garde-Grenadier Regiment and the Kaiser Wilhelm Imperial Cornet Quartet. After a scheduled stop at Southampton on 4 June, the *Rhein* docked at Hoboken on 15 June to a grand reception. That afternoon, the visitors took the Fall River Steamer to Boston, where Strauss's arrival was marred by great disappointment since, owing to a misunderstanding, the entire Strauss Orchestra had been expected.

By any standards, the scale of the Jubilee celebrations, which officially lasted from 17 June to 4 July, was immense. The Coliseum, the hub of the Jubilee concerts, was situated in the Back Bay district of Boston, and was at that time the largest building ever constructed in America. 550 feet (167.64 m) long and 350 feet (106.68 m) wide, it stood 115 feet (35.05 m) high and boasted a seating capacity of 50,000 people. The Jubilee *Handbook* shows that, besides a chorus of some 20,000 voices and a 'regular' orchestra of 809 (including a 'Monster Drum', 12 feet in diameter and weighing almost 600 lb!), there were also military bands from Germany, France and England (the Grenadier Guards, under Dan Godfrey) and twenty-nine separate bands from America, bringing the aggregate of instrumentalists to almost 2000. Among other soloists engaged for the season were the conductor Franz Abt and the pianists Franz Bendel and Arabella Goddard. Invitations were also extended to Hans von Bülow and Giuseppe Verdi, but both had declined.

In this vast auditorium, Strauss took his place on the conductor's platform for sixteen concerts and two balls. As in London, the Waltz King's performances frequently departed from the printed programme, and although he was only committed to play one orchestral item each day there were, inevitably, encores. The works with which 'Strauss the electric' thrilled his American audiences included *On the beautiful blue Danube*, *Artist's Life*, *1001 Nights*, *New Vienna* and the polkas *Pizzicato* and *Kreuzfidel* (op.301). He introduced two novelties, the *Circassian-March* (better known as the *Egyptian March* op.335) and a piece dedicated to Gilmore, the *Jubilee Waltz* (a potpourri comprising several of his earlier waltz melodies, and featuring in the Coda a quotation from *The Star-Spangled Banner*). At least eight other sets of waltzes, apparently composed or arranged for Boston, and published in America, seem not to have been performed there by Strauss.

From Boston, Johann allegedly addressed a letter to the *Neue Freie Presse*, regarding 'my joyful experience in this extraordinary affair'. But his later recollections to a friend tell a different story:

On the concert platform were thousands of singers and instrumentalists, and these I was to conduct! A hundred assistant conductors had been placed at my disposal to control these gigantic masses, but I was only able to see those nearest to me. Although we had rehearsed, an artistic performance, a proper production, was unthinkable. I would have put my life at risk if I had refused to appear . . . Suddenly a cannon fired, a gentle hint for us twenty thousand to begin the concert. *'The beautiful blue Danube'* was on the programme. I gave the signal, my hundred sub-conductors followed me as quickly and as well as they could, and then there broke out a fearful racket that I shall never forget as long as I live! As we had begun more or less simultaneously, my whole attention was now directed towards seeing that we should also finish together. Thank Heaven, I also managed that. The hundred thousand-strong audience roared their approval, and I breathed a sigh of relief when I found myself in the fresh air again and felt the firm ground beneath my feet. The next day I had to flee an army of impresarios, who promised me the whole of California for a tour of America. I had already had quite enough of the music 'festival', and returned to Europe with the very greatest possible speed.

Before returning to Europe, however, Johann braved the train journey from Boston to New York – Jetty later told the *New York Sun*: 'My husband says he'd rather be killed at once, and be done with it, than to take another trip on an American railroad.' At the Academy of Music in New York he earned a further $4500 for three concerts. For the last of these, on 12 July, he arranged another 'potpourri' based on earlier compositions, the *Manhattan Waltzes*, the Coda of which features twenty-three bars from Stephen Foster's song *The Old Folks at Home*. Still pursued by entrepreneurs, 'Mr Johann Strauss, wife and servants' boarded the steamship *Donau* on Saturday 13 July 1872 bound for Bremen, and thence to Baden-Baden. In spite of many offers, Johann never again visited America.

In order to avoid an outbreak of cholera in Vienna, the Strausses extended their stay in Baden-Baden until mid-October. Here, as he had done in 1871, Johann conducted the Spa Orchestra in a number of concerts, while his wife visited the thermal baths. His performances were often attended by the German Emperor and King of Prussia, Wilhelm I, who decorated Strauss for the dedication of his *Kaiser-Wilhelm-Polonaise* (published in Vienna merely as *Fest-Polonaise* op.352). Hans von Bülow also frequented these concerts, and wrote to his mother of

the charming magician Johann Strauss, whose compositions, conducted by himself with such unique grace and rhythmic precision, have given me one of the most stimulating of musical pleasures which I can remember having for a long time.

On the same day (13 September 1872), von Bülow wrote of Strauss to Louise von Welz:

. . . he is a conductor of genius in his small genre, just as Wagner is in the sublime! . . . There is something to be learned from Strauss's style of performance for the *Ninth Symphony*, as for the *Pathétique*.

94

Back in Vienna, Johann took up work on an operetta he had started before his American trip. Entitled *Carneval in Rom* (Carnival in Rome), it was an adaptation by Josef Braun of Victorien Sardou's play *Piccolino*, a romantic tale of a Swiss maiden's love for an artist, set against the colourful backcloth of Italy. First performed at the Theater an der Wien on 1 March 1873 under the composer's baton, and with a cast headed by Marie Geistinger (Marie), Albin Swoboda (Arthur Bryk), Caroline Charles (Countess Falconi) and Jani Szika (Benvenuto Raphaeli), *Carneval in Rom* drew generally favourable comment from the press. The *Fremdenblatt* (2 March), for example, found that, whereas in *Indigo* a profusion of dance melodies had predominated, *Carneval in Rom* revealed depths that were 'finer and more tender', and added:

the popular undertones, so light on the ear, have not been neglected by the composer, and thus his work falls into two parts, of which the one retains the exciting rhythmical tempo of comic operetta, while the second moves into the style of lyric opera.

Strauss himself thought highly of *Carneval in Rom* (later dubbing it 'my polka opera'), and even considered offering it to the Vienna Court Opera, after making various alterations. The operetta achieved wider popularity than *Indigo*, and productions were mounted as far afield as New York and Chicago.

Even at the height of his creativity as an operetta composer, Johann continued to exert an influence on Vienna's concert halls and ballrooms, not only with dances based on melodies culled from his stage works, but also with a number of fine independent compositions. Into this last category falls the waltz *Wiener Blut* (Vienna Blood), first conducted by Johann on 22 April 1873 during a concert in the Musikverein to open a grand festival ball in celebration of the wedding of Emperor Franz Joseph's daughter, Gisela, and Prince Leopold of Bavaria. The performance marked Strauss's début with the renowned Vienna Philharmonic Orchestra.

On 1 May Vienna opened her doors to a World Exhibition along the lines of those already held in London and Paris. Organized on the Prater to promote Austrian trade and industry, this colossal enterprise was scarcely under way when, on 9 May ('Black Friday'), there came the great crash of the Vienna Stock Exchange. Despite this financial disaster, and a renewed epidemic of cholera in the city, more than seven million visitors attended the Exhibition, but it closed on 2 December with a deficit of almost 15 million gulden. As one observer wrote: 'Vienna invited the world to a wedding-feast, which turned into a wake.' Since, at this time, Vienna was literally 'at home' to the world, Eduard Strauss had been justifiably piqued at the Exhibition director's engagement (at Johann's instigation!) of foreign musicians, the Langenbach Orchestra from Germany, as official 'World Exhibition Orchestra', jointly conducted by Julius Langenbach and Johann Strauss.

It was with this orchestra, rather than Eduard's own Strauss Orchestra, that Johann first performed his topically entitled choral waltz, *Bei uns z'Haus* op.361 (At home), with the Wiener Männergesang-Verein in Hietzing's 'Neue Welt' (New World) establishment on 6 August 1873 – this, even though the Neue Welt had a contract with the Strauss Orchestra. Similarly, Johann conducted the Langenbach Orchestra at a charity concert in the Musikverein on 25 October that year, when Marie Geistinger sang a newly composed 'vocal Csárdás', with words by Richard Genée and music by Johann Strauss.

Five days later, *Die Presse* announced that the Waltz King had begun work on a new operetta for the Theater an der Wien.

Vienna's Dianabad–Saal, venue for the first performance of many Strauss family compositions, including the *Blue Danube Waltz*. Charles Maurand's woodcut shows a masked ball in progress.

Johann and Jetty's home at No.54 Praterstrasse, where the *Blue Danube Waltz* was composed in 1867. The apartment was opened to the public in 1978 as a Johann Strauss Museum. Watercolour painting by K. Zajicek.

Title page of the original pianoforte edition of Johann II's waltz, *An der schönen blauen Donau* op.314. Published by C. A. Spina, Vienna, in 1867.

sang-Vereine
widmet.

lauen Donau.

B E R

TE componirt

TRAUSS,

sikdirector.

nd, Frankreich, Belgien, Eigenthum des Verlegers.

A. SPINA

sikalienhandlung

t - Ausstellung   Mailand. Ricordi.

Büttner

Druck Weißel.

Pr. 80 Nkr. / 15 Ngr.

Title page of Johann II's *Promenade Quadrille*, showing Strauss conducting in the Royal Italian Opera House, Covent Garden, during the 1867 Promenade Concert Season. Published by Charles Sheard, London.

Title page illustration of Johann II's waltz *Freuet euch des Lebens* op.340, showing the newly opened Musikverein building in Vienna. Published by C. A. Spina in 1870.

Marie Geistinger as Fantasca in the first production of *Indigo und die vierzig Räuber* at the Theater an der Wien (1871).

The Theater an der Wien, Vienna. Watercolour by K. Zajicek, 1897.

K. k. priv. Theater an der Wien.

Unter der Direktion Geistinger & Steiner.

Sonntag den 5. April 1874.

Zum erstenmale:

Die Fledermaus.

Komische Operette in 3 Akten nach Meilhac und Halevy's „Reveillon", bearbeitet von C. Haffner und Richard Genée. **Musik von Johann Strauss.**
Tänze arrangirt von der Balletmeisterin Frau Therese v. Kilany.
Die neuen Dekorationen des ersten und zweiten Aktes von Herrn Alfred Moser. — Die neuen Kostüme angefertigt vom Obergarderobier Herrn Schulze
Möbel von Aug. Kitschelt's Erben (Rudolf Kitschelt), k. k. Hoflieferant.

Gabriel von Eisenstein, Rentier	Hr. Szika.
Rosalinde, seine Frau	Marie Geistinger.
Frank, Gefängniß-Direktor	Hr. Friese.
Prinz Orlofski	Frl. Nittinger.
Alfred, sein Gesanglehrer	Hr. Rüdinger.
Dr. Falke, Notar	Hr Lebrecht.
Dr. Blind, Advokat	Hr. Rott.
Adele, Stubenmädchen Rosalindens	Fr. Charles-Hirsch a. G.
Ali-Bey, ein Egypter	Hr. Romani.
Ramusin, Gesandschafts-Attaché	Hr. Jäger.
Murray, Amerikaner	Hr. Liebold.
Carikoni, ein Marquis	Hr. Thalboth.
Lord Middleton	Hr. Fink.
Baron Oskar	Hr. Mellin.
Frosch, Gerichtsdiener	Hr. Schreiber.
Yvan, Kammerdiener des Prinzen	Hr. Gärtner.
Ida,	Frl. Jules.
Melanie,	Frl. Kopf.
Felicita,	Frl. Schindler.
Eibi,	Frl. Treuge.
Minni,	Frl. N. Grünfeld.
Faustine,	Frl. A. Grünfeld.
Silvia,	Frl. Künzler.
Sabine,	Frl. Stubel.
Bertha,	Frl. Steinburg.
Lori,	Frl. Donner.
Paula,	Fr. Romani.
Erster)	Hr. Buchner.
Zweiter) Diener des Prinzen	Hr. Kaschke.
Ein Amtsdiener	Hr. Schwellal.

Gäste des Prinzen Orlofski

Herren und Damen. Masken. Bediente.

Die Handlung spielt in einem Badeorte, in der Nähe einer großen Stadt.

Vorkommende Tänze:

1. **Spanisch**, ausgeführt von Frl. Grillich und 8 Damen vom Ballet.
2. **Schottisch**, Frl. Geraldini, Fechtner, Wollschack, Meier und Wiest.
3. **Russisch**, Frl. Angelina-Bonesi, Frl. Stubenvoll, Nagelschmidt, Gwetkofsky, Guhr, Schmidt und Großeli.
4. **Polka**, Frl Walter, Frl. Raab und Anna Thorn.
5. **Ungarisch**, ausgeführt von Frl. Benda und Herrn Couqui.

Anfang 7 Uhr.

K. k. Hoftheater-Druckerei. (B. N. St. G.)

Playbill for the première of *Die Fledermaus* at the Theater an der Wien.

Interior of the Coliseum, Boston, USA, where Johann II conducted at the World's Peace Jubilee and International Musical Festival in 1872. From *Frank Leslie's Illustrated Newspaper*.

Panoramic view of the 1873 World Exhibition buildings on the Prater, Vienna. Line drawing from *The Illustrated London News*, 2 November 1872.

FRITZ LUCKHARDT   K.K.HOFPHOTOGRAPH
LEOPOLDST. TABORSTR. 18   im HÔTEL NATIONAL
WIEN.   WIEN.

Maximilian Steiner and his son Franz, directors of Vienna's famous Theater an der Wien. (Courtesy of the Historisches Museum der Stadt Wien)

F. Zell (Camillo Walzel) and Richard Genée, (*opposite*) the most successful team of libretists in nineteenth-century Viennese operetta.
(Courtesy of the Historisches Museum der Stadt Wien)

The 'Fledermaus Villa' in Hietzing, where Johann II wrote his most famous operetta.

14

*We do not want to praise his operetta to the
skies, but rather keep our feet firmly on the
ground, lest the man become cocksure.*

(Hugo Wittmann, reviewing the première of Johann Strauss's
Die Fledermaus. Neue Freie Presse, 8 April 1874)

WHEN MAX Steiner, co-director of the Theater an der Wien,
acquired the rights to the French vaudeville *Le Réveillon* (1872),
he was confident of repeating its Parisian success in Vienna, and
promptly commissioned the playwright Carl Haffner to prepare a
German version. *Le Réveillon* (Supper on Christmas Eve), written by
Henri Meilhac and Ludovic Halévy – the librettists of Bizet's *Carmen*
and numerous Offenbach operettas – had in turn been based upon a
German comedy of 1851 by Roderich Benedix, *Das Gefängnis* (The
Prison). Steiner dismissed Haffner's effort as unsuitable, however,
and tried in vain to dispose of the French vaudeville to Franz Jauner,
director of Vienna's Carl-Theater. Gustav Lewy, the theatrical
publisher and theatre agent, then suggested that Richard Genée should
rework Haffner's play into an operetta book for Johann Strauss. Genée
accepted, but finding Haffner's version unusable, turned to the French
original for the basis of his libretto. Genée later recalled:

From Haffner's farce . . . I kept only the names of the characters. I also had to
depart drastically from the structure and the characters of the original . . . So
that the trusty writer Haffner would not be hurt, I agreed to have his name on
the playbill as collaborator. I, personally, never saw Haffner.

Strauss's creative imagination was at once sparked by *Doktor
Fledermaus*, as Genée's libretto was first called, and before long a
substantial part of the score had been sketched out – allegedly in just
'42 days and nights'. The *Die Presse* announcement notwithstanding,
documentary evidence now suggests that the major work on
Fledermaus took place between the middle or end of August 1873 and
mid-October of that year, when Johann was permanent in Vienna
with no other pressing commitments. The score may then have been
put to one side, as production of the operetta was originally planned
for September 1874. Because of financial difficulties facing the theatre,
however, it was subsequently decided to bring forward the première

to April 1874, and Strauss's final draft was completed only shortly beforehand. Strauss and Genée worked closely. Genée not only provided the entire song-texts and dialogue but, with his intimate knowledge of writing for the theatre, often assisted Strauss with the elaboration of the score. Indeed, the late Professor Dr Fritz Racek's scholarly analysis of the *Fledermaus* autograph reveals that only the Overture and Rosalinde's Csárdás (as also the alternative csárdás Strauss was to write for the rôle in 1896) are entirely without alterations or additions in Genée's hand.

Die Fledermaus was widely acclaimed by the press following its première at the Theater an der Wien on Easter Sunday, 5 April 1874. Its principal singers were Marie Geistinger (Rosalinde), Caroline Esther Charles-Hirsch (Adele), Jani Szika (von Eisenstein) and Carl Adolf Friese (Frank), while Alfred Schreiber created the rôle of Frosch. The critic of the *Sonn- und Montags-Zeitung* (6 April) spoke of the 'thunderous applause which shook the theatre', while the *Konstitutionelle Vorstadt-Zeitung* wrote:

Almost every number set the audience's hands in motion, and after the end of each act Strauss, bathed in perspiration, could not leave the conductor's desk fast enough in order to thank the friendly audience, from the stage, for its goodwill.

Admittedly, some dissenting voices were raised. The *Fremdenblatt* felt 'it was not the outstanding success that the theatre expected of this new work', while the *Deutsche Musikzeitung* found Strauss's music 'charming, though it lacks élan'. Eduard Hanslick was especially critical of the libretto:

It remains an insoluble puzzle that anyone could have music for such words, and that the musical inspiration in the composer's head doesn't die away before it can cling to such platitudes.

The inaccurate and misleading statement by Strauss's first biographer, Ludwig Eisenberg (1894), that *Fledermaus* was performed in Vienna 'only 16 times in succession', has led innumerable writers to conclude, erroneously, that the work was initially a failure and, as such, was withdrawn. Precisely how Eisenberg derived the figure sixteen remains a mystery. The truth is that when *Fledermaus* opened, the Theater an der Wien was already presenting a season of twenty guest appearances by an Italian opera company, starring Adelina Patti. Thus, the run of *Die Fledermaus* was often interrupted (for the first time on 11 April) by performances of Italian opera, and later by previously scheduled operetta productions. Only after the forty-ninth performance, on 6 June 1874, was *Fledermaus* temporarily withdrawn, owing to the illness of Irma Nittinger in the rôle of Prince Orlofsky. When the work returned to the repertoire that autumn, the cast included a youthful Alexander Girardi as the notary, Dr Falke. Girardi, the creator of many subsequent Johann Strauss rôles, was to become the most celebrated performer in Viennese operetta.

In July 1874 *Die Fledermaus* opened in Berlin, and spread swiftly to other Germany theatres before conquering Europe, America and Australia. In December 1876 it became the first Strauss operetta to be performed in London, and in October 1877 (with a completely new book and revised musical score) it reached Paris as *La Tzigane* (The Gypsy Girl). Gustav Mahler conducted the work at the Hamburg Stadttheater in 1894, and on 28 October that year the 'operetta of all operettas' made its début at the Vienna Court Opera, during the Jubilee celebrations marking Strauss's 'fifty years of artistic activity'.

Less than a month after the Viennese première of *Die Fledermaus*, Johann Strauss left his native city for a series of twenty-one guest concerts throughout Italy with the Langenbach Orchestra. The Strauss Orchestra, under Eduard, was at that time contracted to appear in Vienna, and so was unavailable for the tour. On 9 May, at the Teatro Regio, Turin, Johann introduced an 'especially composed' new waltz entitled *Bella Italia* (Beautiful Italy) which, for his Viennese audiences, he later renamed *Wo die Citronen blüh'n!* (op.364) – a title plucked from the first line of Goethe's famous poem, 'Kennst du das Land wo die Citronen blüh'n?' (Do you know the land where the lemon-trees blossom?)

For his next stage work Strauss seized upon a book by the respected and successful partnership of F. Zell and Richard Genée. The story concerned the eighteenth-century escapades of the real-life alchemist and swindler, Count Alessandro Cagliostro. Strauss was so confident of success with the resulting operetta, *Cagliostro in Wien* (Cagliostro in Vienna), that he performed its Overture even before the première at the Theater an der Wien on 27 February 1875. Perhaps the greatest praise for the *Cagliostro* music came from the composer Johannes Brahms, by that time a frequent guest at Strauss's home. The two men had become acquainted in Vienna on 11 November 1862, and at Baden-Baden in 1871 the acquaintance grew into friendship. At about that time Brahms confided to Hans von Bülow: 'He is one of the few colleagues whom I can hold in limitless respect', and he paid tribute to Strauss in his String Quartet op.51 by interpolating reminiscences of the waltz *Wein, Weib und Gesang!* Brahms regarded Strauss's operettas with especial interest, marvelling particularly at his gift for instrumentation: 'There is now no one who is as sure as he is in such matters', he told the composer Richard Heuberger in 1887. Brahms was enraptured by the score of *Cagliostro*, which he first heard played by its composer on the piano at an informal soirée at Strauss's home. Afterwards, he enthused to the writer Paul Lindau: 'What can one single out – it is all equally wonderful! The man oozes music! He always comes up with something – in that, he differs from the rest of us.'

On the whole, the first-night critics did not share Brahms's enchantment with *Cagliostro in Wien*. The title rôle was taken by Carl Adolf Friese, with Marie Geistinger as Lorenza, Henriette Wieser as Frau Adami, Caroline Finaly as Emilie and Alexander Girardi as Blasoni. The *Fremdenblatt* (2 March) considered that Strauss 'waxes and wanes with the interest of the action; when the right thing is demanded of him, we can trace his streak of genius'. Nevertheless, it conceded: 'When you imagine that Strauss has already played his best cards, he finally produces another waltz which "out-trumps" everything.' *Cagliostro* ran for forty-nine performances at the Theater an der Wien in 1875, but reached comparatively few foreign stages, perhaps because of the very local nature of its subject. Today, the operetta is largely remembered through the dances Strauss arranged on its themes, such as the *Cagliostro-Walzer* (op.370), *Bitte schön! Polka française* (op.372) and *Auf der Jagd, Schnell-Polka* (op.373).

A fascinating glimpse of life behind the closed doors of Strauss's Hietzing villa at this time is given by the German journalist Albert Wolff:

Strauss works 'feverishly': he composes with the same nervous energy with which he conducts the orchestra. His workroom is everywhere. In a velvet suit and top boots, his hair in a mess, he rushes through his apartments . . . Madame Strauss sees to it that in every room there is a table with writing implements . . . Whether Strauss is composing an operetta or a polka, he gets into an indescribable state of nervous excitement. After two or three hours of such work, he is as exhausted as a native bearer . . . Strauss always believes that his best work is already behind him. He belongs to that breed of artists who spend their lives doubting themselves . . .

On 22 March, soon after the *Cagliostro* première, Johann left for Paris to supervise the preparations for the first night of *La Reine Indigo*. Ten days before his departure he wrote to Richard Genée, urgently requesting several numbers from *Carneval in Rom* and *Cagliostro in Wien*, 'which I can insert if necessary . . . I am too <u>weary</u> to get involved in composing new pieces in Paris, and in addition I lack the necessary peace and quiet since I have to hold 4 hours of rehearsals a day. I plan to try and scrape through by these means . . .'

In the event, Johann was delighted at 'the greatest possible success' achieved by *La Reine Indigo*, and he voiced a strong desire to compose a genuine 'French operetta'. Genée straightaway offered Strauss the book of *Fatinitza*, founded on Scribe's *La Circassienne*, but Jetty persuaded him to reject it, fearing a repetition of the plagiarism charges that had been levelled at the unauthorized adaptation of *Le Réveillon*. Suppé, instead, set *Fatinitza* to music, and scored a triumph with it.

Seeing an opportunity to attract Johann Strauss to the Carl-Theater, its director, Franz Jauner, especially commissioned the Parisian librettists Victor Wilder and A. Delacour (the authors of the French adaptation of *Die Fledermaus*) to prepare a book for Strauss. From this, Johann composed much of the score of his new operetta, although he spoke little French and must have relied heavily on Jetty's knowledge of the language. Not until the actor Carl Treumann skilfully revised and translated the French libretto into German did the stage work, *Prinz Methusalem* (Prince Methuselah), eventually reach production. This rather lacklustre, Offenbach-style tale of love and political intrigue in an imaginary princedom was immersed in a wealth of delightful music, combining Viennese verve with Parisian flair. Featured in the principal rôles were Josef Matras (Sigismund, Prince of Trocadero), Caroline Finaly (Pulcinella), Antonie Link (Prince Methuselah), Wilhelm Knaack (Cyprian, Duke of Ricarac) and Therese Braunecker-Schäfer (Sophistica). Strauss conducted the première of his new operetta at the Carl-Theater on 3 January 1877, but was unimpressed by the standard of the resident orchestra and resolved to avoid the Carl-Theater for his subsequent operetta premières. *Prinz Methusalem* was received by the public with rejoicing, but the critics were again mixed in their verdicts. While the *Fremdenblatt* praised the composer's development since *Indigo*, traceable in the 'extraordinarily comprehensive score', others considered that Strauss 'must compose completely independently of the text; for to what could these words and this plot inspire him!' The *Illustriertes Wiener Extrablatt* (5 January) summarized simply: 'The Viennese composer par excellence . . . wanted to become Offenbach the Second, but he remained Strauss the First. Much as he may have wished to, he was unable to deny his own artistic individuality . . .'

Shortly after the *Methusalem* première Johann again travelled to Paris, this time to conduct at the masked balls in the new Paris Opéra building. In March the French rewarded his services to music by conferring upon him the Knight's Cross of the Légion d'honneur. Later that year he returned to Paris to prepare for the première of *La Tzigane*, which took place on 30 October. He left France immediately afterwards. Jetty informed a friend on 20 October: 'Jean is being drawn to Hietzing by his work desk – where, waiting longingly for him, is "Blinde Kuh" . . .' Jetty was never to see this new operetta. After years of persistent and painful illness – she often spoke of herself as 'a poor old cripple' – she died at 11.30 p.m. on 8 April 1878 from a heart attack, reportedly caused by a disturbing letter from one of her illegitimate sons. That same night, alone and in a state of shock, Johann fled the Hietzing villa where Jetty had died, never to return there. Jetty was buried three days later in the local Hietzing cemetery. Johann was absent from her funeral, as he had been from the burials of his mother, brother Josef and Aunt Pepi, and once more left the arrangements to Eduard.

Johann Strauss was unable to face life alone. On 28 May 1878 he remarried, just seven weeks after Jetty's death.

15

You know, I am afraid when I'm alone!

(Johann Strauss to Paul Lindau, shortly after Jetty's death)

JOHANN'S new bride, Ernestine Henriette Angelika Dittrich, was a pretty blue-eyed actress from Breslau, in Prussian Silesia. Known as 'Lili', she was about twenty-five years younger than the composer. The couple are said to have been introduced by Lili's singing teacher, Heinrich Proch, at Vienna's Hotel Victoria, where the 52-year-old Johann had taken up residence after leaving his Hietzing home. There is evidence to suggest, however, that they had already come to know one another during Jetty's lifetime. Whether Lili's motive for marriage was love or infatuation – she later admitted to the writer Julius Bauer that she had adored Strauss's music from her childhood – it cannot be denied that, in Johann, she saw a passport to her ambitions of theatre management.

In 1875 Johann had purchased two adjacent plots of ground in the Wieden district of Vienna, and here Jetty had closely supervised the design and construction of an elegant 'Stadt-Palais', a city home equipped to meet Strauss's every need that was more suited to Johann's position in stylish Viennese society than the villa at Hietzing. Next to music, Johann's passions were billiards and tarot, and his Palais boasted its own billiard-room, stables, and large reception rooms where he entertained eminent guests such as Brahms, Bruckner and Puccini. This Palais, at No. 4 Igelgasse (today, Johann-Strauss-Gasse), was completed shortly after Jetty's death, and it was here that Johann and Lili moved after their wedding in Vienna's Karlskirche. Their honeymoon, at Wyk, on the North Frisian Island of Föhr, was delayed until later in the year to allow Johann time to work on *Blindekuh*. Lili assisted her husband to the best of her rather limited abilities. Like Jetty, she acted as his copyist, but she lacked Jetty's theatrical experience and judgement. Lili soon realized that she had married a compulsive worker whose way of life she was unable to comprehend, and although Johann strove to retain a youthful appearance which denied his years, the fascination he had once held for her began to wane.

Blindekuh (Blind Man's Buff) opened at the Theater an der Wien on 18 December 1878, with Alexander Girardi as Johann, Bertha Olma as Waldine, Hermine Meyerhoff as Betsy and Felix Schweighofer as

Kragel . Strauss had been forced to compose afresh twelve numbers from the operetta which had been mislaid during the move to the Igelgasse. Rudolf Kneisel's libretto, based on his German comedy of the same name, was chiefly to blame for the operetta's unequivocal failure, which neither the music nor Girardi's ability could prevent. *Blindekuh* was withdrawn after only sixteen performances. The *Wiener Pikante Blätter* (22 December) observed keenly: 'Among his other talents, Johann Strauss also possesses that of selecting the worst of the texts put before him.' The satirical *Die Bombe* (22 December) went still further:

Unfortunately, in the choice of his libretto, this time Maestro Strauss is himself playing Blind Man's Buff . . . Johann Strauss personally conducts – the public to the outside of the theatre. That is, the people prefer to avoid the bad text and the dull presentation, and to have the tuneful waltzes of Maestro Strauss played to them in their own homes, in a piano arrangement by Spina.

The 'hit' song of the evening, the Act 2 waltz *Blindekuh! Blindekuh!*, was, however, to achieve remarkable durability when, arranged with a melody from Johann's *Aeols-Töne Walzer* (op.68), it became the haunting *Nun's Chorus and Laura's Song* in Ralph Benatzky's 1928 pastiche-operetta success, *Casanova*.

In February 1879 Johann repeated his Parisian triumph of two years earlier when, again alternating with Olivier Métra, he conducted at the Opéra Balls. That summer, on the advice of his doctors, Johann revisited Wyk with Lili, and here wrote his 'seascape' waltz *Nordseebilder* (North Sea Pictures), which he first performed with the local orchestra. Like so many of his compositions dating from the 1870s onwards, this work was first heard in Vienna at one of Eduard Strauss's regular Sunday Concerts in the Musikverein.

The precarious financial position of the Theater an der Wien in the late 1870s contributed to the serious illness, and eventual death in May 1880, of its director Maximilian Steiner. As Marie Geistinger had chosen in 1875 to exchange her co-directorship for a guest contract, Steiner's son Franz assumed managerial control of the theatre, and for his opening production on 1 October 1880 presented Johann Strauss's seventh operetta, *Das Spitzentuch der Königin* (The Queen's Lace Handkerchief). The author of the original book, Heinrich Bohrmann-Riegen, had intended his work for Franz von Suppé. Learning of this plan, Strauss invited Bohrmann-Riegen to his Palais for a read-through, and was so inspired by this tale of romance and intrigue set in the sixteenth-century Court of Portugal that he spontaneously sketched out what was to become the Act 1 *Trüffel-Couplet*, 'Stets kommt mir wieder in den Sinn'. In the words of one first night reviewer, *Das Spitzentuch der Königin* achieved 'a more enthusiastic reception than any other work since Fledermaus', and there was justifiable praise for the performances of Eugenie Erdösy (The King),

Karoline Tellheim (The Queen), Hermine Meyerhoff (Donna Irene), Ferdinand Schütz (Cervantes), Felix Schweighofer (Count Villalobos) and Alexander Girardi (Don Sancho). Although the libretto was accredited to Bohrmann-Riegen, with assistance from Richard Genée, the critics recorded no less than four co-librettists. At a subsequent court case further 'authors' emerged, each claiming entitlement to a share in the profits of the highly successful *Spitzentuch*! Two of the operetta's most acclaimed numbers, the King's *Trüffel-Couplet* and the poet Cervantes's waltz aria 'Wo die wilde Rose erblüht', figure prominently in Strauss's orchestral waltz on themes from *Spitzentuch*, *Rosen aus dem Süden* op.388 (Roses from the South).

During 1874 work on *Die Fledermaus* had precluded Strauss from composing an original choral work for the Wiener Männergesang-Verein's Fasching Song Programme. Instead, he had arranged his 1864 polka, *'s gibt nur a Kaiserstadt! 's gibt nur a Wien!* op.291 (There's only one Imperial city! There's only one Vienna!), for male chorus, with a text by Genée. On 8 May 1881 he fully compensated the Association for the lapse of seven years when, under his baton, they presented his exquisite choral waltz *Myrthensträusse* (Myrtle Bouquets) – later renamed *Myrthenblüthen* op.395 (Myrtle Blossoms). The performance, given during a festival on the Prater to celebrate the marriage of Crown Prince Rudolf with the Belgian Princess Stefanie (the dedicatees of the waltz), was unfortunately spoiled, as the royal party was prevented from reaching the venue by the jubilant 20,000-strong crowd.

Strauss's desire for a peaceful refuge led him, in 1880, to purchase an imposing country retreat at Schönau-bei-Leobersdorf, in Lower Austria. In these idyllic surroundings he composed his eighth operetta, *Der lustige Krieg* (The Merry War), during the summer months of 1881. Johann had again turned to Zell and Genée for the libretto which, like *Carneval in Rom*, had an Italian setting, a milieu for which Strauss had a predilection. The complex story concerned a bloodless 'war' between two armies, one of them commanded entirely by women. Alexander Girardi, appearing in his fourth Strauss première, was dissatisfied with the extent of his rôle as the Marquis Sebastiani, and threatened to resign his part unless the composer wrote him an additional solo number. Reluctantly Strauss obliged, and at the last moment added to the score the waltz couplet 'Nur für Natur' (Only for Nature), with a text by Franz Wagner – Zell and Genée having declared themselves 'drained'. At the première of *Der lustige Krieg*, on 25 November 1881 at the Theater an der Wien, this number proved the outstanding 'hit' of the evening, and brought the name of Girardi to the front rank of operetta performers. The opening night cast also included Therese Braunecker-Schäfer as Artemisia, Caroline Finaly as Violetta, Rose Streitmann as Else and Felix Schweighofer as the Dutch tulip-grower, Balthasar Groot. *Der lustige Krieg* itself was a triumph, and during the composer's lifetime enjoyed a popularity surpassed only by *Die Fledermaus* and *Der Zigeunerbaron*. In the *Neue Freie Presse* (29 November), Hanslick voiced unwonted approbation for the score:

Strauss, whose orchestral treatment we have always had to praise, has scarcely anywhere else instrumented so finely and elegantly as in 'Lustige Krieg'. In no way does he seek strange orchestral effects, coquettish solos and the like; rather he has worked using the musically firm, mature, sweet orchestral sound which appears so easy, and yet is so difficult to achieve . . . 'Der lustige Krieg' is the work of a brilliant talent, which is conscious of its own limitations, and of the limitations of the chosen genre.

Less than two weeks after the opening of *Lustige Krieg*, on 7 December 1881, Vienna's Ringtheater presented the German-language première of Offenbach's posthumous opera *Hoffmanns Erzählungen* (The Tales of Hoffmann), an event which attracted an illustrious audience. An enthusiastic press response and a public holiday combined to ensure a full house for the following night's performance. Minutes before the curtain rose, an ignition fault with the gas lighting started a fire in the theatre, and 386 people perished in the inferno. The trial which followed blamed the new director, Franz Jauner; he was sentenced and prohibited from holding any further theatre concession, though he subsequently received a pardon from the Emperor. In the immediate aftermath of the Ringtheater tragedy, theatre-going audiences dwindled – only *Der lustige Krieg*, at the Theater an der Wien, continued to draw the crowds. It ran for more than a hundred consecutive performances.

Once more, it was with Zell and Genée that Strauss discussed subjects for his next operetta. According to an oft-quoted anecdote, Johann was offered the choice of two books: one, with a Polish theme, *Der Bettelstudent* (The Beggar Student), the other again set in Italy, *Venezianische Nächte* (Venetian Nights). Reportedly, Johann was persuaded by subterfuge to select the weaker of the two books, *Venezianische Nächte*, to enable Carl Millöcker to secure *Der Bettelstudent*. While this is an interesting tale, reflecting Johann's general inability to recognize the dramatic potential of material placed before him, it remains unproven. Zell later claimed that Strauss's wife, Lili, had demanded an Italian locale (like that of *Lustige Krieg*) for her husband's new operetta; indeed, it was Lili who gave *Venezianische Nächte* its title. Furthermore, in *Kulturgeschichte der Operette* (1961), Bernard Grun rejects the anecdote, avowing that Millöcker was already at work on *Bettelstudent* at the beginning of November 1881, at a time when Strauss was involved with rehearsals for *Lustige Krieg*. Millöcker's detailed personal diary, however, indicates otherwise. Not until July 1882 does Millöcker mention working on the score of *Bettelstudent*, and his previous commitments suggest he is unlikely to have discussed the project in detail much before spring 1882 – when Zell and Genée were already writing *Venezianische Nächte*.

Strauss's delightful *Kuss-Walzer* op.400 (Kiss Waltz), based on melodies from *Lustige Krieg*, is dedicated 'to his beloved wife Angelica' [sic] and is a poignant reminder of the happiness Johann had hoped to find at her side. In reality, frustrated in her theatrical ambition and disenchanted with her marriage – though plainly still feeling an attachment to her husband – Lili had turned her attentions to the 29-year-old theatre director Franz Steiner. Johann was informed of Lili's affair with Steiner by his sister, Anna Strauss, in September 1882, but he appears already to have suspected his wife's infidelity when he wrote imploringly in one of his letters to her in Franzensbad, on 28 July that year: 'Let yourself be well and truly kissed dear Lili, but don't run away from me! Please stay!' Lili did not heed his pleas. On 27 September 1882, she left the Schönau villa for good, and on 9 December the Wiener Landesgericht granted the couple a divorce by consent. After moving into the Theater an der Wien with Steiner, where she worked as his assistant, Lili followed him to Berlin in 1884, but they did not remain together. In Berlin she ran a photographic studio, 'Atelier Lili', later returning to Austria where she opened another studio in Bad Tatzmannsdorf. Here, during the First World War, she fostered two motherless girls whose father had been sent to the Front. Lili often spoke, with remorse, of her parting from Strauss. Upon her death, on 6 May 1919, her foster children showed their gratitude by erecting in her memory a gravestone, bearing the inscription:

> 'Here lies Lili Strauss 1849-1919[*]
> Your goodness is not forgotten.'

[*]Official documents record the year of Lili's birth as 1850.

16

The man who for decades has delighted the music-loving world through his creations, appears now to have reached the zenith of his creative power.

(*Fremdenblatt*, 25 October 1885. Review of Johann's *Zigeunerbaron*)

THE MONTHS leading up to Johann's divorce from Lili had been a time of anguish for the composer. Once again he faced the prospect of being alone. He even felt a temporary alienation from his native Vienna, and accepted as many invitations as possible to conduct his operettas in different cities. Thus, in early November 1882 he conducted the 250th performance of *Der lustige Krieg* in Berlin, and later that month travelled to Pest to conduct the same operetta there. He did not, however, undertake the journey to Pest alone; with him was a 26-year-old widow, Adèle Strauss.

Born Adèle Deutsch in Vienna on 1 January 1856★, she had married Anton Strauss (no relation to the 'Waltz King') in 1874, and the couple had moved into rooms in the capacious Hirschenhaus, occupied by Anton's family since 1849. Albert Strauss, Anton's father, a Stock Exchange agent, had often acted as financial adviser to Johann's family, who were neighbours in the Hirschenhaus. After less than three years of marriage Anton died, leaving Adèle with a two-year-old daughter, Alice Elisabeth Katharina Maria.

Adèle had known Johann for several years, admiring both the man and his music. As a guest in Johann's Hietzing villa, she had observed at first hand the multifaceted rôle his first wife, Jetty, played in his life. Now, with the breakdown of his starcrossed second marriage, Johann turned for consolation to the young and attractive Adèle, who swiftly bewitched the 56-year-old composer. Yet, while Lili lived, there could be no thought of their marrying within Austria, for although the civil authorities recognized and granted Johann's divorce, it was not accepted in the eyes of the Roman Catholic Church to which he belonged. Indeed, Papal consent to the divorce, applied for during the winter of 1882-3, was refused. Adèle's courage and determination were such that, despite this obstacle to her happiness, she took up

★Some uncertainty exists regarding the year of Adèle's birth, as her Jewish birth certificate has been lost. Her gravestone, and most official documents, give 1856, though some sources quote 1858.

residence in the Igelgasse Stadt-Palais with Johann, and confidently set about filling the void left by Jetty. It is significant that even the harshly satirical publication *Der Floh* recognized Adèle's special qualities when it adjudged on 25 March 1883:

Maestro Johann Strauss . . . needs a comfortable, gracious home, if he is to create with a joyful heart, if the refreshing spring of his lovely melodies is to flow unrestricted. Frau Adèle Strauss will offer him such a home; she will have a beneficial effect upon his nervous artistic temperament, and will be happy if she can give again to the honoured and beloved composer the peace of mind and happiness necessary for his creativity.

During the Fasching of 1883 Johann and Adèle were again in Pest, where Strauss had a large number of friends who welcomed the Viennese maestro and his new love into their homes. Among the guests at a banquet held in Johann's honour was Franz Liszt, whom Strauss had met in Vienna in 1856, and to whom he had dedicated his waltz *Abschieds-Rufe* op.179 (Cries of Farewell). Liszt's music had long featured in the repertoire of the Strauss Orchestra, and there existed a mutual respect between the two men. In Pest they played piano duets together and were partners at whist. Their meeting seems to have provided the impetus for one of Strauss's rare forays into the writing of a concert waltz for solo voice. The waltz, *Frühlingsstimmen* op.410 (Voices of Spring), with a text by Richard Genée, was composed for the acclaimed Heidelberg-born coloratura soprano Bianca Bianchi (*née* Bertha Schwarz). First performed on 1 March 1883, at a matinée charity concert in the Theater an der Wien 'in aid of the Kaiser Franz Joseph Foundation for indigent Austro-Hungarian subjects in Leipzig', the waltz drew only polite applause and was considered by the Viennese journal *Die Wacht an der Donau* to be 'decidedly mediocre . . . overloaded with coloratura . . . not very melodious'. Unperturbed, Bianchi repeated the waltz several times in the ensuing weeks, most notably as an additional number in Delibes's opera *Le Roi l'a dit* at the Vienna Court Opera, and as such it was the first opus by Johann Strauss to be performed officially in this building. As a purely orchestral waltz, *Frühlingsstimmen* was first heard on 18 March 1883, when Eduard Strauss conducted it during one of his regular Sunday concerts in the Musikverein. Although the piece gained wider appreciation through the professional whistler 'Baron Jean', the subsequent international popularity of *Frühlingsstimmen* was due primarily to its brilliant performances by the Viennese virtuoso pianist Alfred Grünfeld, to whom Strauss dedicated the first piano edition. Johann greatly admired Grünfeld's playing: 'Only through you do I hear everything that is in my waltzes', he once enthused. In later years, however, Johann confided to the Baron de Bourgoing: 'Nobody plays my waltzes like your uncle does – but, for Heaven's sake, don't tell this to Alfred Grünfeld!'

Another non-operetta work dating from this period is Johann's patriotic march *Habsburg Hoch!* op. 408 (Hail Habsburg!). Written to mark 'the 600 years Commemoration of the Most Illustrious House of Habsburg', and first performed in the Carl-Theater on 27 December 1882 under the composer's baton, the work includes quotations from Haydn's Austrian Hymn, the *Prinz-Eugen-Lied* and the *Radetzky-Marsch*.

Work on *Venezianische Nächte*, by now renamed *Eine Nacht in Venedig* (A Night in Venice), had only proceeded slowly since spring 1882, partly because of Johann's marital problems with Lili, and partly because of Zell and Genée's irritation at Lili's persistent interference in their 'free initiative'. Now, with the divorce behind him, Johann could work unhindered with his librettists on the new operetta. After Zell and Genée had jointly agreed the characters, locations and broad outline of the plot, Zell worked on the dialogue and detailed action while Genée concentrated on the song-texts, in accordance with their customary procedure. In view of Lili's adultery with Franz Steiner, director of the Theater an der Wien, it is not surprising that Johann insisted upon an alternative venue for the première of *Eine Nacht in Venedig*. Discussions with the Carl-Theater and Vienna Court Opera proved unsuccessful, but on 1 May 1883 it was announced that the première would take place that September as the opening production of the recently renovated Neues Friedrich-Wilhelmstädtisches Theater in Berlin – the only one of Strauss's sixteen completed stage works to receive its première outside Vienna. On 10 June Johann and Adèle left Vienna for the tranquility of Strauss's Schönau villa, where the composer could work undisturbed on the operetta. Genée, at his own villa in Pressbaum, periodically received express packages of music in first draft from Strauss, whose frequent practice was to compose musical scenes from a mere summary of the plot. To these drafts Genée would add suitable texts, occasionally filling out the instrumentation and suggesting, or even making, alterations and additions to Strauss's score. His work completed, the scores were then returned to Schönau. It is noteworthy that the extant sections of the *Nacht in Venedig* autograph score reveal also the hand of Adèle as copyist in certain of the song-texts, early proof of her ability and aspiration to become the perfect successor to Jetty Strauss.

Adèle's presence brought a stability and peace of mind to the often restless composer, and the writing of the operetta progressed steadily. On 1 August Johann's old schoolfriend, Gustav Lewy, whose theatrical agency was to promote the new operetta, could announce that 'earnest and purely artistic motives had moved Herr Johann Strauss to overcome objections of a private nature', and that the Viennese première of *Eine Nacht in Venedig* would take place at the Theater an der Wien during the coming season. Further attention was focused on the new stage work later in August when the European press accused Zell and Genée of plagiarism, after a vengeful dismissed employee of the Theater an der Wien revealed that the librettists had poached the book of *Nacht in Venedig* from *Château Trompette*, a comic opera produced at the Paris Opéra-Comique in 1860, with music by François Gevaert and book by Jules Cormon and Michel Carré. Although Zell and Genée recognized the partial veracity of the accusation, Zell at first publicly refuted it, but the pair later agreed to include in the credits: 'With free use of a French subject'.

On 15 September 1883, after a short stay at Bad Ischl in the Austrian Salzkammergut, Johann and Adèle arrived in Berlin, where Strauss immediately threw himself into the rehearsals which had already begun for the world première of *Eine Nacht in Venedig*. Five days later Adèle wrote to Johann's friend and personal adviser, Josef Priester, that Johann was 'pleased with the cast beyond all expectations'. The singers included Sigmund Steiner (Duke of Urbino), Reinhold Wellhof (Pappacoda), Jani Szika (Caramello) and Ottilie Collin (Annina). But, Adèle continued in her letter:

I must tell you, in confidence, that we have every reason to be afraid of the public's verdict with regard to the book. Not a trace of wit, still less of an interesting situation or an absorbing plot. Jean, of course, has long been aware of the book's dismal qualities, but he hoped that they could be overcome in performance. We have the impression, however, that this cannot be expected even from a splendid performance.

Although Johann found director Julius Fritzsche's staging 'wholly satisfactory', he confessed to Gustav Lewy: 'We have been anxious for cuts and improvements in the book, so as to freshen up the libretto into something of consequence.' Sarcastically, he summed up one rehearsal: 'Perhaps encouraged by our applause, the dear director had the macaroni-boy [Pappacoda] kick the fallen lad a few more times up the backside – this, thanks to Fritzsche's intervention, being the most impressive effect in the book.'

It was commonplace with operetta for revisions to the composer's score to continue throughout rehearsals, the definitive version often not being determined until after the first performance. For precisely this reason, the première of *Eine Nacht in Venedig* was postponed until 3 October. This first night drew unanimous praise for director Fritzsche's skilful production, sparkling settings and costumes, but the Berlin press was equally unanimous in its condemnation of what *Der Reichsbote* (5 October) termed 'certain weaknesses of the music and the libretto'. Although the paper acknowledged that the performance 'made a very favourable impression' on the capacity house, the *Vossische Zeitung* (4 October) maintained that 'the reception was mixed; applause vied with disapproval'. The *Berliner Tageblatt* (4 October) was more forthright:

The composer . . . was greeted by the heartiest shouts upon his appearance at the conductor's desk, and every lilting melody in the first act was received with loud applause. But the text of the operetta, a hodge-podge [literally, 'an Italian salad'] of foolishness and tediousness, made it more and more difficult from scene to scene to be receptive to the merry language of the orchestra – and when, in the last act, the silliness outstripped itself when we were told of a roast beef made from the sole of a boot, and were repeatedly assured, to a languishing waltz-tune, that 'At night the cats are grey, at night "meow" they tenderly say' – the audience protested with embarrassing vigour . . .

After effecting a few essential cuts and alterations for the remainder of the Berlin run Johann hastened to Austria, where stage rehearsals for the Viennese première had been under way since 26 September. Putting to good use experience gained from the Berlin fiasco, Strauss, Zell and Genée hurriedly undertook more extensive musical and textual reworkings for the opening night at the Theater an der Wien on 9 October. Among the more significant changes, the Duke of Urbino's 'Lagoon Waltz' – whose 'meow' passage had been so ridiculed in Berlin – was given an entirely new text ('Ach, wie so herrlich zu schau'n') by the Wiener Männergesang-Verein's Franz von Gernerth. This new version was modified by Genée, the waltz song slowed down in tempo and transferred to Caramello, the Duke's personal barber. Sung by Alexander Girardi at the Viennese première, it was one of several vocal numbers which had to be repeated three times. The other alterations made for the Theater an der Wien also proved successful. Upon his appearance at the conductor's desk on the first night, Strauss was greeted by a tumultuous ovation, and according to the *Fremdenblatt* (10 October), 'during the Overture the first waltz theme was welcomed with the liveliest applause . . . Two-thirds of the operetta, ten numbers, had to be repeated.' Other Viennese papers recorded a similar triumph, and lauded the performances of Caroline Finaly (Annina), Josef Josephi (Duke), Alexander Girardi (Caramello) and Felix Schweighofer (Pappacoda). The *Neue Freie Presse* (10 October) concluded its review:

Strauss has enjoyed many brilliant triumphs in his native city and elsewhere, but such stormy applause as reached his ears for a whole evening today must have filled even him, the pampered darling of our city of song, with pride and satisfaction.

The first run of the Viennese production achieved a total of forty-four performances. Most of the changes made for Vienna were adopted by the Friedrich-Wilhelmstädtisches Theater, and on 15 October 1883 Strauss was able to address a letter of thanks to Fritzsche, expressing his delight at 'the fine reception which "Eine Nacht in Venedig" is now having every evening in Berlin'. Productions of the operetta soon followed at other theatres in Germany and throughout Austria-Hungary, and the work was also mounted in New York and Chicago. Over the years, *Eine Nacht in*

113

Venedig has been the subject of numerous revisions, the best-known being that by Ernst Marischka and Erich Wolfgang Korngold (1923). Despite the worthy intentions of those responsible for these many and varied reconstructions, surely none has yet surpassed, or even matched, the vitality and melodic appeal of Strauss's Viennese original.

Even at the Viennese première, however, the revised Zell and Genée libretto had not escaped harsh criticism; after years of successful collaboration with the two men Johann Strauss lost all confidence in their abilities, and composer and librettists parted in high dudgeon. Already, Strauss's thoughts were occupied with plans for his next stage work. Briefly he contemplated *Der junge Herzog* (The young Duke), a libretto adapted from a comedy by the Austrian dramatist Eduard von Bauernfeld, but instead put it aside to develop the germ of an idea which had been sown almost a year earlier – that of composing an Hungarian opera. From his earliest days, Hungarian rhythms had been as much in Johann's blood as Viennese melodies, and during his visit to Pest with Adèle in November 1882 he had not only displayed great interest in the music of gypsy orchestras but had played Hungarian pieces on the piano in the homes of his many friends there. According to Adèle, it was during this stay that she urged Johann to visit the Hungarian writer Mór (Maurus) Jókai to discuss the prospect of an Hungarian stage work. What Johann learned from his meeting with Jókai set his creative mind in turmoil. 'You were right', he told Adèle; 'the man has given me ten subjects for operettas. My head is still burning with all the projects.' Strauss had been particularly excited by Jókai's suggestion that his novel *Saffi* might be suitable for stage treatment. Jókai was unprepared to undertake the work himself, however, and it was agreed that an approach should be made to the Hungarian author and journalist Ignatz Schnitzer, resident in Vienna since 1880. Schnitzer readily accepted the challenge, the more so since in January 1883 an operetta libretto he had submitted to Strauss, though rejected, had drawn the encouraging remark: 'I cannot do other than express the hope that I might receive from your pen something suitable for myself, to which I look forward tremendously.'

Strauss at last completed his work on *Eine Nacht in Venedig* in mid-July 1883. By then, Schnitzer had already drawn up plans for his dramatic treatment of *Saffi*, which Jókai suggested should be called *Der Zigeunerbaron* (The Gypsy Baron). Schnitzer also received from Jókai a draft scenario for the first act, albeit unusable. There are indications that Johann may have set to music Schnitzer's draft texts for Bárinkay's entrance song ('Als flotter Geist') and Mirabella's couplet ('Belgrader Schlacht') even while he was putting the finishing touches to *Nacht in Venedig* – in several instances Strauss spontaneously sketched ideas when he first received libretti, or when

114

situations from operetta scenes were outlined to him. Only a detailed critique of the *Zigeunerbaron* manuscripts may determine an accurate chronology for the writing of the individual numbers.

At all events, news of the Strauss–Schnitzer collaboration hit the Viennese press in February 1884: 'Johann Strauss has started on the composition of a new work. The opera is entitled "Der Zigeunerbaron" . . . The new work will be performed in Vienna at the Hof-Operntheater, and in Pest at the Nationaltheater.' Although the papers reported that Johann had begun composing *Der Zigeunerbaron*, he hesitated for the next few months to begin in earnest on the work, advising Schnitzer of his inability to complete during 1884. The new piece was intended as an opera, and as such the material demanded a treatment very different from the style of his previous stage compositions. Meanwhile, Schnitzer worked quickly, and on 30 June 1884 he sent Strauss the libretto for the third act, advising that 'the book is now complete, with the exception of small alterations to the music-text' which the composer might deem necessary. Schnitzer urged completion by 15 January 1885, since the work was scheduled to be a highlight of the great International Exhibition at Pest during the spring of that year. He further exhorted Strauss to begin on the composition, and issued the ultimatum: 'It is up to you, honoured Maestro, finally to declare yourself.' At the same time he gave the composer the option of returning the *Zigeunerbaron* libretto if he found it insufficiently stimulating. Strauss required no further persuasion. A contract was duly signed, and as Schnitzer later recounted, 'the event was celebrated with goulash and champagne, as customary in the Strauss home'.

Johann once wrote that 'the composer must really sleep in one bed with his librettist, so as to have him by his side even during the night'. It was a maxim he was to stand by more closely with *Zigeunerbaron* than at any other time. Ahead of him lay a period of intensive work, during which time he showed unwonted concern for every aspect of the new work, and repeatedly required revisions to Schnitzer's libretto. He refused to be rushed, and made a point of personal contact with his collaborator at every opportunity to discuss detail. Schnitzer readily complied with almost all of Strauss's wishes. When Johann asked him to rewrite the refrain of the Act 2 duet 'Wer uns getraut?', ensuring that 'in the middle and higher registers the vowels 'a' and 'i' should be predominant – in order to allow the singer a more free delivery', the result was 'Und mild sang die Nachtigall ihr Liedchen in die Nacht: Die Liebe, die Liebe ist eine Himmelsmacht!'

During the autumn of 1883 Strauss had undergone treatment for nicotine poisoning and fainting fits. Now, at the beginning of July, 'owing to risk of brain paralysis', his doctors ordered him to stop composing and to rest. Together with Adèle Johann left for Franzensbad, from where he wrote to Schnitzer on 26 July 1884:

I'm ordered to continue taking the cure here, and not to do any work! None at all! How difficult it is for me to hide from those around me the torment which the enforced leisure is causing me just now. The Zigeunerbaron is the only thought that occupies me – I cannot wait for the moment when I can give it musical life and see it living in front of me!

Progress on the opera was halted again in the autumn of 1884, as Vienna prepared to celebrate in truly festive fashion the 40th Jubilee of Johann Strauss's artistic career, which had begun at Dommayer's Casino. First at the Strauss-Palais to offer his congratulations on the morning of 15 October was the Mayor of Vienna, Bürgermeister Eduard Uhl, who presented Johann with an illuminated diploma conferring upon him the tax-free Freedom of the City of Vienna 'in recognition of his outstanding artistic and humanitarian achievements'. Throughout the day, a constant stream of deputations made their way to the home in the Igelgasse, among them representatives from the Wiener Männergesang-Verein, the 'Concordia' Association, the Theater an der Wien and the Gesellschaft der Musikfreunde. Eduard Strauss, at the head of the entire Strauss Orchestra, was present to add his congratulations, and among the wellwishers who either paid their personal respects or sent bouquets, telegrams or letters were Brahms, von Bülow, Verdi, Suppé, Anton Rubinstein, Bismarck, General MacMahon, and the Archdukes Wilhelm and Johann Salvator – the latter, under the pseudonym Johann Traunwart, was an amateur composer whom Johann Strauss had assisted with waltz instrumentation.

On the evening of the anniversary Strauss conducted, to tumultuous applause, a gala production at the Theater an der Wien, comprising the Overture to *Indigo* and Act 1 of *Eine Nacht in Venedig*. *An der schönen blauen Donau* replaced the advertised waltz from *Blindekuh*. The second half of the programme featured Act 2 of *Die Fledermaus*, in which the guests at Prince Orlofsky's party dressed as characters from other Strauss operettas and sang numbers associated with those rôles. The theatre's celebrations nettled Eduard Strauss. Too late he had written to his brother on 20 September:

You are not celebrating a festival, an anniversary of your activity as an operetta composer – on the contrary, a festival as conductor and of your musical activity as a whole. But 15 October 1844 can only be properly celebrated on 15 October 1884 at the head of the Strauss Orchestra!

There was some consolation for Eduard later that evening, however, as his orchestra provided the music at a festival banquet for Johann held in the Goldenes Lamm (Golden Lamb) Hotel.

Meanwhile, important developments were taking place behind the scenes at the Theater an der Wien. In the summer of 1884 Franz Jauner sold the Theater an der Wien (which he had bought in 1880) to the actress Alexandrine von Schönerer, at the same time dismissing with a generous gratuity the existing lessee-director, Franz Steiner, and his co-director 'companion', Lili Strauss. Since von Schönerer lacked experience in theatre management, she appointed a consortium comprising herself, Alexander Girardi (who was shortly afterwards replaced as artistic director by Jauner) and, as lessee-director and concession holder, Camillo Walzel (better known by his *nom de plume*, F. Zell). Ignatz Schnitzer had also been considered for the post of lessee-director, and during the negotiations had offered the Theater an der Wien an option on the libretto of *Zigeunerbaron*. When, therefore, in January 1885 the press confirmed that Strauss's new work was to be performed at the Vienna Hof-Operntheater (Court Opera), Jauner promptly issued a counter-statement that the Theater an der Wien had bought the libretto and had paid a substantial advance on future royalties. Eventually the matter was resolved, and *Der Zigeunerbaron* was officially secured by the Theater an der Wien. The management of the Court Opera, however, announced that Strauss had 'firmly resolved' to undertake the composition of an opera expressly for them after completing *Zigeunerbaron*.

Zigeunerbaron was itself undergoing major alterations. It had abandoned the confined Hungarian nationality of Jókai's novel for the wider appeal and implications of an Austro-Hungarian subject, reflecting the establishment of the Austro-Hungarian Dual Monarchy in 1867. The work had also altered musically: on 6 July 1885 Johann notified a correspondent that it had been his intention to work Jókai's subject as an opera, but that after encountering obstacles he had been forced to change the style to that of an operetta. *Zigeunerbaron*, nevertheless, still retained something of the opera style in which it had been conceived.

Strauss had earlier announced (21 November 1884) that, because of his still delicate health and to avoid damaging the 'artistic maturity' of the work through haste, *Zigeunerbaron* would not be presented until the autumn season of 1885. Composer and librettist continued their close collaboration, Schnitzer adapting himself with remarkable flexibility to Strauss's ideas. At the end of July 1885 there occurred another interruption when doctors prescribed an immediate change of air for Adèle, who had been suffering from 'intermittent fever', and the couple accordingly travelled via Franzensbad to the coastal resort of Ostend. Here, Schnitzer had found Strauss a quiet villa where the two men could meet and work undisturbed, and he handed Johann his revised and completed Act 3 libretto, saying that it would cost the latter 'at most, a week's work'. Without an assistant, however, Strauss himself had to undertake the time-consuming task of copying. This 'robotry', as Strauss called it, was into its final stages in September when it was interrupted yet again. Johann and Adèle had to leave for Berlin, where Strauss was to conduct three jubilee performances of his operettas at the Neues Friedrich-Wilhemstädtisches Theater – the 300th of *Lustige Krieg*, the 50th of *Nacht in Venedig* and the 400th of *Fledermaus*. From Berlin, Strauss wrote to Schnitzer about the visual aspects of *Der Zigeunerbaron*, displaying an uncharacteristic concern for theatrical detail:

The Entrance March [Act 3] must be imposing. About 80–100 soldiers (on foot, on horse), camp-followers in Hungarian, Viennese (and Spanish) dress, common-folk, children with shrubs and flowers – which latter they strew before the returning soldiers, etc. etc., must appear . . . It must be a scene which is much, – much more splendid that it was in [Millöcker's] 'Feldprediger' – since this time we want to imagine an *Austrian* army – and people in a *joyful* mood over a victory they have won!

Johann ended his letter optimistically: 'I swear to you, dear friend, we can become richer than 100,000 Rothschilds.'

Not until the beginning of October 1885, at Schönau, was *Zigeunerbaron* completed. On 24 October, the eve of Strauss's sixtieth birthday, Johann took his place at the conductor's desk of the Theater an der Wien for the première of the new work. Johann's vision for the staging of his operetta was fully realized in Jauner's munificent production; indeed, Jauner himself had declared: 'Our gypsy camp must look so authentic that everyone who sees it will be forced, instinctively, to hang on to his pockets.' Both Jauner's staging and Schnitzer's libretto found general acclaim, as did the cast, which included Alexander Girardi (Kàlmán Zsupán), Karl Streitmann (Sàndor Bárinkay), Antonie Hartmann (Czipra) and, as the gypsy-girl Saffi, Ottilie Collin, whom Strauss had wooed from Berlin where she had created the rôle of Annina in *Eine Nacht in Venedig*. Girardi was again triumphant, and in having to perform his pig-breeder's couplets ('Ja, das Schreiben und das Lesen') three times utterly confounded Strauss's earlier opinion that Schnitzer's text for this comic song was 'not on quite the same level as the other numbers.'

The *Fremdenblatt* deemed the whole performance 'a great triumph for the composer' and 'an evening of success, in which the artistes and the audience took equal delight'. It continued: 'The riotous applause which . . . broke out after every theme of the Overture repeated itself after every song . . . Fully half the operetta had to be encored.' In adding that he found the *Zigeunerbaron* music 'the score of a romantic comic opera', the critic of the *Fremdenblatt* established common ground with his fellow reviewers. The influential *Die Presse* (25 October) remarked that 'the Maestro has fought his way through to the artistically purer forms of – one might almost say – serious operetta, from which there remains only a short step to opera . . .' Hanslick, in the *Neue Freie Presse* (27 October), likewise praised the 'new step forward for the composer in mastering greater forms and in the finer, and more characteristic, handling of the dramatic', but he warned that 'the expansive way in which the [Act 2] Finale was staged, strayed into the most dangerous proximity of grand opera'.

Der Zigeunerbaron ran for eighty-seven consecutive performances, from the seventy-fifth of which a heightened dramatic effect was achieved at the end of Act 2 by replacing the reprise of Arsena's waltz–song ('So voll Fröhlichkeit') with an ensemble arrangement of the traditional Magyar *Rákóczi March*. It is in this form that the operetta is usually heard today. During Strauss's lifetime *Zigeunerbaron* was seen on about 140 stages around the world, and the composer received additional accolades for the orchestral numbers he arranged on its themes, especially the *Schatz-Walzer* op.418 (Treasure Waltz) and the polkas *Brautschau* (op.417) and *Kriegsabenteuer* (op.419).

The *Neue Freie Presse* (25 October) concluded its first-night review of *Der Zigeunerbaron*:

Strauss was so frequently and so tempestuously called for at the close of each act, and appeared on these occasions so happily preoccupied, everybody supposed that during these intervals he had just completed another new operetta in his head.

Johann's mind, however, dwelt not on any new operetta, but on matters far from the theatre.

On 6 November 1885 Johann Strauss, whose music was the very quintessence of Vienna, applied for unconditional release from his Austrian citizenship.

17

The things one does for a woman!

(Johann Strauss in a letter to Adèle,
shortly before their marriage in 1887)

S O CERTAIN was Johann that in Adèle he had found his partner
in life, he had assured her financial position on 19 April 1883 by
legally bestowing upon her an irrevocable annuity for life of 4000
gulden (today equivalent to £9,118 sterling). By renouncing his
Austrian citizenship, Strauss sought to remove one of the final
obstacles barring his marriage to Adèle.

As early as 1863 Johann had dedicated his polka française *Neues Leben*
op.278 (New Life) to Duke Ernst II of Saxe-Coburg, himself the composer of several operas and an admirer of the Viennese Waltz King.
Johann's choice of dedicatee was to prove fortuitous; not only was he
awarded a decoration, but he established a link with the man who was to
play a vital rôle in his future happiness. Through the recommendation of
his friend, the Archduke Johann, Strauss's marital dilemma was brought
to the attention of Duke Ernst, ruler of the small German dukedom of
Saxe-Coburg-Gotha. On 8 December 1885, Johann Strauss was
officially granted release from his Austrian citizenship 'for the purpose
of acquiring the nationality of Saxony', and on 24 May 1886 he applied
to the City Magistrate of Coburg for 'enrolment on the nationality-
register of the Dukedom of Saxe-Coburg-Gotha, and into the citizenship of the City of Coburg'. He added that he would 'willingly give
expression to his gratitude by means of a donation in favour of the local
fund for the poor', in return for 'an early compliant decision'. By way
of establishing pro forma residence in the city, Strauss rented accommodation in Coburg, and on 24 June 1886 his new German citizenship
was confirmed. On 9 July that year he officially left the Roman Catholic
Church and became a Lutheran Protestant. Adèle, for her part, had
already transferred from the Jewish faith to Protestantism in 1883. On
28 January 1887 Johann took the civic oath of allegiance in Gotha, and on
11 July his marriage to Lili was finally dissolved by Duke Ernst, under
the powers invested in him by Saxony law. Johann and Adèle were
'legitimately joined in law as husband and wife' at the Coburg Registry
Office on 15 August 1887, and later that day in the ducal Hofkirche.

In the year leading up to his marriage, Johann accepted an invitation
from the ladies of the St Petersburg Red Cross Society to travel to

121

Russia in the spring of 1886. Together with Adèle he journeyed via Berlin, where he conducted three performances of *Der Zigeunerbaron*. Despite his seventeen-year absence from Russia, his reception in St Petersburg was no less ecstatic as the public and members of the Court and aristocracy flocked to see him conduct a series of concerts and a performance of *Der Zigeunerbaron*. His repertoire consisted not only of old favourites from his Pavlovsk years, but also featured the first performance of new compositions like *An der Wolga, Polka-Mazur* op. 425, and the waltzes *Les dames de St Petersbourgh* (The Ladies of St Petersburg) and *Adelen* op. 424 (written for his wife-to-be). For a charity concert on 27 April, in aid of the Red Cross Society, Johann wrote his *Marche des gardes à cheval* (March of the Horse Guards), dedicated to Tsar Alexander III and later published in Vienna as the *Russischer Marsch* op. 426 (Russian March). From St Petersburg Strauss was persuaded to give concerts in Moscow where, twenty-eight years earlier, the first of his three scheduled concerts at the Bolshoi Theatre had been so poorly attended that the remaining two were cancelled. In contrast, his 1886 visit was a great success, and he was rewarded with the gift of two magnificent black thoroughbred horses, which for many years he kept in the stables at the rear of the Strauss-Palais.

Upon his return from Russia, Strauss retreated to Schönau for a brief respite. In January 1886 he had discussed a collaboration with Jókai on an opera text with Napoleon as one of its central characters, but nothing had come of this. Now he advised Schnitzer of his desire to compose an operetta with a German subject, citing the success of Viktor Nessler's opera *Der Trompeter von Säkkingen* at the Vienna Court Opera House. Schnitzer suggested a treatment of Heinrich Heine's dramatic poem *Schelm von Bergen* (Hangman of Bergen), whose eponymous hero was a reluctant executioner. Both men were agreed on the eminent suitability of Girardi for the title rôle. Strauss was initially enthusiastic, but throughout the summer and early autumn he wavered as one hindrance after another led him first to withdraw, and then to reconsider the project. In mid-August 1886 he learned that a touring company from the London Savoy Opera was in Berlin, performing *The Mikado* by W. S. Gilbert and Sir Arthur Sullivan, and that it was shortly to open at Vienna's Carl-Theater. Recognizing the remarkable similarity between the peace-loving executioner in the English work and the main character in *Der Schelm von Bergen*, Strauss could see no possible future for his collaboration with Schnitzer, and abandoned the whole idea. In September, however, he recanted, and asked Schnitzer to rework his libretto to suit an opera, confiding:

Operetta, as you know, is starting to get on my nerves – there are always problems, and one cannot follow one's artistic inclinations where one would like. There are no reasonable orchestras, and even singers are becoming scarcer – if they are bad one cannot use them, [and] if they are good they become arrogant. I am fed up with the whole business. In short – I should like to compose a comic opera. At least with that one can hear what one has written, and although the royalties are not so ample, and do not come in as regularly as with operetta, such a work will enjoy a longer life, and for ten or twenty years it provides one with enjoyment and income.

Schnitzer relates that he readily complied with Strauss's wish, and that both men verbally agreed to abstain from writing any operetta before this first Strauss opera had been performed. If we accept Schnitzer's version of events, then Johann certainly behaved less than honourably in his dealings with his librettist: a few weeks later Schnitzer was astonished to learn from the press that Strauss was collaborating on a new operetta with the young Viennese author Victor Léon. The *Schelm von Bergen* project was finally abandoned. Although Schnitzer also discussed with Strauss an opera libretto based on the biblical story of Cain and Abel, this was not developed, and the only fully matured fruit of their partnership remains *Der Zigeunerbaron*.

The new book that had so galvanized Strauss was *Simplicius*, a dramatization of J. J. C. von Grimmelhausen's *Der abenteuerliche Simplicissimus* (Adventurous Simplicissimus), considered by many to be the greatest German novel of the seventeenth century. The story recounts the fortunes of the peasant-boy Simplicissimus during the Thirty Years War, and again the title rôle seemed tailor-made for Girardi. Strauss launched himself straight away into the composition, calling upon unused fragments from *Zigeunerbaron* and material from the near-complete first act of *Der Schelm von Bergen*. To Gustav Lewy, Johann wrote enthusiastically:

As subject-matter, Léon's 'Simplicius' is the most outstanding of all books of modern times . . . I am quite in love with the material . . . From a musical point of view, the operetta as a whole will be handled by me in a much brighter vein than 'Zigeunerbaron'. Just as in 'Zigeunerbaron' I had to make allowances for the Hungarian rhythm, so this time I was very keen to pay homage to the Viennese genre. Something Viennese ought again to appear in my stage work, especially since in the prologue and in several situations I found occasion to strike a more serious note.

As he progressed with the composition, however, shortcomings in Léon's text, which Johann had noted from the outset, became increasingly apparent. These deficiencies demanded of the composer such extensive additional work that he was forced to decline an invitation from the Neues Friedrich Wilhelmstädtisches Theater in Berlin to participate in a cycle of five Strauss operettas during spring 1887. He was also busy at this time editing a seven-volume complete edition of his late father's works for the Leipzig-based publishing firm of Breitkopf & Härtel, for which he further provided a lengthy biographical sketch of the composer.

The first night of *Simplicius* took place at the Theater an der Wien on 17 December 1887. The splendid settings complemented an excellent cast, including Alexander Girardi (Simplicius), Josef Josephi (the Hermit), Karl Streitmann (Armin) and Ottilie Collin (Tilly). The mood of this 'serious operetta' was set by the dramatic overture, and both the prologue and first act met with great applause. A particular favourite in the final act was Josephi's waltz romance, 'Ich denke gern zurück an mein entschwund'nes Glück' (I like to think back to my lost happiness). This was followed by a short dialogue scene. Suddenly a cry of 'Fire!' was heard from the stalls, and the audience, fearing a repetition of the tragic Ringtheater inferno six years earlier, began to panic. Appeals for calm from on stage by director Walzel and Josephi did little to restore order. In the event, a general stampede was only averted by the quick-wittedness of Strauss himself, as evidenced by a letter written to the composer the following day by his close friend, the celebrated sculptor Viktor Tilgner:

Your wonderful music and your presence of mind yesterday saved the lives of thousands of people. If you had not had the idea, and the courage, to direct Josephi to sing the splendid waltz once again – panic would have been inevitable.

The exact source of the alarm remains unclear, but the police report drew attention to the presence of a faint burning smell in the auditorium, apparently the result of a feather plume in the helmet of a supernumerary touching a stage gaslight and beginning to smoulder.

Most of the Viennese papers concurred with the opinion of the *Neue Freie Presse* (18 December) that 'Maestro Strauss has again strewn over his work a true cornucopia of the most delightful melodies'. *Der Floh* (25 December) remarked:

The importunate friends of Maestro Strauss, in their rapturous adoration, stick the Wagner-cap on his head and want to proclaim him as the Richard Wagner of operetta; the sensible Maestro, however, is not only in control of the realms of music, but also of himself.

Nevertheless, despite general approval of *Simplicius*, there was widespread condemnation of Léon's libretto, and the work was withdrawn after twenty-nine performances. Cognizant of the weakness of the text but of the strength of his music, Strauss cooperated on two later reworkings of *Simplicius*, the first undertaken by Ludwig Dóczi (librettist of Johann's next stage work), and the other by Léon himself. Neither attempt matched even the limited success of the original. Once again, it was the individual orchestral numbers, created from the score of the operetta, that found mass appeal. Particularly noteworthy is the exuberant waltz *Donauweibchen* op.427, some of whose themes originated in *Der Schelm von Bergen*, and whose opening waltz features the melody of Josephi's aria 'Ich denke gern zurück'. In view of the debt of gratitude Johann owed to

Duke Ernst II of Saxe-Coburg-Gotha, he insisted that the first piano edition of *Simplicius*, published later, should bear a dedication to the monarch.

Simplicius was the last of Johann Strauss's stage work premières to be conducted by the composer himself. Thereafter, at most he conducted only the Overture before handing over the baton to an assistant. He was finding the physical demands of an entire evening's conducting increasingly strenuous and painful, owing to his worsening arthritic condition. He wrote to his brother Eduard:

On account of my health I must, as much as possible, keep away from conducting . . . because at the end of a number I leave the orchestra as if bathed in sweat, and not as another person who is able to change his underclothes. I have to stay in the same attire for 5–6 hours, until the soaked outfit dries out by itself.

Despite his discomfort, however, Johann willingly acceded to Walzel's request that he conduct the 200th performance of *Die Fledermaus* at the Theater an der Wien on 15 May 1888.

Johann's disappointment with *Der Schelm von Bergen* had not weakened his resolve to compose a full-scale opera, and certain elements of the more serious *Simplicius* can be viewed as a stepping-stone towards Strauss's ultimate goal. This change of direction was noted by the critic of the *Illustriertes Wiener Extrablatt* (23 December 1887), who wrote of the *Simplicius* première: 'The Waltz King tears the crown of diamonds from his head, and makes a pilgrimage to the promised land, but half-way there he turns back . . .' Reassured by such remarks, and encouraged by Adèle, Johann began to search for a suitable opera libretto. He was mindful, too, of his commitment to the Vienna Court Opera, made at the time of *Der Zigeunerbaron* – a commitment he was eager to fulfil in view of his fervent desire to witness the production of one of his stage works at this prestigious house. Strauss finally settled upon a medieval tale, set in a remote corner of Hungary. The work, *Ritter Pásmán*, was to occupy the composer for much of the next three years.

During this period of composition Johann additionally devoted much time to the structural development of the Viennese waltz, producing a series of fine independent concert pieces which perhaps brought the waltz to its consummate form. News of his efforts reached the press, who misinterpreted his intentions. Johann was particularly angered by one journalist who suggested that Strauss wanted to modernize the waltz by slowing down the 'Tempo di valse' to an 'Andante comodo'. In a letter published under Johann's name (*Neue Freie Presse*, 5 March 1890), but actually ghost-written by Hanslick, Strauss declared:

It has never occurred to me, and will never occur to me, to slow down the tempo of the waltz even the slightest. Tempo and character of the waltz are still exactly the same as they were forty years ago. In my latest works – 'Kaiserwalzer' and 'Rathausball-Tänze' – I have only extended the Introduction and Coda, and occasionally mentioned to friends that these sections might be capable of further development. That is what the fable boils down to . . .

On 2 December 1888 Emperor Franz Joseph I celebrated the 40th Jubilee of his reign, the splendour and pomp of which occasion was captured in Johann's magnificent waltz *Kaiser-Jubiläum Jubelwalzer* op.434. It was with *this* waltz, and not as so often stated the later *Kaiser-Walzer* op.437 (Emperor Waltz), that Strauss paid homage to the Imperial Jubilee. Yet jubilation turned to tragedy when, on 30 January 1889 at Mayerling, the heir to the throne, Crown Prince Rudolf, took his own life and that of his mistress, Baroness Mary Vetsera, rocking the Austro-Hungarian monarchy to its very foundations.

In the autumn of 1889 Johann Strauss, Emile Waldteufel and Philipp Fahrbach junior each signed a contract to conduct a week of concerts at the newly opened Königsbau concert hall in Berlin. Before Strauss departed for his engagement he despatched to his Berlin publisher, Fritz Simrock, a new waltz called *Hand in Hand*. This title referred to a recent toast made by the Austrian Emperor during a visit to the German Kaiser Wilhelm II, in which he had stressed the bonds of friendship between their two nations. The astute Simrock, however, proposed the diplomatic change of title to *Kaiser-Walzer*, considering that its ambiguity would satisfy the vanity of both monarchs. Nevertheless, it is the *Austrian* Imperial crown which is emblazoned on the illustrated title page of the original piano edition. Just five weeks after its Berlin première on 21 October, the Vienna *Fremdenblatt* (25 November) commented: 'The "Kaiser-Walzer" already has its place in the Viennese concert repertoire!' There were also words of praise for the waltz from the writer Paul Lindau, who wrote to Strauss on 3 June 1892:

It is no exaggeration when I say that, in my musical view, nothing has been written since the days of Franz Schubert which, for pure melody and unspoiled beauty, can be compared with the first part of your 'Kaiserwalzer'. In the 16 bars there is more music, genuine, unadulterated music, than in many operas that last a whole evening but which leave the heart empty.

Johann Strauss experienced one of his rare musical 'defeats' when, on 12 February 1890, his festive waltz *Rathaus-Ball-Tänze* op.438 (Town Hall Ball Dances) – written for the first 'Ball of the City of Vienna' in the newly opened Town Hall – was overshadowed by C. M. Ziehrer's rousing waltz dedication, *Wiener Bürger* op.419. Johann's waltz, 'dedicated to his beloved Father-City, Vienna', features in its Introduction and Coda themes from his *Blue Danube Waltz*, as well as a brief snatch from Haydn's Austrian Hymn. Of interest regarding

Ziehrer's *Wiener Bürger* is the late Professor Fritz Racek's observation that its syncopated second theme matches, almost note for note, a melody in Strauss's musical sketchbook from the 1870s and 1880s.

Most of the few independent compositions Johann wrote during his intense and protracted work on *Ritter Pásmán* were waltzes. One exception was the *Spanischer Marsch* op.433 (Spanish March), dedicated to Maria Christina, Queen Regent of Spain, a devotee of Viennese music. Owing to his dislike of travel, Johann declined an invitation to give concerts in Madrid, but instead lost little time in writing and despatching this jaunty march to the Queen, a gesture which duly won him a Spanish decoration.

Ten years had passed since Johann Strauss had composed a choral work for the Wiener Männergesang-Verein. Now, for the Association's 1891 Fasching Song Programme, he wrote the waltz *Gross-Wien* op.440 (Greater Vienna), whose text, by Franz von Gernerth, tells of the City of Vienna's expansion through the incorporation of the surrounding suburbs. In the event, the performance by the Association was postponed until the autumn, and the public first heard the waltz in a purely orchestral version on 10 May 1891 in the Sängerhalle on the Prater, played by the 500 musicians of the combined military orchestras of Vienna, under the composer's baton. Among other conductors appearing in this 'Monster Concert' were the military bandmasters Alphons Czibulka, Josef Král, Franz Lehár senior, Carl Komzák and C. M. Ziehrer. The Wiener Männergesang-Verein itself first sang the waltz on 4 October 1891, before an audience of 10,000 Viennese in the Sängerhalle. Strauss was prevented from attending the concert through illness, and the reception given to the new piece was mixed. Nevertheless, one press critic commented:

The waltz is beautifully and artistically formed; the original, unpretentiously simple and fresh nature of the popular Strauss waltzes is less evident. Johann Strauss has become more refined. He is standing at the portal of the Court Opera.

'Burning of the Ring Theatre at Vienna', from *The Illustrated London News*, 17
December 1881.

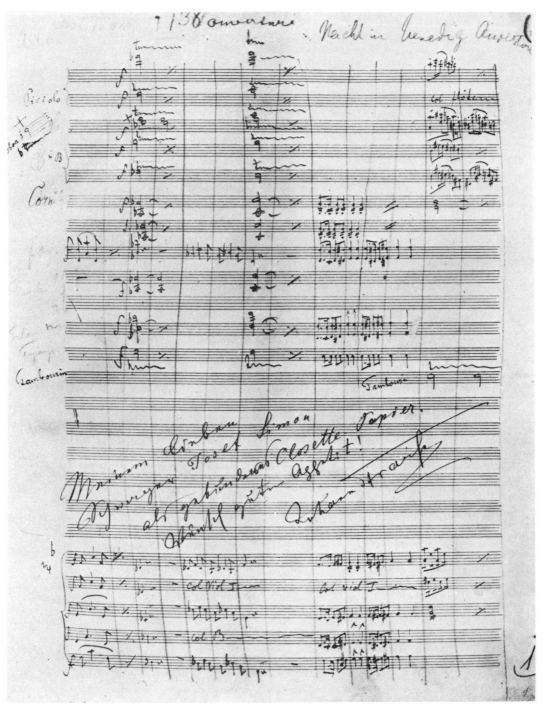

First page of the Overture from the autograph score of *Eine Nacht in Venedig*, with Strauss's sarcastic dedication: 'To my dear brother-in-law Josef Simon as a bound stack of toilet-paper. Hope it goes down well!'

The soprano Bianca Bianchi, who gave the first performance of Johann Strauss II's waltz *Frühlingsstimmen* op.410 (Voices of Spring) in 1883.

Ignatz Schnitzer, librettist of *Der Zigeunerbaron* (The Gypsy Baron).
Photograph by R. Krziwanek, Vienna.

Alexander Girardi as the pig-breeder, Kàlmàn Zsupán, in Strauss's operetta
Der Zigeunerbaron (1885).

'If Kapellmeister Eduard Strauss wants to hear his orchestra now, he has to
pay entrance money.' Viennese newspaper cartoon from 1878, commenting
on Ziehrer's appropriation of the Strauss Orchestra's name.

Johann Strauss II and his friend and admirer Johannes Brahms, photographed in 1894 on the veranda of Strauss's villa at Bad Ischl. Beneath a quotation from the *Blue Danube Waltz*, written by Strauss on a fan belonging to Adèle and Alice Strauss, Brahms wrote: 'Leider nicht von Johannes Brahms' ('Unfortunately not by Johannes Brahms').

Johann Strauss II at his high desk on the veranda of the Bad Ischl villa, circa 1895. (Courtesy of the Historisches Museum der Stadt Wien)

The Strauss villa at No.36 Kaltenbachstrasse, Bad Ischl, photographed in 1953. The building was demolished in winter 1969–70, and a modern block of flats was erected on its site. (Courtesy of Franz Feldkirchner, Salzburg)

Johann Strauss II in October 1898, at the time he was composing the *Aschenbrödel* ballet. Bearing a dedication to the musicologist Professor Robert Fischhof, this is believed to be the last private study taken of the Waltz King. (Courtesy of Simon Marks, Salford)

Detail from the Denkmal, memorial to Johann Strauss II, in Vienna's Stadtpark. Sculpted by Edmund Hellmer, it was unveiled on 26 June 1921, and was partly paid for by public subscription – to which the U.S.A. contributed 30 dollars, while England donated the grand sum of £4 12s.!

(Courtesy of the Rev. Joseph Marmion, Dublin)

Eduard Strauss I in his later years, photographed at his home in Reichsraths-strasse. (Courtesy of the Historisches Museum der Stadt Wien)

Johann Strauss III and his orchestra, circa 1900. Photograph by Atelier Lili (=
Angelika Dittrich), Berlin. (Courtesy of the Wiener Stadt- und Landesbibliothek)

Johann Strauss III, with his wife Maria, and children – Johann, Maria and
Angelika. Photograph probably taken for the birthday of Maria Klenkhart on
13 July 1910. (Courtesy of Frau Elisabeth Strauss, Vienna)

tr preisgekrönten Componistin
Miss Fay Foster

Johann Strauss

zur freundlichen Erinnerung

Johann Strauss

Johann Strauss III (1866–1939). Signed photograph with dedication to Miss Fay Foster, winner of the 1910 International Waltz Competition in Berlin with her composition, *Prairie Flowers*.

Signed publicity photograph of the conductor Eduard Strauss II (1910–69), from the year 1949. (Courtesy of Foto-Knoll, Vienna)

Dr Eduard Strauss, youngest descendant of the dynasty to bear the family name, photographed by the author in October 1982.

18

The smallest success of an opera written by
me *stands higher, in my view, than many*
other [of my successes].

(Johann Strauss, writing to his brother-in-law,
Josef Simon, June 1892)

LIKE THE comic actor who yearns to portray the tragic hero, so
Johann Strauss, whose success lay in the lightness, spontaneity
and melodic appeal of his dance-music and operetta creations, longed
to compose a full-scale opera. His choice of libretto fell to *Ritter
Pásmán*, a dramatization by Ludwig Dóczi of a ballad by the
Hungarian poet, János Arany. Dóczi, himself Hungarian born but
resident in Vienna, combined the occupations of lawyer, journalist
and departmental head at the Foreign Office in Vienna, with that of
successful playwright. Dóczi's totally undramatic book was a
convoluted medieval tale concerning the inevitable misunder-
standings which arise when the newly crowned young King of
Hungary cunningly steals a kiss (on the brow!) from Eva, the beautiful
young wife of the elderly Hungarian knight, Ritter Pásmán. Among
those who offered practical encouragement to Strauss in his ambitious
undertaking was Johannes Brahms, who introduced the composer to
his own publisher in Berlin, Fritz Simrock, in order to ensure
publication of the opera. From late 1889 to early 1893 Simrock was
Strauss's sole publisher, and apart from the *Kaiser-Walzer* was responsible for publishing such waltzes as *Rathaus-Ball-Tänze* (op.438),
Gross-Wien (op.440), *Seid umschlungen Millionen* (op.443) and *Märchen
aus dem Orient* (op.444).

Although *Ritter Pásmán* remains one of the least known of Strauss's
stage works, its genesis is recorded in considerable detail in the 161
letters and two cards Johann wrote to Simrock. Regrettably, this
important collection was not preserved intact when offered for
auction some years ago, and is instead scattered around the globe.

However keen Simrock may initially have been about collaborating
with Strauss on the proposed opera, a letter from February 1890
reveals that he harboured reservations, and that even Strauss's self-
confidence seems temporarily to have waned. Johann had begun work
on *Pásmán* with customary zeal around February 1888, but before
long became dispirited by the poor progress he was making. His
depression was aggravated by lengthy periods of inactivity while he

underwent brine- and mud-bath treatments in the spa-town of Franzensbad, to help alleviate increasingly long and agonizing bouts of gout and neuralgia. In January 1891 Strauss was elated by news of enthusiastic applications from England to buy the opera ('They know very little of the music, as I was only able to play a small part to them, badly . . .'), and he advised his publisher that the Viennese première of the stage work 'will definitely be performed at the Court Opera during the month of April'. On 25 March, however, only days before the date originally set for the première, he gave vent to his growing irritation with Simrock:

I must tell you quite openly that my hopes that our transaction will at long last come to fruition are getting less and less. You often talk of contracts, and by this you seem to understand that you make the arrangements and I have to comply with them, however unreasonable the demand.

After detailing those 'arrangements' he found unacceptable, Johann concluded his letter:

You will understand that, the way things are at the moment, I have no enthusiasm to start writing back and forth about new matters. Now it is a case of completing the opera.

The months ahead were filled with painstaking composition, rewriting and revision. Strauss wrote to Priester on 8 August 1891:

Nothing comes out of writing operas, even when the opera has finally been published. So much torment, so many false temptations in the inventing of melodies . . . By the time I have finished the trips to the spa, 2 full months will have passed without a note being written. The instrumentation requires even more time than the composition. When thoughts of this kind come over me, I cannot but confess that my heroic decision to write an opera not infrequently fills me with distress.

The première was several times rescheduled and postponed, due in part to sickness in the cast. Right up to mid-December 1891, when the full score of the opera was finally completed, Strauss and Simrock continued to disagree over a number of subjects, one being the publisher's intention to put on sale piano and other arrangements of *Ritter Pásmán* before the première. The composer felt that this would *'deal the opera a blow! through debasement and vulgarization'*, leading to a total misunderstanding of the opera itself. Strauss and his contemporaries, writing in the so-called 'Golden Age' of operetta, were naturally eager to popularize their stage works through the performance of selections, but generally only *after* the first night. It is interesting to note that from the time of Kálmán, Lehár and other 'Silver Age' operetta composers writing in the first part of the twentieth century, musical extracts and arrangements were frequently heard *before* the premières to whet the public's appetite – a practice still successfully continued today by writers like Tim Rice and Andrew Lloyd Webber.

Amid all his other anxieties that December, Strauss became involved in a mysterious transaction involving a golden belt studded with diamonds and a large cash payment, apparently given to him in return for his promised services at an exclusive ball in Berlin. Strauss never fulfilled his obligation, and sought to avoid a press scandal, about which he was plainly terrified. In this he was remarkably successful, as the absence of any enlightening detail yet discovered shows only too clearly. We are merely left with Johann's intriguing statement: 'Had I foreseen what I know today, no sum of money would have induced me to give my consent. I have merely fallen victim to [Herr Baron's] urgent entreaties (on repeated occasions), and to my totally false conception of the nature of his balls.'

In the meantime, at the Vienna Court Opera, rehearsals of *Ritter Pásmán* were well advanced. Writing to Adèle Strauss on 6 November, Dóczi predicted:

I am now convinced that it will be a resounding success for Jean, despite all the cuts and bungles which destroy all dramatic effect. The victory, to which I shall in no way have contributed, is guaranteed by the ballet alone.

Later, Dóczi recalled Johann's words as they left a *Pásmán* rehearsal together:

I have heard it just as I had imagined it; the public can make of it what they will. But I have received from this work everything that I could have wished for.

The long-awaited and much-publicized opera *Ritter Pásmán*, which the *Fremdenblatt* previewed as 'a box-office draw that rates alongside *Cavalleria rusticana* and *Manon*', received its première on New Year's Day 1892, conducted by Wilhelm Jahn, Director of the Vienna Court Opera. In the title rôle was the bass Franz von Reichenberg, Bayreuth's first Fafner in Wagner's *Der Ring des Nibelungen*, while the part of Eva, the heroine, was sung by the Graz-born mezzo-soprano Marie Renard. Among the capacity audience, some of whom had bought stalls seats at ten times their value, was Carl Michael Ziehrer. On the visting card he sent to Strauss, he wrote: 'Highly honoured Maestro! In sincere admiration, one of your most ardent and zealous devotees wishes you this evening, with all his heart, an enthusiastic success.' Ziehrer's hopes for the Maestro were, for the most part, fulfilled. There was unanimous respect for 66-year-old Strauss, although many critics held reservations about the venture itself. Ludwig Speidel of the *Fremdenblatt* (3 January) opined:

The opera appears to us to be remarkable through the serious work that it contains, and through the style which is energetically sustained in it. This opera is more than an aesthetic work, it represents a negation of the self for the composer; it is a truly respectable achievement and it commands our greatest admiration, even if it doesn't please us.

The reviewer concluded:

Without a doubt, people will go to *Fledermaus* in order to recover from *Ritter Pásmán*.

In *Die Presse* (3 January) Dr Robert Hirschfeld also sounded a critical note:

Johann Strauss has over-estimated his ability, and thereby failed also in the selection of his model. His own nature could only point him towards the French [opera style], but he took the *Meistersinger* as his pattern.

Strauss held these critics in contempt, and complained to Gustav Lewy:

They are professors! They have to know better than others, and have to be right. Thus, there are many thousands of worms in the world who would remain unnoticed if they did not feel obliged to make themselves noticeable . . . I shit on all professors of music.

Most papers mentioned three highlights in the score: *Pásmán*'s Act 1 drinking-song (*Der Wein, der Wein*), Eva's waltz-aria (*O, gold'ne Frucht am Lebensbaum*) in Act 2, and, as Dóczi had prophesied, the Act 3 ballet music. The latter was considered by Hanslick (*Neue Freie Presse*, 3 January) to be 'by far the brightest crown jewel in this score. None but Strauss could have written it!' He continued:

This incomparable ballet music alone would be capable of making any opera a lasting hit. It awakens in me an often, but vainly, uttered old wish: Strauss might want to present us with a complete ballet.

Another six and a half years were to pass before Johann would satisfy Hanslick's wish. A suggestion by Jahn that the *Pásmán* ballet should be incorporated into Mascagni's opera *I Rantzau* was rejected out of hand by Strauss.

Despite full houses, *Ritter Pásmán* disappeared from the repertoire of the Court Opera after only nine performances. Strauss foresaw the possibility of this when, after the third performance, he wrote to Simrock on 9 January:

It is quite possible – if the Massenet opera [Werther] arrives in the 2nd half of January – that J[ahn] will strive to push Pásmán aside . . .

Johann predicted correctly, and *Werther* opened at the Vienna Court Opera on 16 February 1892. In a later letter to his publisher, on 16 March, Strauss elaborated:

Through Massenet, Jahn received the Légion d'honneur (Knight's Cross) two months ago, and the Officer's Cross today. You will thus understand that it is more important to Jahn to tend to Massenet's interests than to mine

. . . Jahn spies the possibility of receiving the same award from Italy for the cult of Mascagni's operas!!! Pásmán can't provide any decorations for him: thus, discard that which gains nothing for the lapel – his principle. Hitherto, *only* the public has kept us afloat – *we* would have been discarded long ago!"

Although deeply wounded at Vienna's rejection of *Ritter Pásmán*, the ever resilient Strauss resigned himself to the situation and prepared for the opera's first night at Prague. Despite an inadequate rehearsal period and the last-minute discovery of errors in the orchestral parts, Johann felt more confident this time about the fate of *Pásmán*. To Simrock he wrote on 21 April: 'I recognize the opera in Prague as my own work – in Vienna it was a confused affair . . .' The Prague production was certainly more successful than its Viennese counterpart, but neither this, nor subsequent presentations in Berlin, Dresden and Munich, assured *Ritter Pásmán* a permanent place in operatic repertoire. In a letter to his brother Eduard (22 April 1892), Johann confessed:

I only wrote it to prove that I can do more than write dance-music . . . I don't want to blame Dóczi, but to create such a scandal over an innocent little kiss is not acceptable to today's corrupt society. *Nowadays* it would have been more to the audience's liking if the king had *seduced the knight's honourable lady.*

And to Josef Simon he wrote after the Berlin première:

It was very much a fancy of mine for which, unfortunately, my friend Simrock felt inclined to pay 40,000 gulden. Now I literally treat it as a joke, whether the opera appeals or not – the more they insult, the more I like it!

Shortly before the Vienna première of *Pásmán*, Strauss informed Simrock:

Brahms must be honoured with a dedication, by a waltz of my composition. In due course I want to present him with this waltz, popular, yet spicy and peppered, without sacrificing the purpose of a waltz . . .

The title of the new waltz, *Seid umschlungen Millionen* (Be embraced, ye millions), a quotation from Schiller's *Ode an die Freude* (Ode to Joy), had been suggested by Johann's friend Julius Stettenheim, who intended the new waltz for a Journalists' Ball in Berlin. Instead, Strauss promised the waltz to Princess Pauline Metternich as a special attraction during her International Exhibition of Music and the Stage, to be held on the Vienna Prater in May 1892. However, on learning that his composition would be played for the first time by the Exhibition Orchestra, rather than by himself, he preferred to conduct the first performance with the Strauss Orchestra on 27 March in the Musikverein, at brother Eduard's last concert of the season. In so doing, Johann alienated the Princess – the more so as he had also declined her commissions to write an operetta for the Exhibition and a ballet – and *Seid umschlungen Millionen* was not performed at all during the Exhibition. On the eve of the première in the Musikverein, Strauss received from Brahms, the dedicatee of his new waltz, a visiting card bearing the message: 'Tomorrow, your most happy and proud listener!'

Johann Strauss was able to notify Simrock at the end of May: 'Brother Eduard is not one of the sort who is inclined to want to say something that pleases me. However, in his letter of today [written from Germany] he expresses himself as follows: "Your Millionenwalzer is causing a sensation everywhere, I am playing it in every concert".'

In late autumn 1892, Johann wrote to Eduard Strauss:

I have bled myself to death financially through the three years' work on 'Ritter Pásmán'. If financial circumstances did not have to be taken into account, I would never again have subjected myself to the hated work on an operetta. It is certainly not one of the most agreeable of occupations to go to work reluctantly. But, necessity is the mother of invention . . .

The stage work with which Strauss unwillingly rejoined the ranks of the operetta composers was *Fürstin Ninetta* (Princess Ninetta). Its book had been written by the successful Viennese comedy-writing team of Julius Bauer and Hugo Wittmann, respectively editor of the *Illustriertes Wiener Extrablatt* and feuilletonist of the *Neue Freie Presse*. Again set in Italy, this time in Sorrento, the tale was an absurd and confused farce which Strauss considered 'the most miserable libretto ever perpetrated'. Lamenting what he called his return to 'common strumming', the composer informed Josef Simon in spring 1892:

I am already messing around with the operetta . . . I write at this work without inspiration – it will be a real piece of rubbish . . . I shall still succeed in getting people to say: 'he ought rather to write operas'; that would be a triumph!

Strauss eventually completed the score of *Ninetta* in early November 1892, by which time the première had been set for the following January at the Theater an der Wien.

Johann later complained to Paul Lindau* that he had been forced to work from the lyrics alone, and had not had access to the complete libretto and dialogue during his period of writing. When, during final rehearsals, he became acquainted with the whole plot, he was horrified:

The music is completely unsuited to this senseless, inartistic stuff . . . It is a piece of fancy footwork around the author's jokes! . . . I would be even happier if the entire thing were soon committed to a geriatrics' home. They can steal it from me, I shall not shed a tear over it.

Throughout the composition of *Fürstin Ninetta* Strauss and Simrock were in correspondence regarding the complex publishing rights to the operetta. The financial failure of *Ritter Pásmán* had made the

*Johann's views, expressed in an undated letter, are often erroneously taken to refer to *Eine Nacht in Venedig*.

publisher cautious about accepting another Strauss work, and he even turned to Brahms for advice. Strauss found Simrock's delay in reaching a final decision 'intolerable', and on 21 November 1892 he sent the publisher his ultimatum. Simrock decided against taking up his option on the operetta, and it was subsequently published by August Cranz. This outcome was a relief for Johann. As he wrote to Eduard: 'To make a contract with Simrock means selling oneself to the devil.'

Fürstin Ninetta was a complete success at its première on 10 January 1893, much to Johann's astonishment. Even Bauer and Wittmann were congratulated on their witty libretto, and although Strauss remained unenthusiastic about this 'scatterbrained, bombastic tale', he was full of praise for the conductor, Adolf Müller junior, and for the cast, especially Ilka Palmay in the title rôle and Girardi as the Russian-born Egyptian finance minister, Kassim Pascha. Almost four months before the première, Bauer had notified the composer: 'People are eating out of our hands, for they are conscious of the significance of a Strauss work for the Theater an der Wien.' The press seemed to share this viewpoint, *Der Floh* (15 January) remarking that *Fürstin Ninetta* had brought 'the salvation of operetta to the Theater an der Wien for this season'. The critic of the *Neues Wiener Tagblatt* commented that 'the excursion which Johann Strauss made into opera has not remained without effect on his newest work. Everything has become finer, richer and more noble'. There was rather more qualified approbation from the *Deutsche Zeitung* (11 January), which felt that 'not much that is new has occurred to him, but through his masterly skill in instrumentation he knows how to twist and turn many a well-known idea, so that it receives a charm of its own and appears relatively new'. *Fürstin Ninetta* was not, however, without its sterner critics, among them the periodical *Hans Jörgel*:

Sadly, Maestro Strauss has grown old. The dazzling giant reflector of his rich musical inventiveness is no longer functioning; his newest work reminds one of so-called 'official city illuminations'. Everything thoroughly neat and very tidy, but without inner vitality, without breathtaking melodies.

One number which did excite general admiration was the *Neue Pizzicato-Polka* (op.449), which Johann had written during his work on *Ninetta* for a concert series Eduard Strauss was to give in Hamburg in the summer of 1892. Subsequently, Johann inserted this novelty-piece between Acts 2 and 3 of *Fürstin Ninetta* as an entr'acte children's ballet sequence. Quite apart from the jubilation normally associated with the première of a Strauss stage work, the celebratory atmosphere in the theatre was further enhanced on the opening night of *Fürstin Ninetta* by the presence of Emperor Franz Joseph I, making his first visit to the Theater an der Wien for many years. After the final curtain Strauss, now a citizen of Saxe-Coburg-Gotha, was invited into the

Royal Box to receive the personal congratulations of his former sovereign.

Fürstin Ninetta went on to enjoy a total of seventy-six performances at the Theater an der Wien, seventy-four of them consecutive.

Among the panoply of festivities mounted during Vienna's International Exhibition of Music and the Theatre in 1892 was a production of Smetana's opera *Die verkaufte Braut* (The Bartered Bride) at the Sommer-Theater on the Prater. The immense popularity of this joyous work attracted Strauss's attention, and he determined to procure a Slavonic subject for his next operetta. He found the libretto of his choice in *Joschko* – later renamed *Jabuka (Das Apfelfest)* – a story set in Serbian south Hungary during the annual Apple Festival, when young men gather to pick their future brides. Johann's librettists for this three-act operetta were Gustav Davis and Max Kalbeck. Davis (real name David), a former lieutenant and editor of a military journal, concentrated on the plot and the dialogue, while the Breslau-born Kalbeck, a former student of jurisprudence, philosophy and music, worked on the song-texts. Kalbeck, music reviewer for the *Neues Wiener Tagblatt* and a friend of Johann, had earlier unsuccessfully offered the composer a treatment of Shakespeare's *Twelfth Night; or, What you will*, entitled *Viola*.

Johann began work on *Jabuka* in early May 1893, intending to complete the operetta by the end of that year. In the event, agonizing bouts of 'head neuralgia' and bronchial catarrh delayed his 'conquering this giant work', and as winter approached he lived in fear of again succumbing to influenza, from which he had suffered for six months during the previous year. As he later advised Eduard, there were frustrations, too, in his dealings with Kalbeck and Davis:

Working with 2 librettists always involves double the effort for the composer. Each one wants to correct the other, and the upshot results in no improvement . . . In this way, one sketches out an operetta twice!

Throughout the winter of 1893-4 and the following spring and summer, Johann continued work on *Jabuka*. As the date of the première drew closer, Gustav Lewy, who had acquired the rights to the new work, became anxious about the venture. Strauss responded in characteristic fashion:

Today the operetta is not what it will be – don't show the white flag prematurely – save yourself the weeping and wailing for later . . . If it does not succeed – we can hang ourselves next to one another . . . just as long as I can see you swinging before I pull the rope around my own neck.

Girardi, cast as the bailiff Joschko, was 'overjoyed' with his rôle, but rejected his couplet 'Adler, Wolf, Hirsch' (Eagle, Wolf, Stag) with its political allusions, since he did not wish 'to fall out with any party'. Alexander Girardi's participation in a operetta was regarded almost as

136

a guarantee of its success. In March 1883, for example, *Die Presse* proclaimed: 'Today, the operetta recipe of Viennese theatre is very simple: one takes a Girardi, sprinkles in a couplet, and the success is ready . . .' Johann Strauss expressed his own long-felt admiration for the leading tenor in a letter dated 9 September 1894:

There rests on your shoulders, not only every work, but also the existence of the Theater an der Wien. You will understand that all authors who write for this theatre cling to you as tightly as possible – that they grasp you by the head and feet and won't ever let you go. For you alone have to decide over the *to be or not to be*, and thereby [you exercise] the greatest influence.

As if it were not enough that Vienna was awaiting the new Strauss stage work, the city was at the same time preparing itself for an artistic jubilee, the like of which it had not witnessed before. Fifty golden years had passed since Johann Strauss II first appeared at Dommayer's Casino, and to celebrate the achievements of her 'favourite son', Vienna organized several hectic days of festivities. 'Like a swelling festival overture in celebration of the Maestro', *Jabuka* opened at the Theater an der Wien on 12 October 1894. Aside from Girardi, other principal rôles were taken by Jenny Pohler (Jelka), Karl Streitmann (Mirko von Gradinaz), Jean Felix (Vasil von Gradinaz), Josef Josephi (Bambora), Therese Biedermann (Annita) and Alexander Alexy (Mischa). A jubilant audience greeted both composer and operetta with overwhelming enthusiasm and affection, and throughout the evening encores were constantly demanded. The ebullience of the house reached its climax with Girardi's third-act comic song 'Das Comitat geht in die Höh'', to which, after several repetitions, the singer added a topical new verse in praise of the Waltz King. At this point the calls for Strauss to appear on stage were rewarded, and upon his arrival 'the ladies and gentlemen rose from their seats, waved their handkerchiefs and greeted the Maestro with a love and enthusiasm which, even at its most ardent, seemed to flare up even more' (*Neue Freie Presse*, 13 October).

The press was unanimous about the success of the première, the *Neue Freie Presse* describing it as 'electrifying; especially the second and third acts caused a sensation'. *Hans Jörgel*, though endorsing this opinion, noted that the second-night audience 'received this new operetta much more coolly. We think that Johann Strauss would probably never have arrived at such a solemn jubilee if he had only composed operettas like *Jabuka*'. The new work, which the *Neue Freie Presse* found strongly reminiscent of *Der Zigeunerbaron* in mood and music, achieved fifty-seven performances in its first year. Its music was further popularized through the separate orchestral pieces arranged on its themes, like the waltz *Ich bin dir gut!* op. 455 (dedicated to Kalbeck's wife, Julie), the *Živio! Marsch* op. 456 and *Das Comitat geht in die Höh'! Polka schnell* op. 457.

19

The week belonged to Strauss! It was really frantic, but happy and splendid and agreeable.

(Johannes Brahms, writing to Fritz Simrock, Vienna,
16 October 1894)

IN 1890 A POLL conducted to find the 'most popular' European personalities resulted in Johann Strauss being placed third, beaten only by Queen Victoria and Prince Otto von Bismarck. Now, during his Golden Jubilee celebrations four years later, the Waltz King's truly international appeal became apparent as gifts, telegrams, tributes and goodwill messages flooded in from all corners of the world. One of the most original gifts was a magnificent laurel wreath wrought in silver by Tiffany & Co. of New York, presented by two hundred of Johann's American admirers. Each of the fifty leaves was engraved with the title of a Strauss composition, and its six ribbons were inscribed with the Stars and Stripes and the Austrian eagle. Atop the wreath was a lyre-encircled medallion bearing a relief of the composer, cast in solid gold. Not all the presents were so welcome: there was consternation in the Strauss home at the news that two huge giraffes were on their way to the Igelgasse – a tribute from Ismail Pasha, former viceroy and khedive of Egypt! The myriad worldwide tributes from theatre directors and celebrities such as Arthur Nikisch, Ernst Schuch, Carl Goldmark, Carl Millöcker, Anton Rubinstein, Ruggiero Leoncavallo, Mór Jókai, Duke Alfred of Coburg, Prince and Princess Metternich and the Governor of Lower Austria, Count Erich Kielmansegg, were summed up in a letter written to the Waltz King on 6 October that year by Richard Strauss. Having earlier informed Johann of his intention to perform the latter's *Perpetuum Mobile*, the German composer wrote:

May you enjoy one-millionth part of the happiness, and always share in the gaiety, which you have enabled all mankind, and not least the humble writer of these lines, to experience through your inspired compositions during the long period of your artistic activity . . .

Of all the honours heaped upon Johann, the one which afforded him perhaps the greatest satisfaction was the conferment of honorary membership to the Gesellschaft der Musikfreunde – a pinnacle of distinction shared by such masters as Brahms, Bruckner, Liszt, Verdi and Wagner. In recognition of this veneration, Strauss willed his entire estate – almost 850,000 kronen (£35,358 sterling, today equivalent to £988,870) – with certain provisos, to the Society.

On 13 October, the day following the *Jabuka* première, Johann was the guest of honour at the Vienna Court Opera for a performance of a specially composed new ballet, *Rund um Wien* (Around Vienna), an apotheosis of Viennese dance-music ending with *The Blue Danube*, arranged by Joseph Bayer. 14 October heralded two festival concerts in the Great Hall of the Musikverein. At midday the Wiener Philharmoniker (Vienna Philharmonic Orchestra) and the Wiener Männergesang-Verein performed works by Johann Strauss II under the alternating batons of Johann Nepomuk Fuchs, Wilhelm Jahn and Eduard Kremser, and the pianist Alfred Grünfeld played his concert paraphrases on Strauss compositions. In the evening Eduard Strauss led his orchestra in a concert of brother Johann's music, and introduced the *Blüthenkranz Johann Strauss'scher Walzer* op.292, a musical anthology of Johann II's waltzes arranged by Eduard, erroneously described as being 'in chronological order from 1844 to the present day'. The actual day of the anniversary, 15 October, began with an intimate celebration in the Strauss Palais for family, friends and admirers, among them Brahms, Eduard Strauss, Hellmesberger, Dóczi, Kalbeck, Hanslick and, from New York, the composer and theatre director Rudolph Aronson. Deputations from various organizations called to offer their congratulations, and there were speeches by Baron Dr Josef Bezecny, President of the Gesellschaft der Musikfreunde, on behalf of the Festival Committee, and Bürgermeister Dr Raimund Grübl, on behalf of the City of Vienna. Replying, Strauss said:

The distinctions which you bestow upon me today I owe to my predecessors, my father and Lanner. They indicated to me the means by which progress is possible, through the broadening of the forms, and that is my single small contribution . . . I am extraordinarily happy, but feel that . . . you do me too much honour . . .

That same evening Strauss was honoured with a festival banquet at the Grand Hotel, Vienna, attended by some two hundred well-wishers, including composers, writers, representatives of the graphic arts and, unexpectedly, Grand Duke Constantin of Russia. To great applause, Johann responded to the toast given by City councillor Dr von Billing:

If it is true that I have some talent, then I have to thank for its development my dear native city of Vienna, in whose earth my whole strength is rooted, in whose air lie the sounds which my ear gathers, which my heart takes in and my hand writes down . . . Vienna, the heart of our beautiful, God-blessed Austria . . . to her I give my cheer: Vienna, bloom, prosper and grow!

During the period of the festivities, Viennese theatres were not alone in celebrating the Strauss Jubilee. Many European cities also hosted similar special productions. It was, however, the Vienna Court Opera which provided the most fitting coda to the celebrations: on 28 October 1894 this stately building staged its long-overdue first performance of *Die Fledermaus,* and assembled an impressive cast of singers headed by Fritz Schrödter (von Eisenstein), Paula Mark (Rosalinde), Joseph Ritter (Frank), Lola Beeth (Prince Orlofsky), Andreas Dippel (Alfred), Benedikt Felix (Dr. Falke) and Ellen Forster (Adele). This matinée performance was to have been conducted by the composer himself, but ill-health forced him merely to attend as a member of the audience and the operetta was instead conducted by J. N. Fuchs.

Amidst all the eulogizing which accompanied the Jubilee, *Die Presse* (7 October) clearly felt there was room for some plain speaking:

Strauss is nervy and a hypochondriac; he has every possible and impossible illness, especially those from which some acquaintance has just died. In actual fact, there is nothing wrong with him; but one is suffering enough when one is suffering from all the illnesses which one doesn't have.

This interesting statement opens up an area still largely unresearched. The fact that as Strauss grew older he fell prey to neuralgia, arthritis, chronic bronchitis and influenza is not in question. However, as Professor Franz Mailer has observed from his continuing study of the composer's letters: 'Many signs lead one to infer severe psychiatric illness'. Certainly, by 1894 Johann had more and more become a man in flight from himself and his fame, electing to while away the hours in the company of close friends in the 'Coffee-house' salon of his Igelgasse home, enjoying a game of billiards, playing tarot or simply conversing in the convivial atmosphere. Yet his lively spirit was sometimes quite broken, and his joy in living often disturbed by long periods of melancholy. Ignatz Schnitzer relates how the usually jovial and gregarious Strauss could sometimes become suddenly transformed:

Morose, unspeaking, hardly looking up, he would skulk for days or weeks on end unsociably around the house, or kept himself cocooned in his workroom. His own wife scarcely dared to speak to him then, since to be disturbed in this ill-humoured silence could bring him to furious agitation.

Professor Mailer's researches also highlight another facet of Johann's life in later years, namely that the world-famous composer was lonelier in his old age than had previously been imagined. This isolation was not always of his own choosing. From Schönau he once wrote to a friend that he wished his life were different; for almost the entire winter fatigue and pain confined him to his room, which he only left with the greatest reluctance to escort his family to the theatre. Strauss was indeed a complex character, and it is worth diverting at this point to ponder some of the idiosyncrasies of this 'Pied Piper' of Vienna.

Being of the opinion that 'he who composes at the piano is often led, without noticing it, into fields quite different from those which he intended', Strauss shunned the instrument, preferring to compose standing at a high desk and working out some of the more complex orchestrations on a specially constructed harmonium which was installed at the Igelgasse in 1884. From 1892, on his doctors' recommendation, Johann spent the summer months in Bad Ischl, a popular and picturesque spa resort frequented by the Austrian Imperial family and many noted celebrities, like Brahms, Bruckner and Alexander Girardi. Here he rented the imposing Villa Erdödy (named after the original owner), and in June 1897, together with his brother-in-law Josef Simon, he purchased the property. In fine weather Johann could be seen working at his high desk on the veranda, although he had a distinct preference for composing in inclement weather. To Girardi, for example, he wrote on 9 September 1894:

Only now does it become beautiful in Ischl. People disperse, and according to what I hear – it's never going to stop raining. A splendid prospect for me! I love it when I can work in a pleasant house, in stormy, yes (for others) gloomy weather. This is true delight for me; in a night of stormy weather I write twice as much as in the most beautiful summer night.

Beside the work desk in his Igelgasse home was a bell which would ring upstairs should the composer wish to summon Adèle to hear some new melody he had created. Johann composed mainly at night, though inspiration could come, unbidden, at any time. This he sometimes found disconcerting, as he once informed Adèle:

Suddenly, while I was working on a highly dramatic scene, there passed through my mind, like a flash of lightning, an absolute belter of a waltz which almost surpassed the [Nur für] Natur waltz – since it displayed a shameless audacity in its geniality. When it came to me I cursed and thought: wretch, I cannot use you now – be off with you!

The many night hours Johann spent working on his manuscripts gradually impaired his eyesight. In mid-October 1894 he wrote to Eduard:

I see everything double – if I take a toothpick, I always see two before me. Should I have the misfortune to go blind – I shall shoot myself. Of all physical ailments, this is the most insurmountable. Not to read – [or] be able to write, would take away from me all joy of life.

Not only did Johann harbour an almost obsessive fear of death, as evidenced by his absence from the funerals of his close family, but he also developed a phobia of contact with disease. While he doted upon Adèle's daughter, Alice, as if she were his own child, Adèle's family recalls that Johann strictly forbade the child to invite her friends into the Strauss homes for fear of catching their childhood ailments. This testimony was further corroborated by Josef Strauss's daughter, Karoline.

Despite his transient periods of gloom, Johann never lost his sense of humour, and many of his letters, even those written shortly before his death, show his lifelong readiness to tease his family and friends, all in harmless fashion. For a short time around 1864 Johann took instruction in landscape painting from the popular Viennese artist Anton Hlaváček. Unlike his brother Josef, however, Johann lacked innate artistic ability in this medium, but he found relaxation in spontaneously sketching caricatures of people around him, often adding, as an extension of his humorous letter-writing, cheerfully sarcastic or impertinent commentaries.

Perhaps the greatest irony of all was that Johann Strauss, the man who made the whole world waltz, was himself unable to dance. He admitted as much to Adèle, and during one of his early visits to Russia he told a friend how he was frequently called upon to dance to his own waltzes and polkas: 'But you know very well that I have never been a dancer, and have to give a decisive "no" to all the really tempting and attractive "Invitations to the Dance".'

20

*The Muse of the seventy-year-old Strauss
sits herself down here and there, and takes a
rest. But she has by no means become the
quietly dozing old chaperone at the ball . . .*

(*Wiener Tagblatt*, 5 December 1895 reviewing
Strauss's operetta, *Waldmeister*)

JOHANN HAD begun work on *Waldmeister* even before the *Jabuka* première. On 12 September 1894 he advised Priester:

The first scene of Waldmeister not only drafted – but partly instrumented as well . . . The opening of the operetta Waldmeister is so full of genuine feeling – exceedingly charming, that I could not stop working on it. I lost interest in Jabuka long ago!

His sometimes irksome dealings with the two *Jabuka* librettists were still on his mind when, earlier in 1894, he notified his brother Eduard:

Now I want to begin on a new composition with *one* librettist. The unfortunate fellow's name is Davis – now this one will have his problems with *me*.

Johann had a high regard for the abilities of Gustav Davis, and he eagerly accepted the book of *Waldmeister* when the author offered it to him. 'Never in my youthful years did I work so indefatigably', Johann was to write to Alexandrine von Schönerer, who secured the new work for the Theater an der Wien. Certainly Strauss seems to have been inspired by the plot of *Waldmeister*, as he had been with *Die Fledermaus*, and a number of critics drew parallels between the 'subtle and piquant' orchestrations of the two stage works. As champagne was an essential ingredient of *Fledermaus*, so was another intoxicating beverage central to *Waldmeister*. The 'Waldmeister' of the title is known in English as woodruff, a sweet-scented plant of the genus *Asperula*, used to flavour 'Maitrank' (May Bowl). 'As delectable knockout drops', wrote the *Musical Courier* (2 November 1895) of this wine-based drink, 'there is nothing so marvellous as this Teutonic concoction'. The comic story of *Waldmeister* concerns the inhabitants of a small village in Saxony who suffer the effects of imbibing, either consciously or inadvertently, woodruff-laced infusions.

Not surprisingly, it was for Girardi that Davis shaped the leading character of Erasmus Müller, the dialect-speaking Professor of Botany. The increasingly temperamental Girardi, however, required considerable persuasion before he would condescend to accept the part, and the humorous weekly paper *Figaro* consequently dubbed the operetta *The Girardi Crisis*. *Waldmeister* was, in fact, the last Strauss première in which Girardi would appear: in summer 1896 he left the Theater an der Wien and joined the Carl-Theater. This rival theatre was by then under the directorship of Franz Jauner, who had himself quit the Theater an der Wien at the close of the 1895 season.

On 4 December 1895 the curtain of the Theater an der Wien rose on *Waldmeister*, Strauss's penultimate operetta. It proved to be the most successful of the composer's last stage works, enjoying eighty-eight performances before disappearing from the theatre's repertoire. At the première the sparkling Overture was conducted by the composer, who then relinquished the baton to the capable hands of Adolf Müller junior for the remaining three acts. Cast and orchestra combined to produce a performance which Hanslick found 'not merely creditable, but magnificent'. His enthusiastic review in the *Neue Freie Presse* (6 December) observed:

'Waldmeister' is full of merriment from one end to the other. That differentiates it from its predecessors, 'Zigeunerbaron', 'Simplicius', 'Pásmán', 'Apfelfest', which, at least in some scenes, teeter on the dangerous brink of tragic or sentimental style . . . 'Waldmeister' turns back much more to the familiar paths of Strauss's most effective operetta, 'Die Fledermaus', not only in its innocuous middle-class material, but also in the consistently maintained comedic nature of the music.

Despite his earlier reservations, Girardi was again triumphant. Hanslick considered him 'the comic soul of the entire piece'. Apart from the popular tenor's three couplets, several numbers attracted special praise from the first-night press. Among these was the Act 1 duet 'Denkt doch nur, ich sitze hier ganz allein', for Pauline and Tymoleon (Annie Dirkens and Josef Josephi), and the Act 2 Lawn Tennis ladies' chorus with its English cries of 'Ready all! Hollah, play!' The greatest acclaim, though, was reserved for what one reviewer called 'that cascade of irresistible splendour' from the intoxicating Act 2 Finale, the waltz song 'Trau', schau', wem?', which also closes the final act and figures prominently in the Overture. Towards the end of the Overture this main waltz theme reappears, played by the woodwind accompanied by a delicate violin countermelody. There is an old anecdote that Brahms, who was in the audience for the *Waldmeister* première, went to the conductor's desk during the first interval and wrote this countermelody into the autograph score, adding the words 'Contrapunkt von Brahms!' ('Counterpoint by Brahms!'). Charming though this story may be, the original score (now in the Archives of the Gesellschaft der Musikfreunde) shows no trace of these additions, and a calligraphic examination reveals only the hand of Strauss. Johann certainly required no such technical assistance, a fact ably demonstrated by the counterpoint passages in many of his earlier compositions, notably in the waltz *Johannis-Käferln* op.82 (1850). We do know, however, that Brahms was enchanted by the *Waldmeister* score, and remarked at the première to Hanslick how Strauss's orchestration reminded him of Mozart.

During May 1895 Johann and Adèle had travelled to Munich at the request of the eminent German artist Franz von Lenbach, in order to sit for portraits which were later presented to them. In return, Johann dedicated to Lenbach his 'Waldmeister-Walzer', *Trau, schau, wem!* op.463 (Take care in whom you trust!). Of the five other orchestral works Strauss arranged on themes from *Waldmeister*, the *Klipp-Klapp Galopp* op.466 and the march *Es war so wunderschön* op.467 were especially successful.

Apart from his work on *Waldmeister*, Johann also created a number of interesting independent pieces during 1895. On 6 January he gave the first performance of his *Gartenlaube-Walzer* op.461 (Bower Waltz), which he dedicated to the readers of an illustrated family periodical of that name in Leipzig, and in which publication the waltz first appeared as a special supplement. The year also marked the 25th anniversary of the opening of the new Musikverein building. In celebration, the Gesellschaft der Musikfreunde organized a festive evening on 18 April, at which Johann conducted the Strauss Orchestra, with soloist Olga von Türk–Rohn, in the première of his new vocal concert waltz *Klug Gretelein* (Clever little Gretel), dedicated to the organizing Society. The text to this waltz was provided by Dr Alfred Maria Willner, co-librettist of Johann's next operetta. *Klug Gretelein* (op.462) possesses the lyrical grace and pensiveness typical of many of the composer's last works. Among these later creations is to be found a pair of 'symphonic poems' of such exquisite beauty and originality that one might be forgiven for assuming that they were, instead, the work of one of the serious Masters of the Romantic period. Posthumously published as *Traumbilder I* (dedicated to Adèle Strauss) and *Traumbilder II*, these 'Dream Pictures' are musical portraits of the composer's family. Informing Eduard Strauss of the personalities he planned to portray, Johann quipped : 'It will be your turn too; nobody is immune from my cruelty.'

In these later years the publishers often displayed an almost insulting lack of interest in Johann's compositions, and at times he could find no publishing outlet for his music. Yet, by his own admission, it was just this neglect which allowed him the time, and freedom from constraint, to devote himself to such 'musical wanderings' as *Traumbilder I* and *Traumbilder II*, *Auf der Alm* and *Auf dem Tanzboden* op.454 – the last being a musical illustration of Franz Defregger's painting of the same name. Johann was also able to add to his already sizeable collection of decorations when, in 1895, he somewhat belatedly received the insignia of the Turkish Medjidye Order from Sultan Abdülhamid Khan, dedicatee of Strauss's waltz *Märchen aus dem Orient* op.444 (Fairy Tales from the Orient), written three years earlier.

On 27 February 1896 Adèle's daughter, Alice, married the distinguished painter Wilhelm Franz Josef, Marquis de Bayros, in the historic Deutsche Ritterordenskirche in Vienna. Alice had invited Johannes Brahms to act as witness to her marriage, but he had reluctantly declined, confiding to Richard Heuberger his aversion to public appearances, adding: 'I can already see myself in the dreadful dress-suit, with white gloves and top hat – no, that's impossible!' For this family occasion Johann Strauss wrote his touching *Hochzeits-Präludium* op.469 (Wedding Prelude), scored for organ, solo violin and harp. The groom, Franz de Bayros, had been responsible for the famous oil painting *Ein Abend bei Johann Strauss* (An Evening with Johann Strauss), depicting a gathering of the composer's friends and relations. The picture had been Adèle's present to Johann on his Jubilee in 1894. Sadly, Alice's marriage foundered, and so incensed was Adèle that she ordered Bayros's face to be overpainted with a different likeness. From a second marriage, in 1899, Alice produced two sons, and before her death in 1945 she is known to have married at least once more.

With the death of Viktor Tilgner, on 16 April 1896, Johann lost another close friend from his circle of intimates. 1895 had already seen the passing of Camillo Walzel, Josef Weyl, Franz von Suppé, Richard Genée and Josef Schrammel, and Strauss was growing ever more isolated. Johann took Tilgner's death particularly badly, and in an effort to distract her husband from his thoughts, Adèle asked the writer Paul Lindau to revive earlier proposals for a collaboration with Johann on a ballet. Enthusiastic though Strauss was, he declined Lindau's suggestion, as his publisher and theatre agent were stressing the better business prospects afforded by the composition of a new operetta. Lindau lost the day. On 22 July 1896 Johann advised Alexandrine von Schönerer that he had accepted from A. M. Willner and Bernhard Buchbinder a libretto for an operetta entitled *Die Göttin der Vernunft* (The Goddess of Reason).

Completion and delivery of the new stage work were patently a long way off, and serious differences of opinion soon arose between the composer and his librettists. Strauss was far from happy with the milieu of the operetta – set in the time of Robespierre's reign of terror during the French Revolution – and in August he attempted to dissociate himself from the undertaking. Willner and Buchbinder, however, would 'in no way assent to the abrogation of the contract', and insisted on fulfilment of the agreement. Thus, under protest, Johann worked on towards the première, which eventually took place at the Theater an der Wien on 13 March 1897. Even then the operetta was still without an overture, which Strauss failed to provide until the twenty-fifth performance.

The atmosphere of the capacity first-night house was appropriately festive. Even Brahms struggled to the theatre, despite his suffering from the cancer which was to bring about his death three weeks later. Only one eagerly awaited celebrity was absent: owing to a bout of bronchial catarrh, Strauss was confined to his home and was unable to attend the première of his new work. Nevertheless, he kept in touch via bulletins telephoned through to him from the theatre at the close of each act. When the appreciative audience called for the composer at the end of Act 1, an announcement was made regarding his indisposition. This news, according to the *Fremdenblatt* (14 March), 'spread like a crape over the mood of the house . . . We can only attribute it to the effect of this mood, that the sparkling musical numbers in the second and third acts were not such a great success as might have been expected under normal circumstances'. The paper went on to enumerate the many highlights in the score, particularizing 'a rich booty for the music-lover' in the Act 1 Finale and throughout Act 3. By comparison, Richard Heuberger, in his review, felt Strauss had been 'economical' in his inspiration, and he noted the excellence of only two or three individual numbers.

Willner and Buchbinder appeared on stage to acknowledge the applause of the audience, but the critics were sceptical of the morality of a libretto which sought to juxtapose burlesque comedy and the cruel days of the French Revolution. 'Can you disguise a blood-red guillotine with flowers?', asked the *Neue Freie Presse* (14 March). Moreover, the confused state of the libretto led the press to nickname the operetta *Die Göttin der Unvernunft* (The Goddess of Absurdity). The *Fremdenblatt* wrote: 'The librettists seem to have put the emphasis more on the colourfully interwoven situations than on a logical organization of the action.' For all this, the paper concluded: 'Without a doubt, the "Goddess of Reason" will reign for a considerable time at the Theater an der Wien.' Notwithstanding praiseworthy contributions from Julie Kopácsi-Karczag (who played Ernestine, the 'Goddess of Reason'), Karl Blasel (Bonhomme), Josef Josephi (Colonel Furieux) and Karl Streitmann (Captain Robert), *Die Göttin der Vernunft* passed out of the repertoire after just thirty-six performances. After Strauss's death its music was resurrected and married to a completely new text by Ferdinand Stollberg, whereupon in December 1909 it achieved considerably greater success as *Reiche Mädchen* (Rich Girls) at Vienna's Raimund-Theater. Triumphant in the rôle of Michael Karinger, the self-made millionaire in this reworking set in contemporary Vienna, was the 59-year-old Alexander Girardi.

The score of *Die Göttin der Vernunft* yielded ample material for the separate orchestral numbers which Strauss arranged on its themes. At the forefront of these pieces stands the spirited march *Wo uns're Fahne weht!* op.473 (Where our banner flies!), surely one of the most rousing of all Strauss marches.

Although *Die Göttin der Vernunft* was to be Johann's final operetta, he was to play a key rôle in two further stage works – neither completed during his lifetime. As early as February 1893, Johann had unsuccessfully discussed with Alfred von Berger, former Artistic Secretary of the Hof-Burgtheater, the idea of constructing a new stage work using music from Strauss's earlier operettas. Newly discovered correspondence shows that similar discussions, involving Johann's earlier dance-music, took place with Alexandrine von Schönerer of the Theater an der Wien, with the theatre's own Adolf Müller junior as musical arranger. The correspondence suggests that the costs of this project eventually became prohibitive to von Schönerer, at which point Franz Jauner, director of the Carl-Theater, assumed responsibility for bringing the new operetta, *Wiener Blut*, to the stage. This course of events would explain the apparent irregularity of the Carl-Theater using a rival theatre's resident conductor as arranger of this new work, which received its première at the Carl-Theater on 26 October 1899, almost five months after Strauss's death. Eduard Steinberger played Prince Ypsheim-Gindelbach, Prime-Minister of Reuss-Schleiz-Greiz, with Julius Spielmann as Count Zedlau, Ilona Szoyer as Franziska Cagliari, Valerie Stefan as Pepi Pleininger and Louis Treumann as Josef. The proposals for *Wiener Blut*, which took its title from Johann's waltz (op.354) of that name, had received the composer's blessing, a fact which seems to be confirmed in an undated letter written by him to an unnamed correspondent:

Am truly delighted with your prospective plan, although an old, already forgotten, waltz does not deserve to be glorified by such a charming, poetic pen . . .

Set at the time of the Vienna Congress of 1814–15, the amusing libretto of *Wiener Blut* was the work of Victor Léon and Leo Stein, a team who were to achieve their greatest success in 1905 with *Die lustige Witwe* (The Merry Widow) for Franz Lehár. Jauner's gamble failed. The lavish and colourful staging of *Wiener Blut* attracted only a lukewarm reception from the public. After thirty consecutive performances it made way for the acclaimed Sidney Jones operetta, *The Geisha*, and in the coming months saw just six more performances at the Carl-Theater. Jauner was bankrupted. On 23 February 1900 he shot himself dead at his desk in the Carl-Theater. Five years later, in April 1905, a production of *Wiener Blut* was mounted at the Theater an der Wien. It immediately caught the public imagination, and the operetta has retained its popularity ever since on stages around the world.

Strauss had been content to leave the principal selection of the music for *Wiener Blut* to Adolf Müller junior, as at about this time he had himself finally consented to undertake the composition of a full-length ballet score. On 5 March 1898 the Viennese weekly, *Die Wage*, announced details of a sensational 'Prize Competition':

For many years, friends of the Maestro Johann Strauss have tried to persuade him to compose a ballet. He has now determined to fulfil this request, and hopes to acquire a suitable text by way of the prize-competition.

Johann's final acquiescence was doubtless influenced by the distinguished names on the panel of judges. Apart from Strauss himself and the editor of *Die Wage*, the adjudicators comprised Nicolaus Dumba (former Chairman of the Wiener Männergesang-Verein, and dedicatee of Johann's waltz *Neu-Wien*), Professor Dr Eduard Hanslick and, for Strauss the most influential of them all, the then Artistic Director of the Vienna Court Opera, Gustav Mahler. The success of the competition exceeded all expectation. By May 1898 seven hundred entries had been received, and the prize was eventually awarded to a modern version of the classic fairy tale, *Cinderella*, submitted by one A. Kollmann from Salzburg. It soon transpired, however, that 'A. Kollmann' was a pseudonym. The collection of the 4000 kronen★ prize money (today worth about £4900 sterling) was effected through a lawyer, and to this day nobody has succeeded in penetrating Kollmann's anonymity. Although initially unenthusiastic about the already overworked story, albeit updated and set in a department store in 1900, Johann set to work without delay. 'I have my hands full with the ballet – I write my fingers to the bone, and still make no headway, I am on the 40th sheet (full score) and have only managed 2 scenes', he informed Eduard Strauss in the summer of 1898. In spite of this claim, progress was swift, as Strauss looked forward to the forthcoming première of his ballet, *Aschenbrödel*, at the Vienna Court Opera House.

On 28 June 1898 the Wiener Männergesang-Verein sang the first performance of a choral march Strauss had written especially for the 'Emperor's Jubilee and Fifth Austrian Federal Shooting Competition'. The piece, entitled *Auf's Korn!* op.478 (Take aim!), had a sentimental text by Vincenz Chiavacci in praise of the marksmen, Vienna and the old Emperor Franz Joseph. Dedicated to the competition's central committee, the new work was performed in the great Schützenfesthalle (Shooting Festival Hall) on the Prater. The chorus of the Wiener Männergesang-Verein was accompanied by the Vienna Cyclists' Orchestra who, in Strauss's absence, were conducted by Eduard Kremser. This was to be the last occasion on which the Choral Association gave the première of a new work by Johann II.

By late autumn 1898 Johann had completed the rough draft of *Aschenbrödel*, intending to fill out the orchestrations as time permitted. Sadly, he was destined never to finish this work, and after his death the

★Following a reorganisation of the Austrian monetary system in 1892, the 'Krone' (=Crown) was adopted as the new monetary unit.

task of completing the score from Strauss's material fell to Joseph Bayer, then Director of Ballet at the Vienna Court Opera. Through a series of misfortunes, not the least of which was a complete volte-face by Mahler, the world première of *Aschenbrödel* took place at the Königliches Opernhaus (Royal Opera House) in Berlin on 2 May 1901, 'in the presence of the Kaiser [Wilhelm II] and a sparkling audience' (*Vossische Zeitung*, 3 May 1901). The performance was conducted by Dr Karl Muck, with Antonietta dell'Era* in the title rôle, Berthold Zorn as Gustav, Emil Burwig as Franz and Gertrud Spiering as Madame Leontine. Not until 4 October 1908 was the ballet staged in Vienna, when Mahler's successor as Director of the Court Opera, Felix Weingartner, introduced the enchanting work into the repertoire, with principal rôles danced by Marie Kohler (Grete/Cinderella), Carl Godlewsky (Gustav), Alfred Rathner (Franz) and Rosa Schimanek (Madame Leontine).

On Whit Monday, 22 May 1899, Johann interrupted progress on his ballet in order to conduct the Overture to a special matinée performance of *Die Fledermaus* at the Vienna Court Opera House. Afterwards he returned to his home in the Igelgasse, and there resumed his orchestral revisions of *Aschenbrödel*. Three days later, on 25 May, after catching cold at a soirée, Strauss suffered a stomach and intestinal disorder. On the evening of Saturday 27 May he took to his bed with severe shivering fits and vomiting, which developed into a fever. His condition worsened, and the family doctor summoned the assistance of a distinguished specialist, Professor Dr Hermann Nothnagel. At first a recurrence of Strauss's old bronchial ailment was suspected, but soon pneumonia was diagnosed. On 1 June Johann became delirious. Adèle recalled that in one of his lucid moments her husband, smiling wearily, had feebly sung the familiar strains of *Brüderlein fein*, an old song by his former teacher, Joseph Drechsler. A medical bulletin on the morning of 3 June finally put an end to all hopes of a recovery:

The inflammation has reached its peak, and has attacked both lobes of the lungs in their entirety. The fever is very high; the patient is unconscious.

Shortly after four o'clock on the afternoon of Saturday 3 June 1899, Johann Strauss passed away in the arms of his devoted wife.

That same afternoon, Eduard Kremser was conducting an open-air festival concert in the Vienna Volksgarten in aid of the Lanner-Strauss father Memorial Fund. When news of Johann's death reached him, he made a brief announcement to the large audience, before turning to the orchestra and leading them quietly into *The Blue Danube Waltz*. No further words were necessary.

Silent mourners lined the route followed by Johann Strauss's

*Italian-born ballerina, best remembered for creating the rôle of the Sugar Plum Fairy in Tchaikovsky's *Nutcracker* at the Maryinsky Theatre, St Petersburg, in 1892.

funeral cortège on the afternoon of 6 June. From the Igelgasse the coffin was taken, via the Theater an der Wien, to the Evangelical Church in the Dorotheergasse. After the consecration service, the procession made its way past the Hof-Operntheater and Musikverein buildings to the Zentralfriedhof (Central Cemetery), where Strauss was laid to rest in a grave of honour close to the tombs of Beethoven, Brahms and Schubert. Funeral orations were delivered at the graveside by Dr Karl Lueger, Mayor of Vienna, and by representatives from the Vienna Musicians' and 'Concordia' Associations. Many were the other tributes paid to the memory of Vienna's Waltz King, but perhaps the most fitting, serving as a lasting epitaph to 'this missionary of gladness', was made three years earlier by the Director of Berlin's Lessing-Theater:

For fifty years Johann Strauss has, although unseen, been present at almost every joyous function of the civilized world; wherever parties of happy people have gathered for carefree pleasure Johann Strauss's spirit has pervaded. If we could estimate the amount of happiness and enjoyment contributed to the world by his creations, Johann Strauss would be regarded as one of the greatest benefactors of the century.

(Oskar Blumenthal, 2 May 1896)

21

The calling which I have practised . . . and which wholly fulfils and satisfies me, is to take Viennese music, and above all the immortal music of my immediate ancestors, out into the world, and to interpret it as it should be.

(Johann Strauss III. Vienna, January 1928)

EDUARD STRAUSS did not attend his brother Johann's funeral. He had been detained on a summer concert tour, a preliminary to the final great artistic undertaking of his career.

In 1890 he had made a triumphant twenty-nine week tour through sixty-two North American towns, giving concerts daily. Over the next nine years Strauss made concert tours to Germany, Russia, Holland and England, besides fulfilling engagements in his native Vienna. The financial yield from his endeavours, particularly from his work outside Austria, was substantial. In 1897, however, Eduard was suddenly confronted by the stark realization that the greater portion of this wealth, so assiduously gathered, had been shamefully squandered by his immediate family. In a period of three-and-a-quarter years from 1894, his two sons, with the cognizance of their mother, dissipated a total of 738,600 kronen (£30,749 sterling, today equivalent to £888,879). From London Eduard wrote to his friend, Jacques Kowy, on 21 July 1897:

I do not know if you have heard about the limitless distress which I suffer due to the prodigality of the members of my family, and the position and the circumstances force me to stand completely alone! I *no longer have* a family! Let me not dwell on this unspeakably sad situation any longer . . .

In the face of such deep personal disappointment and heartache, it is a tribute to the character of Eduard Strauss that, at the age of sixty-four, he set about rebuilding his lost fortune in preparation for his retirement.

In autumn 1899 Eduard signed a contract for a second concert tour of North America, comprising daily concerts and twice-weekly matinées from 22 October 1900 to 12 February 1901. During this expedition Strauss and his forty-two-piece orchestra repeated the

155

success of their former trip, despite a number of mishaps. In New Orleans, Chicago and San Francisco Eduard had to be treated for malaria, while in Montreal his concerts were boycotted by the large French-speaking community, who were angered because his agent had only placed advertisements in the English-language press! In the early morning of 7 February 1901 Strauss dislocated his right collarbone when the train on which he was travelling was involved in a collision as it pulled into Pittsburg. As a result of this injury, Eduard was forced to conduct with his left hand for the five remaining engagements in America. After 106 concerts throughout North America, the tour ended in New York with a benefit ball. Eduard recalled the occasion:

As I laid down my baton at the ball, and the orchestra-servant placed it in the violin case with the violin, I knew that I had now conducted for the last time, and I cannot describe what feelings came over me in this moment when, after 39 years' work with all its unpleasantness, rancour, troubles, sorrows, deprivations and exertions . . . I had now reached my goal, the provision for my old age. My first duty on the following morning was to make my way to the cathedral in New York to offer thanks to the Almighty.

At eleven o'clock on the morning of 13 February 1901 Eduard disbanded the Strauss Orchestra, founded by his father almost seventy-six years earlier and which he himself had managed for the last thirty years of its existence. 'I was overjoyed to have nothing more to do with this category of men', he later admitted in his family biography. Upon his return to Vienna Eduard relinquished his duties as k. k. Hofballmusik-Direktor and retired from public life. That November he was awarded the Austrian Grosse Goldene Salvator-Medaille for his services to music. Ironically, the invitation to the presentation incorrectly named the recipient of this honour as *Johann* Strauss – the very man in whose shadow Eduard had laboured for so much of his life.

Although Eduard was no longer an active participant in Vienna's musical life, from his home at No. 9 Reichsrathsstrasse in the heart of the city he observed the passage of events with a sometimes critical eye. He was, for example, deeply resentful that neither he, nor his surviving sister, Therese, were consulted about the design for the Lanner–Strauss father Memorial to be unveiled in Vienna's Rathaus-Park in summer 1905. 'For how many people are still alive who were acquainted with my father, *or even who only saw him*?', he wrote angrily to the sculptor Franz Seifert in February 1904.

1906 saw the publication of Eduard's memoirs, *Erinnerungen* (Reminiscences), an always interesting, if not wholly accurate, account of the activities of his family. Eduard refers in passing to a 'social contract' made between Josef Strauss and himself in 1869, whereby, in return for assuming responsibility for the other's widow,

156

all rights to performing material would be vested in the surviving brother. Moreover, wrote Eduard, 'should he give up his musical activity, then [the surviving brother] should destroy all the arrangements of the deceased', as well as making provision in his will for the subsequent destruction of his own music. Such an agreement, he argued, would prevent valuable Strauss material from falling into the hands of unscrupulous persons who might avariciously claim the works as their own. On 22 October 1907 Eduard arrived at the premises of a furnace manufacturer in Vienna's Mariahilf district, together with a vehicle laden with 'several hundred kilos of waste paper', which he had arranged to burn. Suddenly realizing that the 'waste paper' was, in fact, the extensive music archives of the Strauss Orchestra, the factory owner attempted in vain to dissuade Strauss from such an act of folly. Seating himself in an armchair in front of the two large pottery-firing kilns, Eduard looked on as the workmen opened the packets in front of him and scattered the sheets of music into the flames. A decade later, the proprietor recollected the scene for the *Neues Wiener Journal*:

Strauss was visibly moved by particular parcels of music which held special family memories. He stood up, looked away, or went back into the office for a while. He only left the factory, however, after the last sheet of music was burned. One can perhaps visualize the extent of the archives when I say that the burning of the music – which included original manuscripts and unpublished works – lasted from 2 o'clock in the afternoon until 7 o'clock at night.

Only subsequently was it learned that Eduard had destroyed two further vehicle-loads of music at a factory in the Porzellangasse.

Fortunately, through the activities of bodies such as the Johann Strauss Societies of Sweden, Great Britain, France, Germany, Japan and, of course, Vienna, many of the published orchestral parts of these pieces, long out of print, are being painstakingly reassembled and made available again, allowing new generations to appraise for themselves the long since forgotten works of the Strauss family. As we gradually rediscover the delights of the neglected published scores, one cannot but reflect upon the large amount of unpublished material that must have fallen victim to Eduard's irrevocable actions.

After several successive illnesses, Eduard Strauss suffered a fatal heart attack on the night of 28 December 1916, and passed away in the arms of his faithful housekeeper. At the age of eighty-one, and virtually alone, the last of the great triumvirate of Strauss brothers was dead. A golden epoch of Viennese musical history had been brought to a close.

With the disbandment of the Strauss Orchestra in 1901 the family music tradition was upheld by Eduard's eldest son, Johann III. Like his two uncles, Johann III (who was known variously as Johann Strauss junior and Johann Strauss grandson) attended the Wiener Schottengymnasium, where he was a student from 1876 to 1884. During his early boyhood he was taught piano and violin, and later studied musical theory under Professor (Karl?) Nawratil, despite Eduard's wish that he should not become a professional musician. Upon his matriculation, Johann junior studied law at Vienna University for a few terms before leaving to take up a post as an accounts official in the Ministry of Education and Instruction. His career flourished, and he duly received promotion. But as he later recalled,

I had music in my blood, and I longed to get away from the prose of the public functionary. It was my paternal uncle, Johann, who especially understood my bent for music. He supervised my efforts as a composer, he even let me transcribe his own orchestral compositions for piano, and he encouraged my musical studies in every way.

Eduard, however, repudiated this statement, claiming that 'my brother never bothered about the upbringing or education of my sons'. Eduard also strenuously denied that he himself had forced his son into legal studies, maintaining that, after matriculation, Johann junior had been given complete freedom in the choice of his career. On 17 April 1894 Johann III married Maria Emilie Karoline Hofer, the 26-year-old daughter of a Viennese theatrical costumier. Four children were born of the marriage – Johann Eduard Maria (1895–1972), Eduard Lambert Maria (1-3 March 1897), Maria Pauline Anna (1900-86) and Angelica Maria Pauline (1901-79) – none of whom was to pursue a musical career. With the breakup of his parents' marriage, following the disagreements of 1897, Johann III and his father became almost totally estranged.

Early in 1898, while still employed by the Ministry, Johann began work on a three-act operetta, *Katze und Maus* (Cat and Mouse), and the following year he quit the Civil Service to devote his life to music. The libretto for *Katze und Maus* was furnished by Ferdinand Gross and Victor Léon. Uncle Johann was plainly impressed. On 30 May 1898 he wrote to Eduard: 'The book is considered to be excellent. Schönerer is quite delighted with it. For years I have been looking for a good book, but cannot find one. Str[auss] junior is more favoured by fortune than me – his very first (perhaps also last) is a real winner.' *Katze und Maus* received its première at the Theater an der Wien on 23 December 1898. It survived just seventeen performances. The press could fault neither the opulent staging nor the excellence of a cast that included Josef Josephi (to whom Strauss dedicated the operetta), Julie Kopácsi-Karczag, Therese Biedermann, Karl Streitmann and Karl Blasel. The libretto, a treatment of Scribe's comedy *Der Damenkrieg* (The Ladies' War), was widely recognized as clever and amusing. But to the young composer's contribution there was a quite different reaction, one that at times bordered on hostility. Though acknowledging the welter of pleasant, if undistinguished, melodies in the score, the music critic of the *Neue Freie Presse* (24 December) complained:

The plot, which needs to progress quickly, is continually interrupted by the numerous long songs, and suffers greatly for it . . . Many sharp words were heard in the auditorium to the effect that the composer should have examined himself more closely, for the sake of the famous name he has received, before he appeared publicly. This name, it was said, should not become a shop-sign behind which inferior goods are to be found. Also, if Herr Strauss, by some delusion, should believe that he has real and greater talent, it would have been more appropriate to have appeared modestly under a pseudonym, and to see whether he would be able to gain recognition . . .

Strauss was aware of this animosity towards him, and wrote to a friend after the fourteenth performance on 6 January 1899: 'That under such circumstances I could experience fourteen performances at all, I certainly have only the eminent production to thank.'

To coincide with the première of *Katze und Maus*, Johann III's only operetta, the Viennese music publishers Ludwig Doblinger (Bernhard Herzmansky) issued several piano and orchestral arrangements from its score. Among these were the waltzes *Sylvianen* (op. 1) and *Leonie* (op.2), *Comme il faut, Polka française* (op.3), *Rococo-Gavotte* (op.4), *Empire, Polka-Mazur* (op.5), *Schlau-Schlau, Polka schnell* (op.6), *Dragoner-Marsch* (op.7), *Katze und Maus Quadrille* (op.8) and *Musette* (op.9).

Strauss made his conducting début in Budapest on 12 February 1900 with his waltzes *Gruss aus Wien* op.24 (Greeting from Vienna) and *Dem Muthigen gehört die Welt* op.25 (The World belongs to the Brave). During that year he undertook a seven-month concert tour through Austria and Germany. From Krefeld, in Germany, he wrote on 10 July to Jacques Kowy:

Yesterday I completed my *70th concert*! My artistic successes are – touch wood – quite extraordinary, the material ones unfortunately not satisfactory, because I have had to play in concert halls again and again because of continuously miserable weather! – Now I have 82 more concerts to go! Then, with God's assistance, it's back home to my dear ones!!

He appeared for the first time in Vienna at the head of his own orchestra on 3 November 1900, for a festival concert in the Sofienbad-Saal in aid of the Lanner–Strauss father Memorial Fund. He was joined on this occasion by two virtuosi – the pianist Alfred Grünfeld and the harpist Sophie Geraldini-Lanner, who was the granddaughter of Joseph Lanner and a member of the Ziehrer Orchestra.

From 1901 to 1906 Johann III directed the music at the balls of the Imperial Court in Vienna, still presided over by Emperor Franz Joseph I. While Strauss junior might well have expected to inherit the coveted title of k.k. Hofballmusik-Direktor upon the retirement of his father in 1901, issues in his private life were to foreclose this possibility. In both 1897 and 1901 Johann III had been under preliminary investigation for bankruptcy, but these enquiries were dropped. But on 5 October 1904 he stood before a Court of Law, accused of bankruptcy incurred through negligence, and was eventually convicted in November 1906. With liabilities amounting to 175,000 kronen (£7291 sterling, today about £197,490), he was sentenced to a week's imprisonment on charges of defrauding his creditors. Eduard Strauss felt deeply that dishonour had been brought upon the family name by his eldest son's irresponsible behaviour, and if at any time the old man had wavered in his resolve to destroy the family archives, his bitterness at this affair would surely have persuaded him to carry out his alleged promise to Josef.

Although the trial highlighted Johann III's extravagant lifestyle, it also disclosed that misfortune had dogged his early tours. In 1902, for example, during his tour of Romania, Bulgaria and Turkey (where he played before Sultan Abdülhamid II at Yıldız Palace, Istanbul), his concert entrepreneur in Sofia absconded with 5000 francs. That same year, Johann was engaged with his orchestra for the concert and dinner to be given in London on the occasion of King Edward VII's coronation, for which he composed his *Krönungs-Walzer* op. 40 (Coronation Waltz), dedicated to the King and Queen Alexandra. Owing to the King's sudden illness, the coronation was postponed, and Strauss suffered a considerable financial loss from the cancellation of the festivities. He was, however, made a member of the Royal Victorian Order (Honorary 4th Class) by Edward VII in October 1903 following the King's visit to Vienna earlier that year.

In 1907 Strauss junior turned his back on his native city and moved with his wife and family to Berlin, which became his centre of operations for the remainder of his life. In the years immediately before his departure, Johann III participated in several notable Viennese musical events, such as the festival concert in April 1903 to celebrate C. M. Ziehrer's sixtieth birthday. On the morning of 13 March 1904 – one day before the centenary of Strauss father's birth – Johann junior joined Adèle and Therese Strauss, Ziehrer, Ludwig Eisenberg and others at the unveiling of a commemorative tablet at No. 11 Kumpfgasse, the house in which Johann I had died in 1849. That evening, Johann III conducted a Strauss concert in the Sofienbad-Saal, held in his grandfather's memory. The next day, in the company of his father, Aunt Therese and the Lanner–Strauss Committee, Johann junior attended a wreath-laying ceremony at the grave of Strauss father in Döbling Cemetery. On 21 June 1905, Eduard Strauss and his sister, Therese, together with other family members, were present at the unveiling of the Lanner–Strauss father Memorial in the Rathaus-Park. At this ceremony, which was also attended by Lanner's daughter and granddaughter, the 'Kapelle Johann Strauss junior' performed an arrangement entitled *Perlen aus Lanners Walzern* (Pearls from Lanner's Waltzes).

From their base in Berlin, Strauss and his orchestra became a familiar sight on their annual tours of the Continent. True to family tradition, Johann III usually conducted from the violin. With the outbreak of the First World War in 1914 concert halls in Germany were requisitioned as military hospitals, and Strauss was forced to disband his orchestra. From autumn 1915 until the end of May 1916 he performed with a smaller chamber ensemble, but thereafter worked mainly as a guest conductor. Aware that he was the guardian of a great name and a great heritage, he continued with admirable singlemindedness to keep the family's music alive in a crisis-torn world, and in the face of new musical forms dominated principally by the American Jazz influence. In July 1914 he declined an offer from Rudolph Aronson for an American tour, and not until November 1934 did he make the first of his two concert trips to that country. Even in 1925 he had stated:

I have certainly made the observation that the interest in negro music everywhere has started to slacken, but I am nevertheless not travelling to the homeland of jazz until I can be completely certain that the last bacillus has disappeared, and my music again has a place to fill with the public.

During his career Johann conducted extensively throughout Europe, and he reckoned to have performed with 187 different orchestras in Germany alone between 1921 and 1925.

In April 1903 Johann III brought the Strausses into the new age of technological entertainment, when the Deutsche Grammophon AG of Germany issued eight single-sided records of the conductor directing the 'Johann Strauss Orchestra, Vienna' in works by his family. The list included his own highly popular waltz *Dem Muthigen gehört die Welt* – sadly, he was to record only four of his own compositions for posterity. It should be mentioned that the young man had in fact been anticipated in the field of 'recording' by his father: on 28 October 1889 the Eduard Strauss Orchestra had made a demonstration cylinder of A. Leonhardt's *Prinz Eugen-Marsch* for the Edison Company, one day before the 'Phonograph' made its public début in Vienna.

Further records featuring 'Johann Strauss's Vienna Orchestra under the personal supervision of Johann Strauss' appeared from the German Homophon Company in 1906-7, but in 1909 Johann III signed an exclusive contract with Thomas Alva Edison's National Phonograph Company for the recording of wax cylinders. Under the terms of the agreement Strauss not only made recordings with his orchestra but also acted as critic and adviser at Edison's Berlin Recording Laboratory. During the three-year period of their association with Edison, Strauss and his orchestra made not less than 158 cylinder recordings, performing music by composers such as Franz Lehár jun.,

161

Waldteufel, Lincke, Suppé, Ziehrer, Berlioz, Chopin, Saint-Saëns, Flotow and Auber, besides works by the Strauss family. Johann's own march, *Mit vereinten Kräften* op.29 (With United Strength), features in the Edison catalogue. More records were issued around 1910 by the Pathé Company, but it was in London, in 1927, that Strauss was to make the recordings for which he is best remembered today. Between 24 April and 2 June 1927 'Johann Strauss & Symphony Orchestra' recorded eighteen titles for the Columbia label at the company's studios at Petit France, Westminster, and in the Wigmore Hall. The 'Symphony Orchestra' was presumably that which Strauss conducted at his Royal Albert Hall concert on 24 April, and which comprised players from the London orchestras. In 1931 'Johann Strauss and his own Viennese Orchestra' recorded eight titles for the Parlophon label in Berlin, among them the composer's own exhilarating *Im Galopp* op.34 (At a Gallop). Although, combined with his tours, these recordings added greatly to Strauss's international reputation and popularity, they lack the youthful vitality and exuberance of the earlier Edison cylinders.

As a composer, Johann III wrote some thirty orchestral dances and marches, though the numbering of his works is misleading since the opus numbers 10–23 inclusive remained unallocated. While his waltzes, in particular, reflect the more 'modern' style and orchestrations of 'Silver Age' composers like Franz Lehár jun., his galops and quick polkas clearly betray more than a hint of his father's dash and stylishness.

Johann and his family returned to Vienna in 1916, shortly before Eduard Strauss's death, but less than two years later they moved back to Berlin. Thereafter, Johann made only occasional visits to his native city. On 1 August 1931, for instance, he conducted an orchestra of 800 instrumentalists at an open-air concert in the new Vienna Municipal Stadium. Five years later, on 1 March 1936, shortly after his seventieth birthday, he conducted a programme of Strauss music in the Musikverein, which was broadcast by several European radio stations. During this concert the Wiener Männergesang-Verein gave the première of his specially composed choral waltz *Lob der Heimat* (In Praise of the Homeland), dedicated to the Association. With its text by Josef Weinheber, the unpublished *Lob der Heimat* remains the only Strauss family composition with verses written by a genuine poet. The following year, Strauss directed another concert broadcast from Vienna, this time celebrating the seventieth anniversary of his uncle Johann's waltz *An der schönen blauen Donau*.

While actively engaged in preparing new touring plans, Johann Strauss III died in Berlin on 9 January 1939. In its obituary notice for the composer, the *Neue Freie Presse* (16 January) wrote:

With him died an emissary of Viennese musicality, who, with a modesty which was proof of greatness, put his own creative ambitions after his service to the work of his great ancestors and, as a conductor of Strauss music, gave to the world joy, elation and the inspired spirit of Vienna.

The fourth generation of Strauss family musicians stemmed not from Johann III but from his younger brother Josef. Born on 20 September 1868, Josef evidently showed early talent as a pianist, but chose to become a garage proprietor rather than enter the music profession. On 14 October 1907 he married an Austrian girl, Cäcilie Žak, who bore him three children – Josef Maria (1907–88), Maria Theresia Cäcilia (1908–) and Eduard Leopold Maria (1910-69). To the youngest child, Eduard, fell the task of continuing the family music tradition.

Eduard Strauss II was born on 24 March 1910 at No. 7 Kliebergasse, Vienna. Like his uncle Johann III, he received his first violin lessons when he was six years old. After attending elementary school in Vienna's Argentinierstrasse he went to the Walterrealschule, and thence to high school at the Handelsakademie in Albertgasse. Setting his sights on a musical career from the age of twelve, Eduard took instruction in piano, horn, violin and singing, both privately and at the Vienna Academy of Music (today known as the 'Hochschule für Musik und darstellende Kunst in Wien'). Before his enlistment for military service in 1939 he worked as an accompanist at the Auer-Weissgerber singing school in Vienna. From 1946 to 1956 he was employed as teacher and répétiteur in the opera class at the Konservatorium der Stadt Wien (Vienna Conservatory). Eduard II made his public conducting début in 1949, the year marking the centenary of the death of Johann I as well as the semicentennial of Johann II's death. On 4 June, during the 'Strauss Festival Week' organized by the Johann Strauss Society of Vienna, the 39-year-old Eduard conducted the Tonkünstler-Orchester of Lower Austria for a 'Johann Strauss Ball' held in the Vienna Town Hall. Later that year he attracted further attention conducting performances of ballet and operetta in the Volksoper. A concert by the Vienna Symphony Orchestra took place under his baton on 24 September 1949 in front of the Lanner-Strauss Memorial in the Rathaus-Park.

On 27 December 1950 Eduard Strauss married Elisabeth Josefa Pontes, a young Polish-born soprano who studied under him at the Vienna Conservatory. Upon their marriage Elisabeth abandoned her own promising singing career, and devoted her time to her husband and to their only child, Eduard Josef, born on 21 April 1955.

Eduard II's artistic career flourished amid great personal popularity. He won many admirers with his good looks and self-effacing manner, combined with the elegance he brought to his interpretations of music by the Strauss family and composers such as Mozart and Schubert. Like Johann III he was not content merely to trade on his famous ancestry: 'It is not easy to bear this name', he once said. 'It signifies, and demands, justification.'

In May 1954, soon after conducting the Vienna Symphony

Orchestra in a Musikverein concert celebrating the 150th anniversary of the birth of Johann I, Eduard Strauss II embarked on his first tour. Together with the Neue Wiener Konzertverein he gave a week of concerts in Germany and Switzerland, returning there in October 1955 with the Wiener Männergesang-Verein and the Vienna Symphony Orchestra. There were to be many further tours, which took him to such locations as Manila (1956), Seoul (1958, 1962), Moscow (1960), Cairo (1961), Paris (1962, 1964), London (1963, 1964, 1966), Athens (1963), Gothenburg (1964) and Warsaw (1967). Of his varied artistic achievements, perhaps none is more significant than his series of six major tours of Japan with the Tokyo Symphony Orchestra between 1956 and 1967. Eduard conducted a total of 137 concerts in thirty-six Japanese cities, and recordings from this period show the remarkable results of his patient rehearsals with an orchestra unfamiliar with Western musical styles. After the conductor's untimely death in 1969, tribute was paid to him by Professor Toyofumi Murata, President of the Japanese-Austrian Society:

Without him the Japanese would never have learned to understand and love the Viennese waltz. He taught us that Mozart's music is like a flower-filled garden, Beethoven's music like a great cathedral, but the music of the Strauss family has united the hearts of all mankind. We have indeed lost a true friend.

A major event in 1966 was the formation of the Wiener Johann Strauss Orchester, under the auspices of the late Professor Oskar Goger and Austrian Radio (ORF). Eduard Strauss was invited to be founder-conductor of this ensemble, whose players were drawn from the Vienna Radio and other leading Viennese orchestras, with the aim of recreating the touring Strauss Orchestra of the late 1800s. There followed a highly successful whirlwind tour of Canada and the United States of America from 17 October to 11 December 1966. Of the many reviews published, one in the *Daily Collegian*, reporting on Eduard's concert at the Masonic Auditorium, Detroit, on 27 November, concisely expressed the views of the majority:

And when the necessary attention to nuance and rhythm came through, it was as if all the schmaltz that conductors have allowed to clog the pores of these delightful pieces over the years had finally been melted away. No soggy tempi, no monotonous ONE-two-three beat, no racing to the finish line: in short, excellent Strauss.

Eduard's personal credo, regarding the interpretation of Strauss waltzes, was simple – the melodies should be allowed to unfold 'like a flower'. He also held that the waltz should not be played too quickly: 'Always remember, people must be able to *dance* to it smoothly.' The conductor was characteristically modest about his own attempts at composition. In conversation with a colleague in June 1966, he admitted that he had put some ideas down on paper, 'but I was not at all satisfied that they were of any value, and therefore threw them away'.

164

In early October 1966 Eduard recorded a programme for BBC Television in London, in which he conducted the BBC Concert Orchestra and personally introduced one of the numbers. The film was broadcast on 12 March 1967, during 'Blue Danube Centenary Year'. Throughout this and the following year, he was kept busy with concerts at home and abroad. On 19 January 1969 he conducted the Grand Orchestre Symphonique at the Namur Festival, Belgium. This was destined to be his final public engagement. Eduard Strauss II died suddenly in Vienna, on Easter Sunday, 6 April 1969, from an aortic embolism.

This gifted conductor left us a rich heritage of recordings, with numerous orchestras, by which to assess his stylish interpretations of his family's music. Among these, *Johann Strauss Première*, recorded for Philips (GBL 5600/G 03086 L–deleted) with the Vienna Symphony Orchestra, is especially treasured by devotees. It was Eduard's intention to make a comprehensive series of Strauss recordings for Vox Productions Inc. of New York, but regrettably his concert engagements claimed priority. Only the first of the projected series, *The Unknown Johann Strauss* (Turnabout TV 34328), was completed. The sessions for this record, undertaken in February 1969, proved to be his last. We can only regret that this gentle 'Ambassador of Viennese Music' was not granted the time to fulfil his ambition.

22

To be called Eduard Strauss, and live in Vienna: you cannot imagine the pressure!

(Dr Eduard Strauss, interviewed in *Classical Music*.
London, 24 December 1983)

AT THE TIME of this publication, Eduard Strauss II represents the dynasty's last professional musician. Academic study into the music and history of the Strausses continues within the family, chiefly through the work of the conductor's widow, Elisabeth, and their 34-year-old son, Eduard. Both have lectured at home and overseas, and Eduard (III) – the family reserves the 'numbering system' exclusively for its professional musicians – made his début as radio presenter on 22 October 1983 at Hereford, England, as compère of BBC Radio 2's concert, *The Vienna of Strauss and Friends*. Subsequently he has fulfilled several further broadcasting engagements.

This youngest Strauss descendant received his four-year elementary education at the private Diözesan Übungsschule, over which period he also learned piano at the Vienna Conservatory. He entered the Wiener Schottengymnasium at the age of ten. From October 1973 to December 1978 he was a student in the law faculty of Vienna University, becoming a Doctor of Law on 1 February 1979, shortly before his twenty-fourth birthday. From 1 October 1982 to 31 December 1986, Herr Richter Dr Eduard Strauss was a practising judge at the District Court of Wiener Neustadt. Since then he has been a judge at the County Court in the same town, some 50 kilometres south of his home in Vienna. On 13 September 1986 Dr Strauss married Susanne Charlotte Kienast, an Austrian pharmacist, at St Jakob's Church, Vienna. This followed their civil wedding at the Standesamt, Hietzing, on the previous day. The first child of the marriage was born on 28 July 1988 at the 'Goldenes Kreuz' clinic in Vienna: mindful of the earliest days of the Strauss family, the couple chose to name their son Michael Johann.

Outside his legal career, Dr Strauss continues the connection between his family and the Wiener Männergesang-Verein: on 29 May 1975 he was honoured by an invitation to join the Association, and he sings regularly in the baritone section. His uncle Josef, who died in October 1988, was also a Doctor of Law. An active member of the Wiener Männergesang-Verein's committee from 1951 to 1972, Josef was its chairman for twelve of these twenty-one years.

The Strauss dynasty has been delighting the world with live musical entertainment for over a century and a half. Is it really conceivable that the last of the professional musical line has been reached? Dr Eduard Strauss himself has firmly dismissed any thoughts of a musical career, despite obvious pressures for him to reconsider. Yet, perhaps through him, or through another branch of the family, concert posters may one day proclaim again:

HEUT' SPIELT DER STRAUSS! – STRAUSS PLAYS TODAY!

BIBLIOGRAPHY

Apart from contemporary letters, documents, newspaper reports and articles, the author has drawn upon the following works of reference:

BAUER, Anton: *150 Jahre Theater an der Wien*. Amalthea-Verlag, Zürich-Leipzig-Wien, 1952.

BIBA, Otto: *Johann Strauss und Johannes Brahms*, in 'Programm des Neujahrskonzert der Wiener Philharmoniker'. Wien, 1983.

DECSEY, Ernst: *Johann Strauss. Ein Wiener Buch*. Deutsche Verlags-Anstalt, Stuttgart, 1922.

EISENBERG, Ludwig: *Johann Strauss. Ein Lebensbild*. Breitkopf & Härtel, Leipzig, 1894.

ENGEL, Erich Wilhelm: *Johann Strauss und seine Zeit*. Kalendar. Verlag der k.u.k. Hof-Verlags-Buchhandlung Emil M. Engel, Wien, 1911.

GRUN, Bernard: *Kulturgeschichte der Operette*. Georg Müller Verlag GmbH, München, 1961.

HÜRLIMANN, Martin: *Die Walzer-Dynastie Strauss. In Zeugnissen ihrer selbst und ihrer Zeitgenossen*. Manesse Verlag, Zürich, 1976.

JACOB, Heinrich Eduard: *Johann Strauss und das neunzehnte Jahrhundert. Die Geschichte einer musikalischen Weltherrschaft*. Querido-Verlag, Amsterdam, 1937.

JÄGER-SUNSTENAU, Hanns: *Johann Strauss. Der Walzerkönig und seine Dynastie*. Verlag für Jugend und Volk, Wien-München, 1965.

KEMP, Peter: *From the Danube to the Thames – the Strauss family in Britain* (in preparation).

KYDRYŃSKI, Lucjan: *Jan Strauss*. Polskie Wydawnictwo Muzyczne, Kraków, 1979.

LANGE, Fritz: *Johann Strauss-Ausstellungskatalog*. Wien, 1931.

LANGE, Fritz: *Josef Lanner und Johann Strauss. Ihre Zeit, ihr Leben und ihre Werke*. Julius Pasternak, Wien, 1904.

LIEN, Michael Thomas: *The American Concert Appearances of Johann Strauss, with an Emphasis on the 1872 World's Peace Jubilee and International Musical Festival in Boston*. M.A.Thesis, University of Minnesota, May 1980.

LINDAU, Paul: *Nur Erinnerungen*. Band II. J. G. Cotta'sche Buchhandlung Nachfolger, Stuttgart-Berlin, 1917.

LOEWY, Siegfried: *Johann Strauss, der Spielmann von der blauen Donau*. Lebensfragmente. Wiener Literarische Anstalt, Wien, 1924.

MAILER, Franz: *Das kleine Johann Strauss Buch*. Residenz Verlag, Salzburg, 1975.

169

MAILER, Franz: 'Man tut mir zuviel Ehre an', in *Österreichische Musikzeitschrift* No.5/6 (1975). Elisabeth Lafite, Wien.

MAILER, Franz: *Joseph Strauss. Genie wider Willen.* Jugend und Volk, Wien, 1977.

MAILER, Franz: *Johann Strauss (Sohn). Leben und Werk in Briefe und Dokumenten.* Band I. Hans Schneider, Tutzing, 1983.

MAILER, Franz: *Die Persönlichkeit Johann Strauss' im Spiegel seiner Briefe.* Beitrag zum Internationalen Meeting der Johann Strauss-Gesellschaften, Wien, 1983.

MILLÖCKER, Carl: *Das Tagebuch Carl Millöckers.* Herausgegeben von Fritz Racek. Verlag für Jugend und Volk, Wien, 1969.

OSGOOD, James R. and Co.: *Hand-Book of the World's Peace Jubilee and International Musical Festival.* Boston, 1872.

PROCHÁZKA, Rudolph Freiherr von: *Johann Strauss.* 'Harmonie' Verlagsgesellschaft für Literatur und Kunst, Berlin, 1900.

RACEK, Fritz: Revisionsbericht, in *Johann Strauss (Sohn) Gesamtausgabe:* Serie II, Band 9 – 'Eine Nacht in Venedig'. Doblinger and Universal Edition, Wien, 1970.

RACEK, Fritz: Revisionsbericht, in *Johann Strauss (Sohn)* Gesamtausgabe: Serie II, Band 3 – 'Die Fledermaus'. Doblinger and Universal Edition, Wien, 1974.

RACEK, Fritz: *Johann Strauss zum 150.Geburtstag.* Ausstellungskatalog der Wiener Stadtbibliothek, Wien, 1975.

REICH, Willi: *Johann Strauss-Brevier. Aus Briefen und Erinnerungen.* Werner Classen Verlag, Zürich, 1950.

ROGERS, Robert J.: 'Des Wanderers Lebewohl', in *Tritsch-Tratsch* No.12 (1970). The Johann Strauss Society of Great Britain.

RUFF, D. Dr Philipp: 'Sendbote der Walzerdynastie Strauss. Erinnerungen an Kapellmeister Eduard Strauss', in *Rathaus-Ball-Tänze* No.2 (1979). Wiener Johann Strauss-Gesellschaft.

SCHEYRER, Ludwig: *Johann Strauss's musikalische Wanderung durch das Leben.* Wien, 1851.

SCHNEIDEREIT, Otto: *Johann Strauss und die Stadt an der schönen blauen Donau.* VEB Lied der Zeit Musikverlag, Berlin 1975.

SCHNITZER, Ignatz: *Meister Johann. Bunte Geschichten aus der Johann Strauss-Zeit.* Bände I & II. Halm und Goldmann, Wien–Leipzig, 1920.

SCHÖNHERR, Max & REINÖHL, Karl: *Das Jahrhundert des Walzers. Ein Werkverzeichnis. I. Band, Johann Strauss Vater.* Universal Edition, London–Wien–Zürich, 1954.

SCHÖNHERR, Max: 'An der schönen blauen Donau. Marginalien zur 100.Weiderkehr des Tages der Uraufführung', in *Österreichische Musikzeitschrift* No.1 (1967). Elisabeth Lafite, Wien.

SCHÖNHERR, Max: 'An der schönen blauen Donau in Paris', in *Österreichische Musikzeitschrift* No.2 (1968). Elisabeth Lafite, Wien.

SCHÖNHERR, Max: *Carl Michael Ziehrer. Sein Werk, sein Leben, seine Zeit.* Österreichischer Bundesverlag, Wien, 1974.

SCHÖNHERR, Max & MAILER, Franz: *Lanner-Strauss-Ziehrer. Synoptisches Handbuch der Tänze und Märsche.* Doblinger, Wien-München, 1982.

STRAUSS, Adèle: *Johann Strauss schreibt Briefe.* Verlag für Kulturpolitik, Berlin, 1926.

STRAUSS, Eduard: *'Erinnerungen'.* Franz Deuticke, Leipzig-Wien, 1906.

STRAUSS, Johann (Vater): *Gesamtausgabe. Herausgegeben von seinem Sohne Johann Strauss.* Lieferung I. Breitkopf & Härtel, Leipzig, 1887.

WAGNER, Richard: *My Life.* Volume I. Constable & Co., London, 1911. (Authorized translation from the German)

WEINMANN, Alexander: *Verzeichnis sämtlicher Werke von Johann Strauss Vater und Sohn.* Musikverlag Ludwig Krenn, Wien, 1956.

WEINMANN, Alexander: *Verzeichnis sämtlicher Werke von Josef und Eduard Strauss.* Musikverlag Ludwig Krenn, Wien, 1967.

WHITTEN, Dr John: 'Johann Strauss und der Wiener Männergesang-Verein', in *Österreichische Musikzeitschrift* No. 10 (1975). Elisabeth Lafite, Wien.

Index of the printed compositions by the Strauss Family

JOHANN STRAUSS-VATER
(1804–1849)

op.

1 Täuberln-Walzer
2 Döblinger Reunion-Walzer
3 Wiener Carneval-Walzer
4 Kettenbrücke-Walzer
5 Gesellschafts-Walzer
6 Wiener Launen-Walzer
7 Alpenkönig Galoppe Nr. 1, Nr. 2
8 Champagner-Galopp
9 Seufzer-Galopp
10 Alte und neue Tempête. Altdeutscher Polstertanz. Altvater-Galoppade und Sauvage
11 Walzer (à la Paganini)
12 Krapfen-Waldel-Walzer
13 Die beliebten Trompeten-Walzer
14 Champagner-Walzer
15 Die so sehr beliebten Erinnerungs-Ländler
16 Fort nach einander! Walzer
17 Gesellschafts-Galoppe
18 Lust-Lager-Walzer
19 IIte Lieferung der Kettenbrücke-Walzer
20 Chineser-Galoppe
21a Carolinen-Galopp
21b Kettenbrücke-Galopp
22 Es ist nur ein Wien! Walzer
23 Josephstädter-Tänze [Walzer]
24 Hietzinger Reunion-Walzer

25 Der unzusammenhängende Zusammenhang, Potpourri
26 Frohsinn im Gebirge, Walzer
27 Erinnerungs-Galoppe
28 Hirten-Galopp
29a Wettrennen-Galopp
29b Wilhelm Tell-Galopp
30 Sperls Fest-Walzer
31 Des Verfassers beste Laune, Charmant-Walzer
32 Schwarz'sche Ball-Tänze . . . Cotillons nach beliebten Motiven aus der Oper: »Die Stumme von Portici« [D. Auber]
33 Benefice-Walzer
34 Gute Meinung für die Tanzlust, Walzer
35 Einzugs-Galopp
36 Ungarische Galoppe oder Frischka [Nr. 1, 2 u. 3]
37 Wiener Tags-Belustigung, Potpourri
38 Souvenir de Baden, Helenen-Walzer
39 Tivoli-Rutsch-Walzer
40 Wiener Damen-Toilette-Walzer
41 Fra Diavolo. Cotillons
42 Sperl-Galopp
43 Der Raub der Sabinerinnen. Characteristisches Tongemälde

175

176

(ausgenommen Walzer-Komposita)

Wiener Bürger-Märsche des 1.
Regiments:
Nr. 1 Original-Parade-Marsch
Nr. 2 Marsch nach Motiven der
  Oper: »Zampa« [Hérold]

Nr. 3 Marsch nach Motiven aus der
  Oper: »Robert der Teufel«
  [Meyerbeer]
Radetzky-Bankett-Marsch
[Unvollendete Skizze von Johann
Strauß-Vater. Für Pianoforte
eingerichtet]

JOHANN STRAUSS-SOHN
(1825–1899)

op.

1 Sinngedichte, Walzer
2 Debut-Quadrille
3 Herzenslust, Polka
4 Gunstwerber, Walzer
5 Serailtänze, Walzer
6 Cytheren-Quadrille
7 Die jungen Wiener, Walzer
8 Patrioten-Marsch
9 Amazonen-Polka
10 Quadrille nach Motiven der
  Oper: »Der Liebesbrunnen«
  von M. W. Balfe
11 Faschings-Lieder, Walzer
12 Jugend-Träume, Walzer
13 Czechen-Polka
14 Serben-Quadrille
15 Sträusschen, Walzer
16 Elfen-Quadrille
17 Jux-Polka
18 Berglieder, Walzer
19 Dämonen-Quadrille
20 Austria-Marsch
21 Lind-Gesänge, Walzer
22 Die Oesterreicher, Walzer
23 Pesther Csárdás
24 Zigeunerin-Quadrille
25 Zeitgeister, Walzer
26 Fidelen-Polka
27 Die Sanguiniker, Walzer
28 Hopser-Polka

29 Odeon-Quadrille
30 Die Zillerthaler, Walzer im
  Ländlerstyle
31 Quadrille nach Motiven aus
  der Oper: »Die Belagerung
  von Rochelle« von M. W. Balfe
32 Irenen-Walzer
33 Alexander-Quadrille
34 Die Jovialen, Walzer
35 Industrie-Quadrille
36 Architecten Ball-Tänze.
  Walzer
37 Wilhelminen-Quadrille
38 Bachus-Polka
39 Slaven-Potpourri
40 Quadrille nach Motiven der
  Oper: »Die Königin von
  Leon« von Boisselot
41 Sängerfahrten, Walzer
42 Wilde Rosen, Walzer
43 Explosions-Polka
44 Fest-Quadrille
45 Erndte-Tänze. Walzer
46 Martha-Quadrille
47 Dorfgeschichten, Walzer im
  Ländlerstyle
48 Seladon-Quadrille
49 Fest-Marsch
50 Klänge aus der Walachei,
  Walzer

179

181

468	Waldmeister-Quadrille	473	Wo uns're Fahne weht! Marsch
469	Hochzeits-Präludium	[474]	Da nicken die Giebel, Polka-Mazurka*
470	Deutschmeister Jubiläums-Marsch	[475]	Frisch gewagt. Galopp*
		476	Quadrille*
471–476	*Nach Motiven aus der Operette: »Die Göttin der Vernunft«*	477	An der Elbe, Walzer
471	Heut' ist heut', Walzer	478	Auf's Korn! Bundesschützen-Marsch
472	Nur nicht mucken! Polka française	479	Klänge aus der Raimundzeit. [Musikalisches Vorspiel]

HAUPTWERKE OHNE OPUSZAHL
(ausgenommen Walzer-Komposita)

Abschieds-Walzer. (F-Dur). Nachgelassener Walzer Nr. 1
Altdeutscher Walzer aus der Operette: *Simplicius*
Aschenbrödel-Walzer nach Motiven des gleichnamigen Balletts
Aufzugsmarsch aus der komischen Oper: *Eine Nacht in Venedig*
Autograph Waltzes
Csárdás aus der Operette: *Die Fledermaus*
Csárdás aus der Ballettmusik der komischen Oper: *Ritter Pásmán*
Centennial Waltzes (Säcularfest Walzer)
Einzugs-Marsch aus der Operette: *Der Zigeunerbaron*
Engagement Waltzes
Entre-Act. Vorspiel zum III. Act des Balletts *Aschenbrödel*
Erster Gedanke von Johann Strauß [Walzer]
Eva-Walzer nach Motiven aus der komischen Oper: *Ritter Pásmán*
Freiwillige vor! Marsch
Hommage au public russe. Potpourri
Ischler-Walzer. (A-Dur). Nachgelassener Walzer Nr. 2
Jugendliebe. Walzer nach Motiven der Operette: *Simplicius*
Liebesbotschaft, Galopp nach Motiven des Balletts *Aschenbrödel*
Liebeslieder aus Rußland, Polka-Mazurka
Odeon-Walzer (Nachgelassenes Werk)
Pásmán-Polka aus der Ballettmusik der komischen Oper: *Ritter Pásmán*
Pásmán-Quadrille über Motive aus der komischen Oper: *Ritter Pásmán*
Pásmán-Walzer aus der Ballettmusik der komischen Oper: *Ritter Pásmán*
Piccolo-Marsch nach Motiven des Balletts *Aschenbrödel*
Potpourri Quadrille
Probirmamsell, Polka française nach Motiven des Balletts *Aschenbrödel*

---

* Angekündigt: Erscheinen nicht nachweisbar

Promenade-Abenteuer, Polka-Mazurka nach Motiven des Balletts
Aschenbrödel
Serbischer Marsch
Tauben-Walzer nach Motiven des Balletts *Aschenbrödel*
Quadrille nach Motiven der Oper: »Des Teufels Antheil« von Auber
Traumbilder I u. II

ORIGINAL BÜHNENWERKE
VON JOHANN STRAUSS SOHN

Erstaufführung

Indigo und die vierzig Räuber	10. Februar 1871	Theater an der Wien
Der Carneval in Rom	1. März 1873	Theater an der Wien
Die Fledermaus	5. April 1874	Theater an der Wien
Cagliostro in Wien	27. Februar 1875	Theater an der Wien
[La Reine Indigo	27. April 1875	Théâtre de la Renaissance, Paris]
Prinz Methusalem	3. Jänner 1877	Carl-Theater, Wien
[La Tzigane	30. Oktober 1877	Théâtre de la Renaissance, Paris]
Blindekuh	18. Dezember 1878	Theater an der Wien
Das Spitzentuch der Königin	1. Oktober 1880	Theater an der Wien
Der lustige Krieg	25. November 1881	Theater an der Wien
Eine Nacht in Venedig	3. Oktober 1883	Neues Friedrich-Wilhelmstädtisches Theater, Berlin
	9. Oktober 1883	Theater an der Wien
Der Zigeunerbaron	24. Oktober 1885	Theater an der Wien
Simplicius	17. Dezember 1887	Theater an der Wien
Ritter Pásmán	1. Jänner 1892	Hofoperntheater, Wien
Fürstin Ninetta	10. Jänner 1893	Theater an der Wien
Jabuka (Das Apfelfest)	12. Oktober 1894	Theater an der Wien
Waldmeister	4. Dezember 1895	Theater an der Wien
Die Göttin der Vernunft	13. März 1897	Theater an der Wien
Aschenbrödel [Ballett, vollendet von Joseph Bayer]	2. Mai 1901	Königliches Opernhaus, Berlin
	4. Oktober 1908	Hofoperntheater, Wien

JOSEF STRAUSS
(1827–1870)

1 Die Ersten und Letzten, Walzer
2 Vergissmeinnicht, Polka-Mazurka
3 Sturm-Quadrille
4 Mille Fleurs-Polka
5 Flinserln, Walzer
6 Tarantel-Polka
7 Vielliebchen, Polka-Mazurka
8 Bachanten-Quadrille
9 Punsch-Polka
10 Bauern-Polka-Mazurka
11 Rendez-vous-Quadrille
12 Die Ersten nach den Letzten, Walzer
13 Wiener Polka
14 Avantgarde-Marsch
15 Titi-Polka
16 Die Vorgeiger, Walzer
17 Maiblümchen, Polka-Mazurka
18 Wiegenlieder, Walzer
19 Lustlager-Polka
20 Schottischer Tanz
21 Policinello-Quadrille
22 Sehnsucht, Polka-Mazurka
23 Joujou-Polka
24 Kais. Königl. Oesterreichischer Armee-Marsch
25 Kadi-Quadrille
26 Die guten alten Zeiten, Walzer
27 Jucker-Polka
28 Sylphide, Polka française
29 Die Veteranen, Walzer
30 Ball-Silhouetten, Walzer
31 »Herzbleamerl«, Polka-Mazurka (im Ländlerstyle)
32 Dioscuren-Quadrille
33 Masken-Polka
34 Mai-Rosen, Walzer
35 Une Pensée, Polka-Mazurka
36 Liechtenstein-Marsch
37 Csikós-Quadrille
38 Gedenke mein, Schnell-Polka
39 Perlen der Liebe, Concert-Walzer
40 La Simplicité, Polka française
41 Wallonen-Marsch
42 La Chevaleresque, Polka-Mazurka
43 Steeple-chase, Schnell-Polka
44 Fünf Kleeblad'ln, Walzer
45 Parade-Quadrille
46 Musen-Quadrille
47 Frauenblätter, Walzer
48 Harlekin-Polka
49 Die Amazone, Polka-Mazurka
50 Nymphen-Polka
51 Zeit-Bilder, Walzer
52 Matrosen-Polka
53 Defilir-Marsch
54 Flora, Polka-Mazurka
55 Bon-Bon, Polka française
56 Liebesgrüße, Walzer
57 Moulinet-Polka (Polka française)
58 Bivouac-Quadrille
59 Oesterreichischer Kronprinzen-Marsch
60 Laxenburger-Polka
61 Wiener Kinder, Walzer
62 Flattergeister, Walzer
63 Wald-Röslein, Polka-Mazurka
64 Lanciers-Quadrille
65 Caprice-Quadrille
66 Wintermärchen, Walzer
67 Minerva, Polka-Mazurka
68 Soll und Haben. Handels-Elite-Balltänze [Walzer]
69 Saus und Braus, Polka (schnell)
70 Die Kokette, Polka française
71 Schwert und Leyer, Walzer
72 Amanda, Polka-Mazurka
73 Symphathie, Polka-Mazurka
74 Elfen-Polka
75 Sturm-Polka
76 Adamira-Polka
77 Die Naive, Polka française
78 Gurli-Polka
79 Waldbleamln, Ländler
80 Stegreif-Quadrille
81 Cupido-Polka (française)

HAUPTWERKE OHNE OPUSZAHL

EDUARD STRAUSS
(1835–1916)

1 Ideal, Polka française
2 Die Kandidaten, Walzer
3 Sonette-Polka (française)
4 »Gut Heil«! Marsch
5 Eldorado, Polka française
6 *Unbesetzt*
7 Quadrille nach Motiven der Operette »Mannschaft an Bord« von G. von Zaytz
8 Carnevals-Gruss, Polka-Mazurka
9 Iris-Polka (française)
10 Fitzliputzli-Quadrille nach Motiven der Operette: »Fitzliputzli« von G. von Zaytz
11 Lebenslust, Polka (schnell)
12 Masken-Favorite, Polka française
13 Die Evolvirende, Polka française
14 Helenen-Quadrille über Motive der komischen Oper »Die schöne Helena« von J. Offenbach
15 Cascoletto-Quadrille nach Motiven der gleichnamigen Operette von J. Offenbach
16 Paragraphen-Polka (française)

17 Gruß an die Heimath, Polka (française)
18 Hesperiden, Walzer
19 Dornröschen, Polka-Mazurka
20 Gazelle, Polka (schnell)
21 Colibri, Polka (française)
22 Pirouette, Polka (française)
23 Lieder-Kranz, Quadrille nach Motiven von Franz Schubert
24 Pariser Leben, Quadrille nach Motiven der gleichnamigen Operette von J. Offenbach
25 Apollo, Polka française
26 Memoiren einer Ballnacht, Walzer
27 Herz an Herz, Polka-Mazurka
28 Kreuz und Quer, Polka (schnell)
29 Fleurette, Polka (française)
30 Tanz-Parole, Polka (française)
31 Wiener Stereoskopen, Walzer
32 Carnevals-Blume, Polka-Mazurka
33 Studentenliebchen, Polka française
34 Die Ballkönigin, Polka (française)

35 Nachtrag, Polka (française)
36 Harmonie, Polka (française)
37 Wunderblümchen, Polka-Mazurka
38 Jugendlust, Polka (française)
39 Freie Gedanken, Walzer
40 Devise, Polka française
41 Wiener Genre-Bilder, Walzer
42 Thauperle, Polka-Mazurka
43 Froh durch die ganze Welt! Polka (schnell)
44 Lanciers-Marsch
45 Bahn frei! Polka (schnell)
46 Vom Tage, Polka-Mazurka
47 In Künstlerkreisen, Polka française
48 Studentenstreiche, Polka française
49 Sardanapal, Quadrille nach Motiven des gleichnamigen Balletts von F. Hertel
50 Sängers Liebchen, Polka française
51 Pegasus-Sprünge, Polka (schnell)
52 Flüchtige Skizzen, Walzer
53 Über Stock und Stein, Polka (schnell)
54 Die Biene, Polka française

HAUPTWERKE OHNE
OPUSZAHL
(ausgenommen Walzer-Komposita)
Die Wienerin, Polka française
Greeting Waltz, on English Airs
Im hypnotischen Schlummer,

Walzer-Intermezzo
Mes Sentiments. À Jean Strauss.
Polka française (identisch mit
Ideal, Polka française op. 1)
Zehn Mädchen und kein Mann,
Quadrille

GEMEINSAME WERKE DER
BRÜDER STRAUSS

JOHANN STRAUSS-SOHN
UND JOSEF STRAUSS
Hinter den Coulissen, Quadrille
nach beliebten Motiven
Monstre-Quadrille
Pizzicato-Polka
Vaterländischer Marsch

JOHANN STRAUSS-SOHN,
JOSEF UND EDUARD STRAUSS
Schützen-Quadrille
Trifolien-Walzer

JOHANN STRAUSS-ENKEL
(1866–1939)
1–9 Nach Motiven aus der Operette
»Katze und Maus«
1 Sylvianen-Walzer
2 Leonie-Walzer
3 Comme il faut, Polka française
4 Rococo-Gavotte
5 Empire, Polka-Mazurka
6 Schlau-schlau, Polka schnell

7 Dragoner-Marsch
8 Katze und Maus-Quadrille
9 Musette
10–23 *Unbesetzt*
24 Gruß aus Wien, Walzer
25 Dem Muthigen gehört die
Welt, Walzer
26 Budapester-Polka
27 Frisch durch's Leben, Galopp
28 Rosige Laune, Mazurka
29 Mit vereinten Kräften, Marsch
30 Unter den Linden, Walzer
31 Die Schlittschuhläuferin,
Walzer
32 Wiener Weisen, Walzer
33 Mariana Valse
34 Im Galopp
35 Ludmilla, Mazurka
36 In der Blütezeit, Walzer
37 Mit freudigem Herzen, Polka
38 Dichterliebe, Walzer
39 Wilhelminen-Walzer
40 Krönungs-Walzer

BÜHNENWERK VON JOHANN
STRAUSS-ENKEL

Erstaufführung
Katze und Maus   23. Dezember 1898   Theater an der Wien

INDEX

200